I0810589

IMAGES
of Rail

TOOELE VALLEY RAILROAD

On the Cover: In this iconic photograph from 1951, the Tooele Valley Railroad proceeds through the intersection of Vine and Main Streets in signature style: caboose first, engine pushing from behind. A horn on the caboose warned motorists of the approaching train. The buildings in the background still stand, though the intersection now has a traffic light instead of a train. (Courtesy of the Utah State Historical Society.)

IMAGES
of Rail

Tooele Valley Railroad

Emma Louise Penrod

ARCADIA
PUBLISHING

ISBN 978-1-4671-3026-4

Published by Arcadia Publishing
Charleston, South Carolina

Printed in the United States of America

Library of Congress Control Number: 2013946960

For all general information, please contact Arcadia Publishing:
Telephone 843-853-2070
Fax 843-853-0044
E-mail sales@arcadiapublishing.com
For customer service and orders:
Toll-Free 1-888-313-2665

Visit us on the Internet at www.arcadiapublishing.com

For Jeff Barrus, the mentor who thought I could write a book.
Looks like you were right.

Contents

ACKNOWLEDGMENTS

History does not happen in a vacuum, and so I owe my ability to write this book to those who recorded and preserved the memory of the Tooele Valley Railroad. I am especially indebted to Jean Mogus, the current caretaker of the Tooele Valley Railroad Museum. Without her, this book would not have been possible. Gary Bevan also assisted us in collecting and identifying many of the photographs compiled in this book.

I also owe thanks to Tim Booth and James Bevan, with the Sons of Utah Pioneers, and to David Bern, the editor of the *Tooele Transcript-Bulletin*, for assisting me with my research.

Additionally, I am indebted to a great number of local historians who I never had the privilege to meet in person: Claude Atkin, Larry Deppe, Don Lee, and numerous others whose names unfortunately are not so frequently mentioned by the historical record, though they are no less important. I am especially grateful to all those who served on the original board that oversaw the creation of the Tooele Valley Railroad Museum. Without them, the vast majority of the railroad's history would be lost today.

On the writing side of things, I owe special thanks to Brigham Young University for providing the creative works and research grant that made the creation of this book possible, and to Quint Randle, my faculty mentor, for keeping me on track throughout the process.

Last but not least, my editor at Arcadia, Jeff Ruetsche, deserves my gratitude for his unending patience in the face of numerous setbacks.

To all those family members, friends, fellow writers and historians, and readers who continue to support me: thank you. I hope the work I produce lives up to your faith in me.

INTRODUCTION

Stories about the Tooele Valley Railroad begin with its sister company, International Smelting. Utah Consolidated Mining, a conglomerate of mines pursuing wealth in the ore-laden Oquirrh Mountains, founded these sibling companies on the same day in 1908. For the mines, this was a matter of strict self-interest: smoke litigation in the Salt Lake Valley had cost the company its primary smelter. To turn a profit, the mines needed an immediate, cost-effective smelting solution.

While seeking an escape from the mounting tide of litigation that came with Utah's agrarian and urban centers, the mining executives discovered Tooele. This desert town, settled in a choice canyon on the western slopes of the Oquirrhs, presented Utah Consolidated with exactly the location it desired. Some 32 miles of scrubby wasteland, a salty lake, and the Oquirrh Mountains separated Tooele from the majority of nearby population centers. But industrialization had not left the town untouched. Mining booms had swelled nearby communities, such as Mercur, to populations near 10,000 in the recent past. The modern conveniences that came with a wealth of silver and gold—electricity, communications, and railroads—remained in place next door. Most importantly, vacant land in Pine Canyon could be found just opposite Utah Consolidated's mines in Bingham Canyon. Several mountain peaks stood in the way, but this obstacle seemed readily surmountable when compared to the costly pollution controls Salt Lake City now required.

Utah Consolidated found Tooele in something of an adolescent state—a developing city of 1,200 at odds with itself. Mormon pioneers originally settled the valley in 1849, hoping to establish a self-sustaining agricultural community after the pattern of older Mormon colonies. But the area's soil proved too saline and the climate too dry for substantial crop production. Ranching became the industry of choice, but the population's limited success with its herds sustained little growth and left locals impoverished. Mining came to the valley in 1864 thanks to prospecting by the US army, but Tooele City's Mormon majority initially rejected this development. By 1900, with the population divided by political and economic ideals, a perpetual identity crisis embroiled the community.

The tipping point came in 1908. After fighting judicial law in Salt Lake City for two years, seeking peace with lifelong competitors, and attempting to pacify litigious farmers with out-of-court financial settlements, Utah Consolidated ran out of alternatives. Company administrators scrambled to set up shop in Pine Canyon, knowing that every day of construction meant decreased productivity and lost profit. They still faced a number of problems not solved by the Pine Canyon location, including the absence of an obvious route for transporting ores to the new smelter. The nearest railroad station, called the Tooele or Warner station, serviced the Western Pacific, the Rio Grande Western, and the Union Pacific, but it was about six miles southwest of the smelter site. Utah Consolidated solved this problem with the creation of the Tooele Valley Railway.

The mines company conceived a short-line railroad that was essentially the shortest distance between two points: the International smelter and the station at Warner. The line spanned 6.235 miles, beginning at Warner, turning east to follow Vine Street through downtown Tooele, then angling gradually northward to meet the International rail yard. A railroad depot constructed at 35 North Broadway—the intersection of Vine Street and Broadway—would serve as a third station and as the Tooele Valley Railway's company headquarters.

What political wrangling occurred in the fall of 1908 remains untold, but Utah Consolidated procured a right-of-way down the middle of Vine Street, one of the busiest roads in town, in relatively short order. In November, a little over a month after Utah Consolidated made the decision to move smelting operations to Pine Canyon, it incorporated two spinoff companies: the International Smelting Company, which later came to be known as International Smelting and Refining; and the Tooele Valley Railway Company, which many locals call the Tooele Valley Railroad, though it conducted official business under the "railway" name.

One final barrier stood between Utah Consolidated and the realization of its plans: Tooele's population. For the company to maintain its ambitious construction schedule, it planned to hire 600 workers at the smelter, 70 for the railroad, and another 200 to build a 20,000-foot-long aerial tram that would connect International directly to the mines in Bingham. The three projects could have employed 72 percent of the entire population living in Tooele City at the time.

A swarm of surveyors and company officials descended on Tooele that November to prepare the town for its overnight transformation. In December, E.P. Mathewson, the newly installed general manager of International Smelting, met with city officials to request the construction of 2,000 new homes.

Limited railroad services came online four months after construction began, and official operations commenced on October 15, 1909. The International smelter—which cost more than $2 million, paid in full by Utah Consolidated—took another year to finish, opening in the summer of 1910. Gov. William Spry lit the first furnace during a ceremony in July.

After more than doubling Tooele's population in a matter of months, business at the smelter quickly took a turn for the worse. Coincidently, ore supplies in Bingham dropped off without warning the same year the smelter opened, sending International scrambling for independent clients. To diversify its services, the company installed a lead smelter in 1911. The $500,000 investment paid off in July, when a group of mines in Ely become the smelter's first major customer outside Bingham, sending International nearly 900 tons of ore per month.

Operating as an independent smelter in the 1920s brought International its greatest success, and the Tooele Valley Railroad profited alongside it. In April 1926, the Interstate Commerce Commission counted four locomotives, 60 freight cars, and seven passenger cars in the railroad's possession.

The Tooele Valley purchased many of its original steam engines during these golden years. Engines No. 11 and No. 12 both came to Tooele in 1912. The exact origin of these sister engines is unknown, but according to Orrin Miller in *Mining, Smelting and Railroading in Tooele County*, the American Locomotive Company evidently built the two 2-8-0 engines in April 1910 for the Buffalo & Susquehanna Railroad. However, the New York railroad did not retain the engines for long. After changing hands a number of times, the Tooele Valley Railway bought both, and they remain in Tooele to this day. No. 10 arrived in Tooele in 1916. It was the oldest on the Tooele Valley Railroad, having been built in 1907, and was acquired secondhand from the Butte, Anaconda & Pacific Railroad (BA&P). The railroad did not acquire No. 9 until years later, in 1925, although American Locomotive had also built the 2-8-0 in 1910. It had worked on the BA&P as No. 29 before receiving its final number in Tooele.

Both the train and the smelter weathered the Great Depression and carried numerous Tooele City residents with their success. Unemployed men who had not found work for months would buy a 5¢ ticket for the Tooele Valley Railway and join a long line at the smelter, where they could, if they were lucky, land a day's work if a regular employee failed to arrive. "There would be long lines of men who wanted work," Claude Atkin wrote in *Mining, Smelting and Railroading in Tooele County*. "They'd take your job in a minute, and that meant you'd keep your head down and your backside up, and keep that pick and shovel going."

As the Great Depression wound to a close, a new face arrived with grand plans for reuniting the Tooele Valley Railway with the mines in Bingham. James Elton, then the general manager of the

International Smelting and Refining Company, believed he could restore the mines' productivity and bring the prosperity of the early 1920s to Tooele once more. His plan involved a merger that would bring the various industrial entities in the area under a single name and use their combined capital to fund an ambitious project: a 4.5-mile tunnel beneath the Oquirrh Mountains that would drain the underground mines and directly link them with International. Once Elton successfully united four mine companies, including Utah Consolidated itself, under the National Tunnel and Mines umbrella, he announced his plan and began excavation on April 9, 1937.

Had all gone as planned, Elton would have finished his tunnel in 1939, but the mountain had other ideas. An undiscovered fissure complicated the construction effort, and by the time the tunnel opened in 1941, Elton had spent $1.5 million on the project. Despite opening-day promises of dramatic growth and economic salvation, the Elton Tunnel proved an immediate failure. Two world wars carried International through the 1940s, but the unreturned investment on the tunnel caught up with the company when metals subsidies ended; in 1948, the entire holdings of the bankrupt National Tunnel and Mines went up for auction.

Anaconda Copper, a competitor that had long coveted International, stepped up to buy the ailing company for eight percent of its estimated value. This purchase brought change beyond new administration. The Tooele Valley ceased 24-hour operation in 1950, and visible downsizing began that same year when the No. 9 was officially retired and scrapped.

This trend continued in 1955, when the Tooele Valley Railway decided to make the transition to diesel power. The railroad acquired engine No. 100, an SW1200 built by General Motors, in June 1955. Soon after, engine No. 10 was sold for scrap, and engine No. 12 met a similar fate a year later. Executives kept No. 11 in service for another decade. Its final run, in 1963, made it Utah's last steam locomotive in common carrier service. The decision to condemn the boiler on No. 11 left the Tooele Valley without an alternate engine, forcing it to rent a locomotive from the Union Pacific and causing numerous delays. A second diesel, engine No. 104, an SW900 built by General Motors in 1959 and acquired secondhand from the Pickering Lumber Corporation, replaced the retired steam engine in 1966.

Smelter closures throughout Utah continued to change the state's industrial dynamics, but they granted International one last spurt of success. Anaconda also saw potential for further development in the Tooele area and began exploratory drilling in Pine Canyon for a new mine that would be known as Carr Fork.

Trouble in Chile, where Anaconda Copper had been a central figure, brought the local monopoly and the promise of a new mine to a screeching halt in the early 1970s. Anaconda lost millions almost overnight when the Chilean government nationalized its copper industry. Anaconda executives systematically identified unprofitable properties to be sold or closed, and the International smelter made the short list. With the closure came additional downsizing at the railroad, which resulted in the transfer of engine No. 100 to Anaconda Aluminum Works.

Anaconda gave Tooele little notice of the impending closure, publicizing its intent just two months before shutting down the smelter in the first few weeks of 1972. Without an economical option for smelting, 30 nearby mines were also unable to continue operations and had to close their doors. The Tooele railroad, however, managed to stay in business, hauling scrap from the decommissioned smelter, running odd jobs around town, and occasionally serving the needs of the new Carr Fork project.

Carr Fork opened in 1974 but did not begin producing ore until 1979. Meanwhile, Atlantic Richfield bought Anaconda in 1977, and although it allowed Anaconda a measure of autonomy, the new parent company soon grew tired of the fragmented projects remaining in Tooele. After months of below-capacity productivity, Carr Fork began laying off miners, beginning with a wave of 100 pink slips in June 1981. The problem, according to Anaconda executives, was the price of copper, which had continued to fall through the 1960s and bottomed out in the mid-1970s near 58¢ per pound. Feasible operations at Carr Fork required prices near $1.10 per pound.

This time, the railroad found itself on the chopping block as well. Try as it might, Atlantic Richfield could not come up with a use for a railroad that had not found a paying customer since

July 7, 1980. In June 1981, the company announced its intentions to formally abandon the line and all three stations.

The announcement punctuated a dark time for Tooele, which only worsened in May 1982 when Carr Fork laid off another 800 employees while the railroad stood by, waiting to hear if Atlantic Richfield's petition to abandon the line would be approved. With the rest of Utah's mining industry faring nearly as poorly, Carr Fork miners found alternate jobs few and far between. Unemployment in Tooele flirted with 11 percent; a year later, more than 60 percent of former Carr Fork employees remained out of work.

Though the Interstate Commerce Commission approved Atlantic Richfield's petition in 1982, a band of Tooele historians and former railroad employees formed an official coalition to preserve this portion of the town's heritage. The company listened readily to their requests and, in July, donated engine No. 11, several railcars, and the railroad's main passenger station to Tooele City for the creation of a museum.

Perhaps the most remarkable thing about this coalition was that it consisted of individuals descended both from the valley's original settlers and from those who had come to Tooele for the mines. Through years of success and hardship, the Tooele Valley Railway saw the community mature from a town of 1,200 to a growing city of 14,000. And though the tracks no longer traverse Vine Street, their mark remains. Today, Tooele stands as a unique symbol of both the rural and industrial west.

One

Foundation and Construction

Pre-1910

Tooele's turn of fate began on the other side of the Oquirrh Mountains, in the Salt Lake Valley. In 1906, an association of farmers filed suit against the area's mining and smelting companies because increasing pollution damaged crops and threatened the livelihood of a traditionally agrarian populace.

While a legal battle that spanned nearly two years continued, Salt Lake City farmers and Utah Consolidated, which stood to lose thousands if its mines in Bingham Canyon lost access to the Highland Boy smelter, met privately for negotiations. In December 1907, Utah Consolidated rejected a proposed $200,000 settlement and, unable to afford the expensive pollution controls required by a new district court ruling, shortly thereafter lost the Highland Boy.

For the better part of the next year, the company explored potential alternatives. Rumors in the local papers suggested that Utah Consolidated had set its sights on a parcel of land in Pine Canyon, a few miles east of Tooele. Speculators thought it a rather logical choice, given Pine Canyon's proximity to Bingham, and the company had begun to protect its Pine Canyon properties rather fiercely, even threatening to prosecute locals caught logging in the area. However, news that Utah Consolidated was talking with the American Smelting and Refining Company, which owned the sole smelter still operating in the Salt Lake Valley, derailed some of this building excitement.

Everything came together in the later months of 1908. The negotiations with American Smelting and Refining fell through on September 29, just 24 hours before the option on the Pine Canyon site was set to expire. A month later, Utah Consolidated gave birth to twin companies, both officially incorporated on November 18—the International Smelting and Refining Company and the Tooele Valley Railway. Construction on the railroad began on December 8, and construction on the smelter began the following day.

Industrialization would transform Tooele almost overnight. The railroad came online in a matter of months, as Utah Consolidated expedited the process to speed construction at the smelter. By July 1909, limited passenger service to Salt Lake was available. By the end of October, the railroad, the smelter, and all the associated construction had created 900 new jobs. That same month, when International listed its first one million shares, they sold for $134 each. Business boomed.

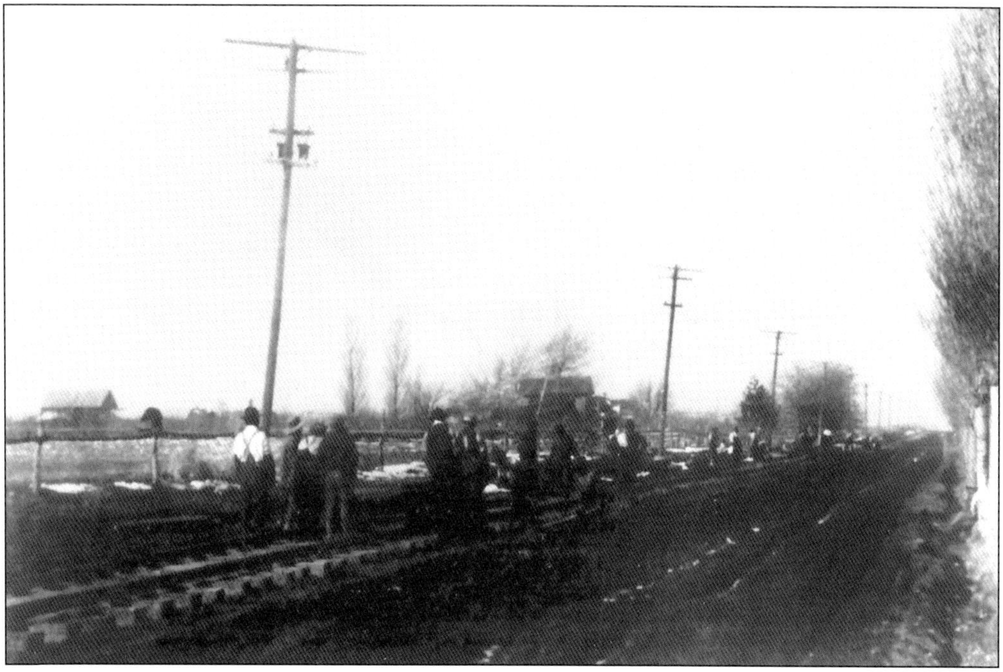

Work crews lay track down the center of Vine Street. This photograph is undated, but construction on the downtown portion of the railroad began in December 1908 and continued through the spring of 1909. Judging by the trees and the lack of snow, these men had not been at it long. (Courtesy of the Tooele Valley Railroad Museum.)

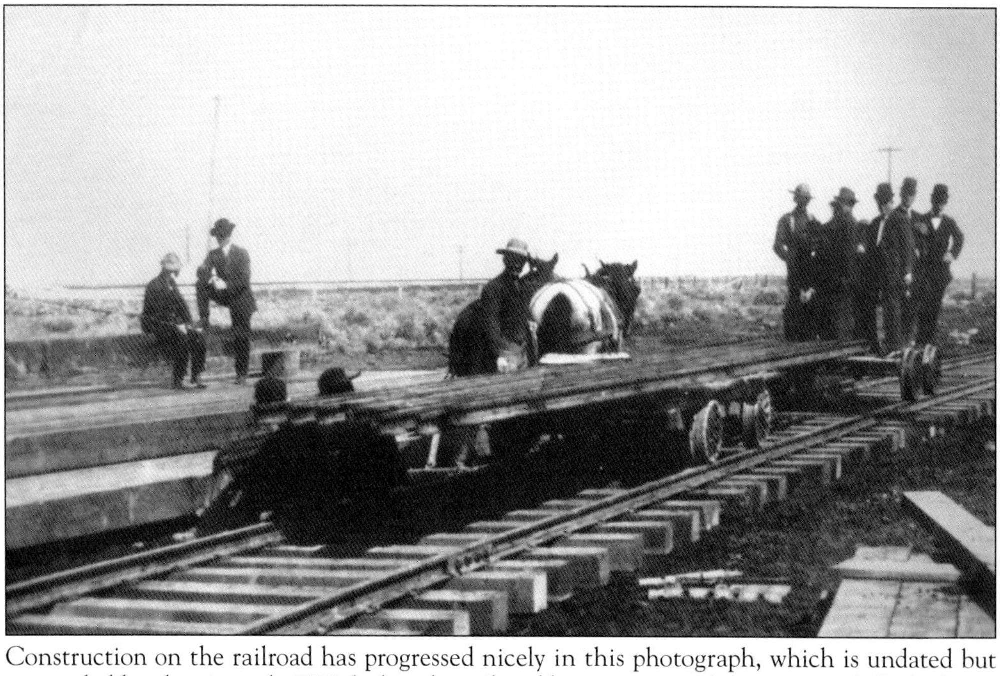

Construction on the railroad has progressed nicely in this photograph, which is undated but was probably taken in early 1909, before the railroad began running locomotives. A flatbed cart carries lumber, but it is pulled by the old-fashioned type of horsepower because the rails are not yet ready for an engine. (Courtesy of the Tooele Valley Railroad Museum.)

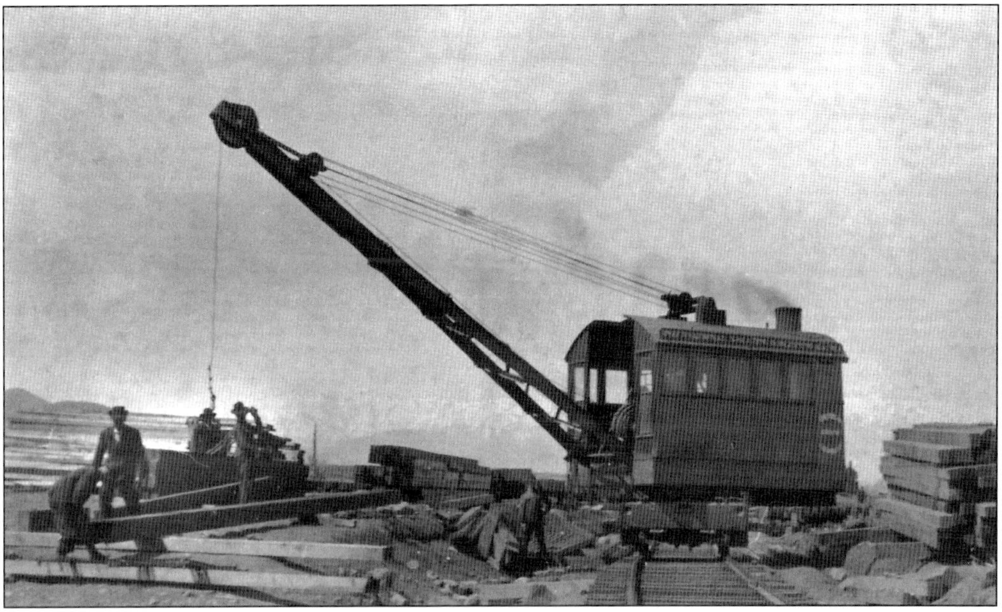

A crane helps construction crews move lumber into position near the site of the future smelter. Access to such heavy equipment was limited in pre-1910 Tooele, and construction required a host of horses and hundreds of hands-on laborers. The Tooele Valley Railway retained more than 70 construction workers in October 1909, even with the bulk of the track complete. (Courtesy of the Tooele Valley Railroad Museum.)

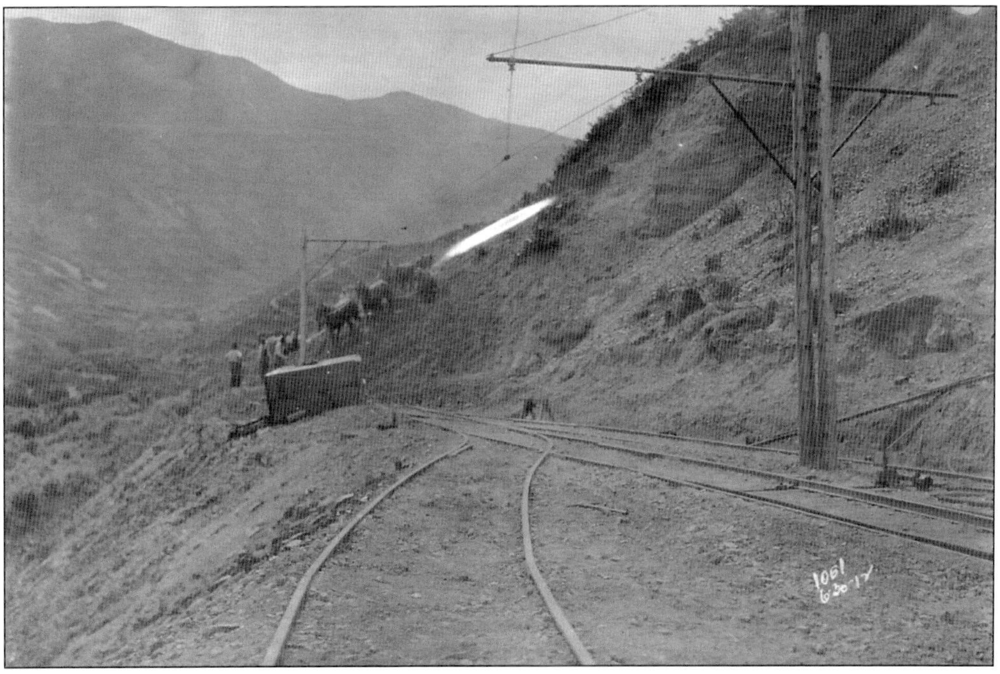

Men and horses take a break from their work on unfinished track near the mouth of Pine Canyon. The date on the photograph reads June 30, 1912, but the railroad became fully operational in October 1909. Most likely, the work seen here contributed to a railroad siding above the smelter site. (Courtesy of the Tooele Valley Railroad Museum.)

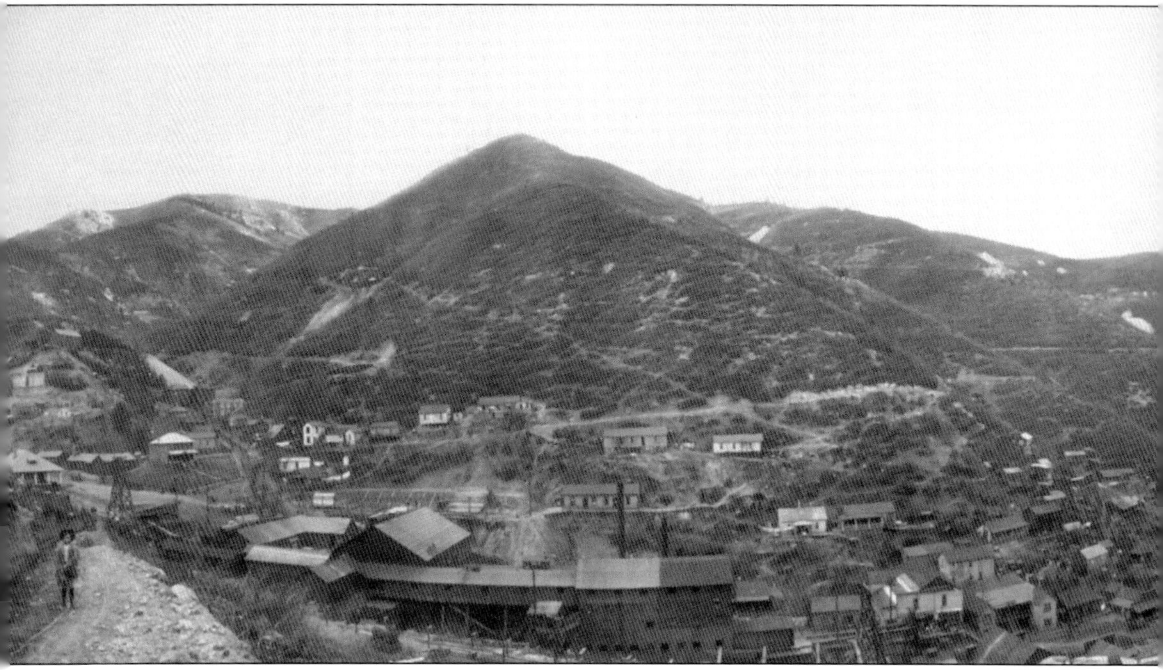

This panoramic photograph shows a settlement in Bingham Canyon on the east side of the Oquirrh Mountains. The buildings in the foreground belong to the Highland Boy mine. Most Bingham Canyon mines relied on the Highland Boy smelter in Murray, until smoke litigation

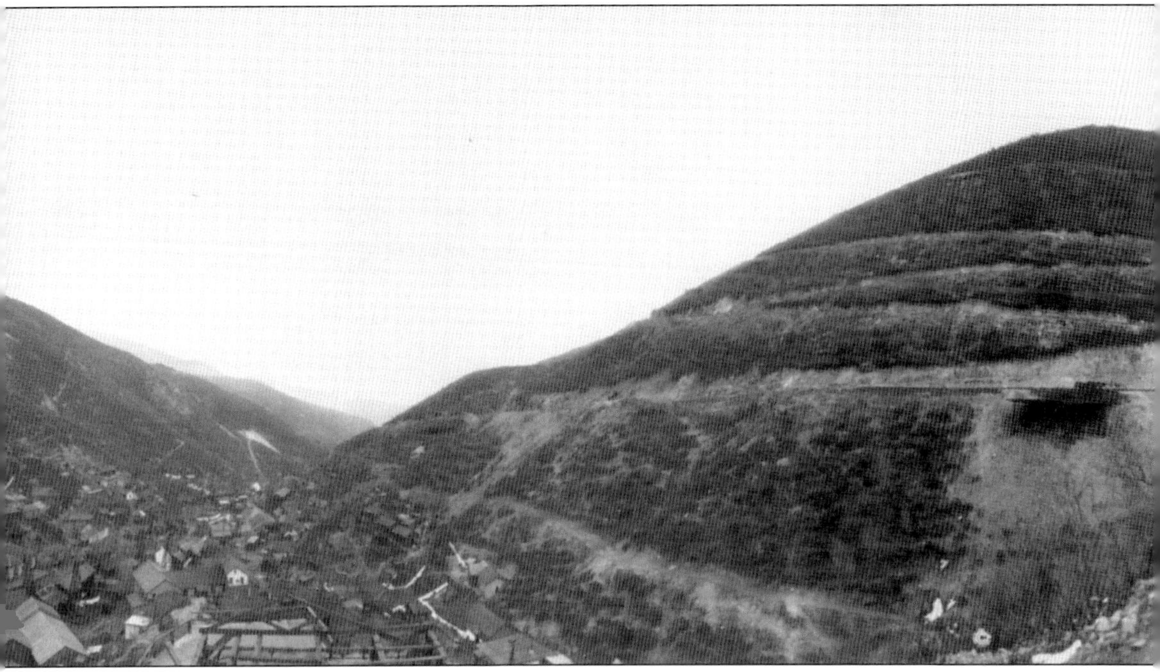

made smelting in the Salt Lake Valley nearly impossible. Today, Bingham Canyon is the site of an open pit mine so large it can be viewed by the naked eye from orbit. (Courtesy of the Library of Congress.)

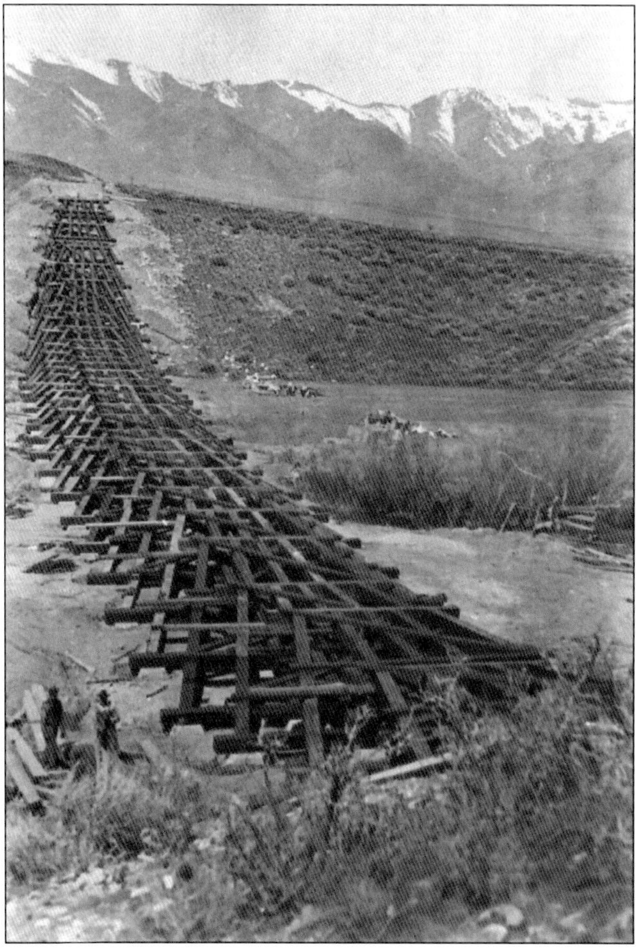

The shortest route for International's railroad took the track over this dry gorge below Middle Canyon. Instead of extending the track to avoid the natural barrier, engineers designed a large wooden trestle to bridge the gorge. Here, crews have just begun to assemble the structure's base. (Courtesy of the Tooele Valley Railroad Museum.)

This is a view of the trestle's completed base from above the gorge. Constructing the Middle Canyon trestle proved far more complex than laying the rest of the short line's track. While the train began carrying freight and passengers below Middle Canyon as early as July 1909, service across the trestle was not available for another three months. (Courtesy of the Tooele Valley Railroad Museum.)

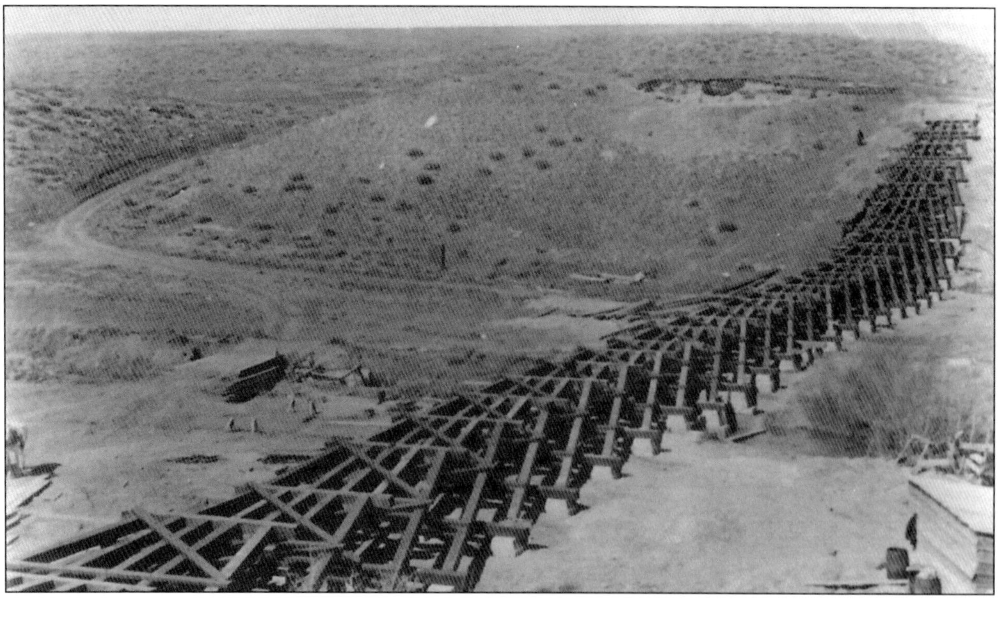

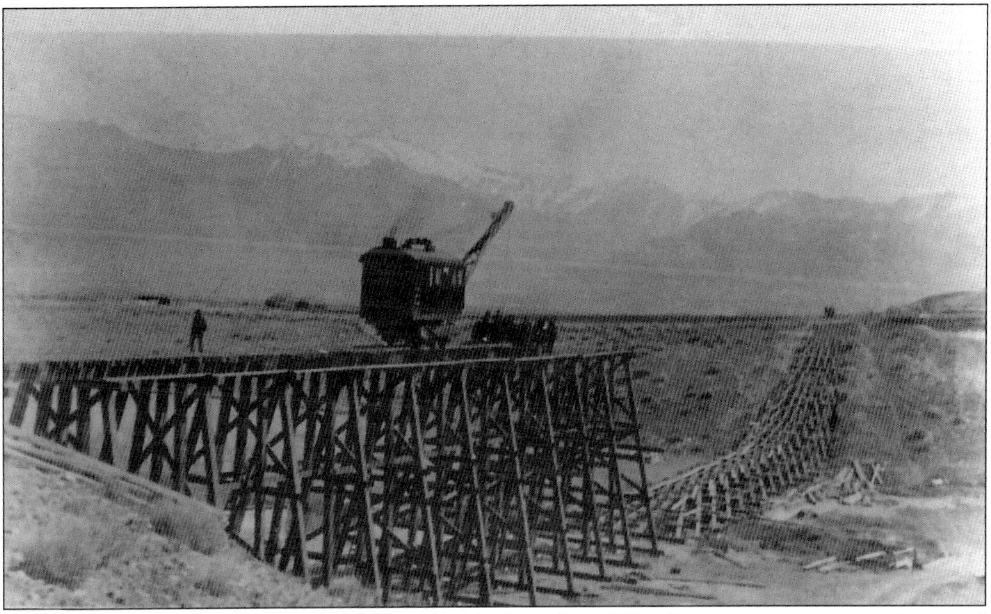

A steam-powered crane creeps onto the half-finished trestle in 1909. Construction crews implemented a novel method of assembling the trestle that required heavy equipment. Support structures were assembled off site and then laid out across the gorge in the correct order before the crane lifted each into position. (Courtesy of the Tooele Valley Railroad Museum.)

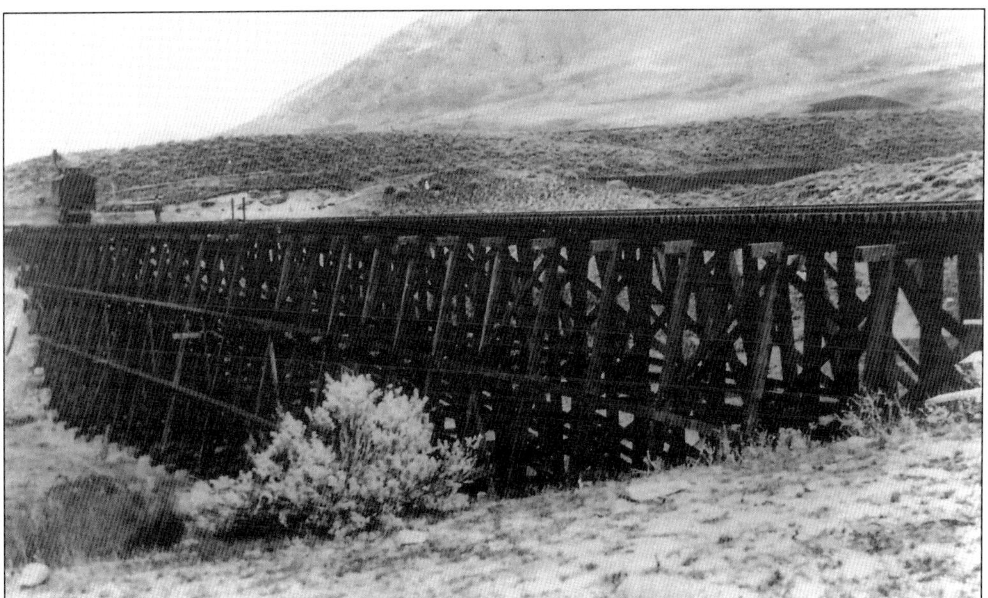

With the trestle nearly completed, a crane crosses to the opposite side with ease. After construction crews finished assembling the top part of each segment, the crane would inch forward to lift the next set of half-complete supports into position. The height of the bridge made speed restrictions necessary for passing trains. (Courtesy of the Tooele Valley Railroad Museum.)

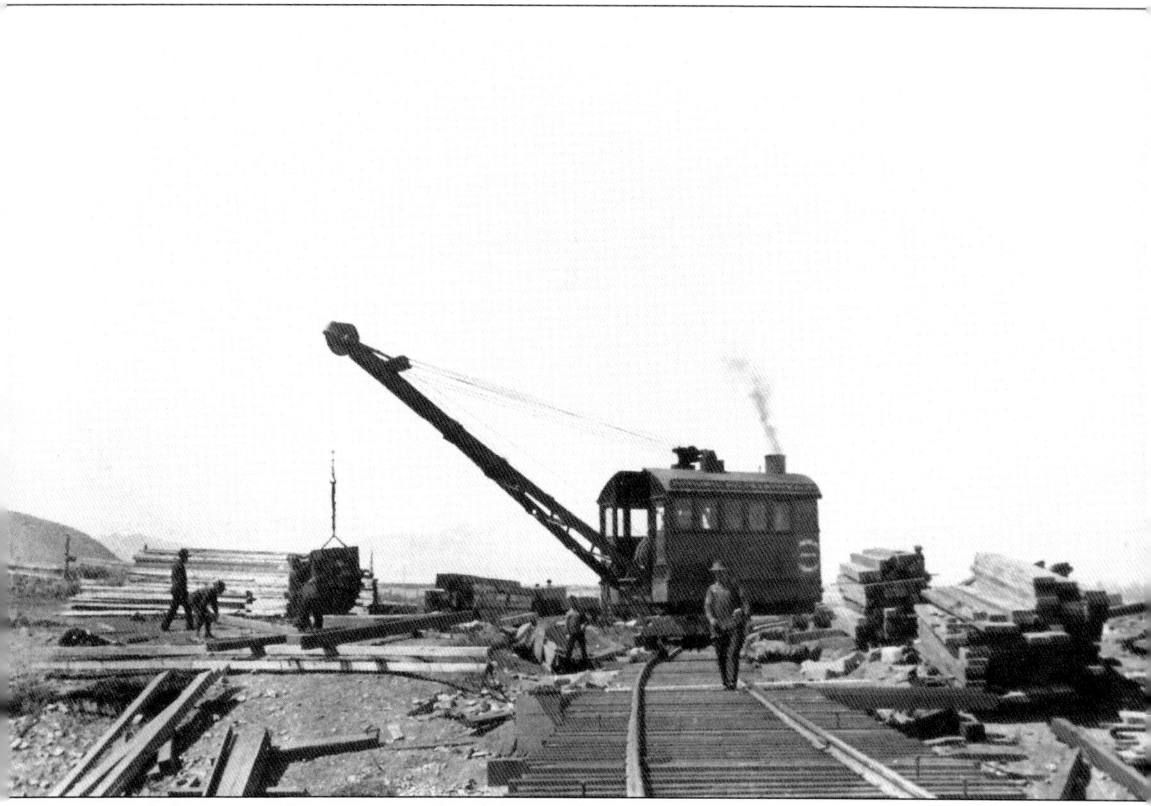

Work begins on the opposite side of the trestle beneath the smelter site, with the steam crane still in use. The line curved southeast after crossing the trestle, a feature locals referred to as the Big Curve. The radius of the turn caused the wheels of passing trains to screech as they passed. (Courtesy of the Tooele Valley Railroad Museum.)

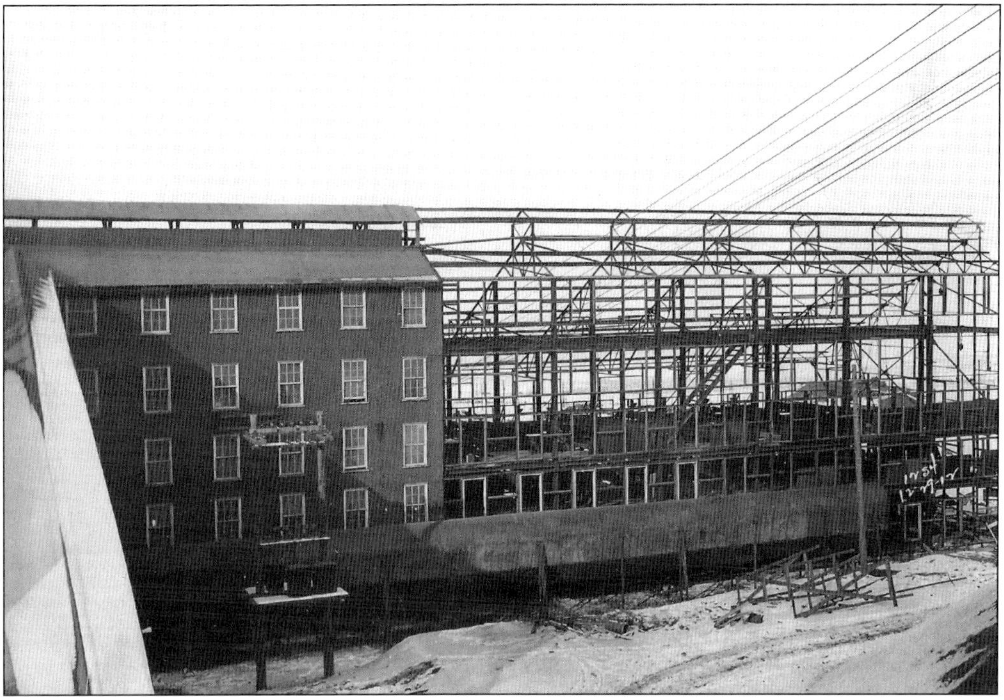

These photographs show work progressing at the International smelter. Construction at the smelter began on December 9, 1908, but moved slowly until the railroad brought freight operations online and began hauling supplies from Warner to International. The first ore arrived on July 14, 1910, but construction continued well beyond that date alongside limited smelting operations. Crews continued work on the copper smelter through the summer of 1910, and many remained to erect the lead smelter when it was announced shortly after the plant opened in the first months of 1911. (Both courtesy of the Tooele Valley Railroad Museum.)

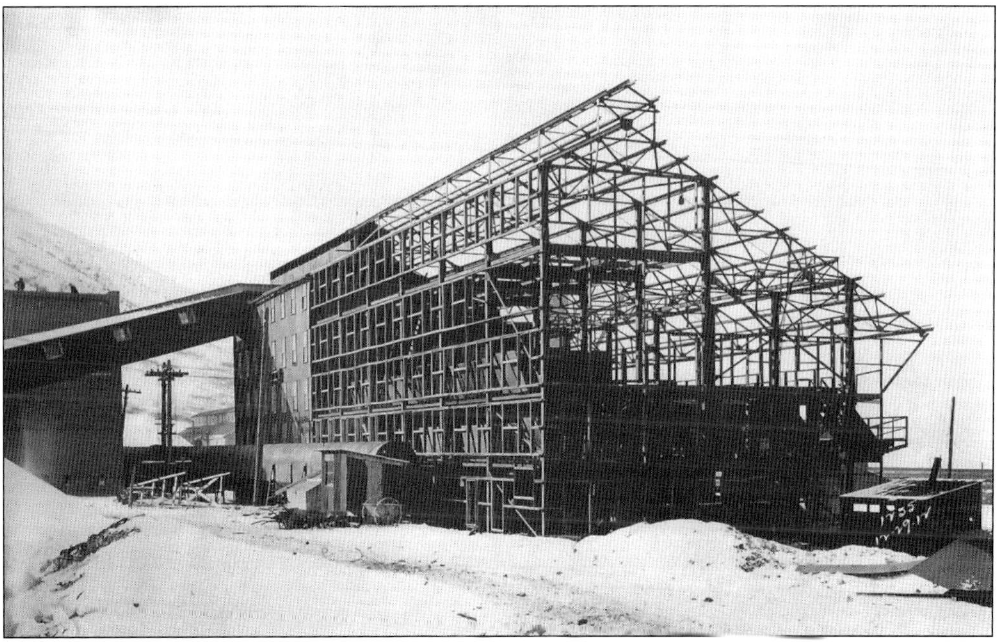

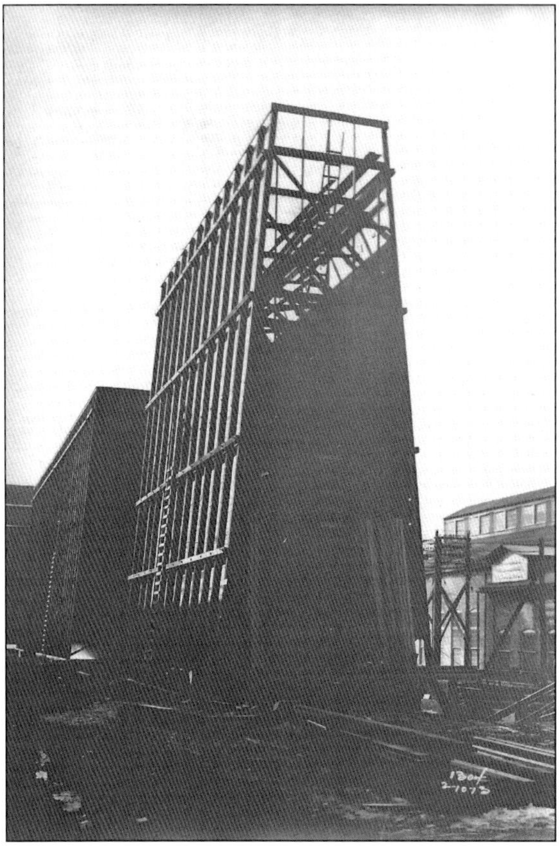

Scaffolding anticipates the arrival of a new structure at the International smelter site in the early 1900s. International hired the Oscar Daniels Company of Chicago to oversee the construction of the smelter, but also hired a number of full-time construction workers itself. On October 21, 1909, International had 601 full-time employees on its monthly payroll. (Courtesy of the Tooele Valley Railroad Museum.)

The assembly of interior smelter apparatuses began in the early 1900s. The construction, over the course of three years, required 200,000 cubic yards of excavation—removed by steam shovel, or, more likely, mule teams—and the installation of 26,000 cubic yards of plain and reinforced concrete. (Courtesy of the Tooele Valley Railroad Museum.)

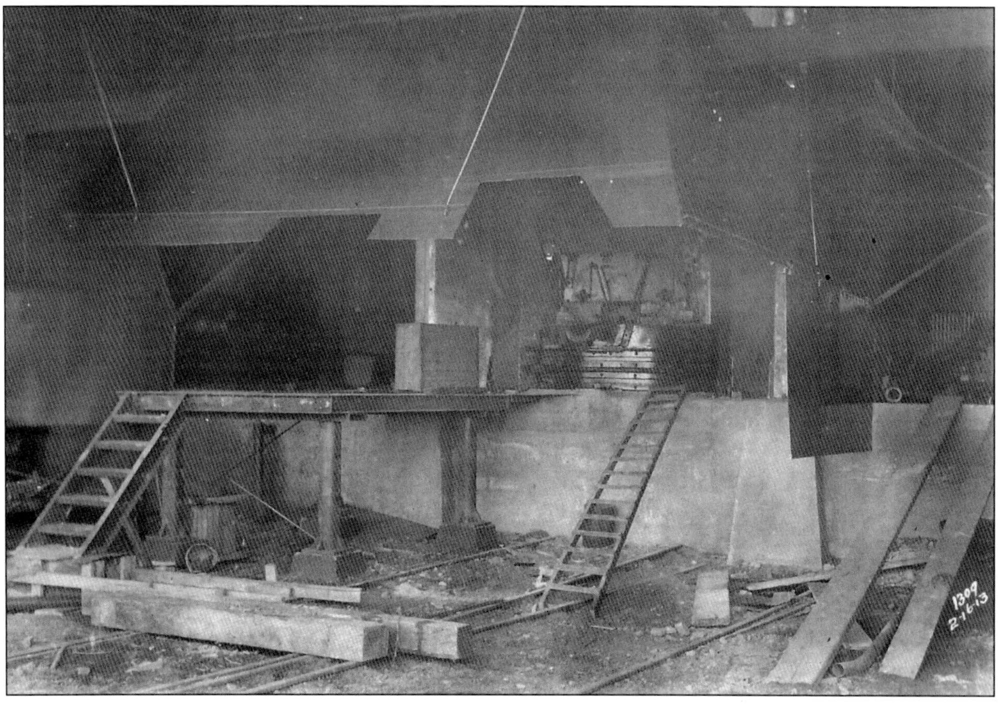

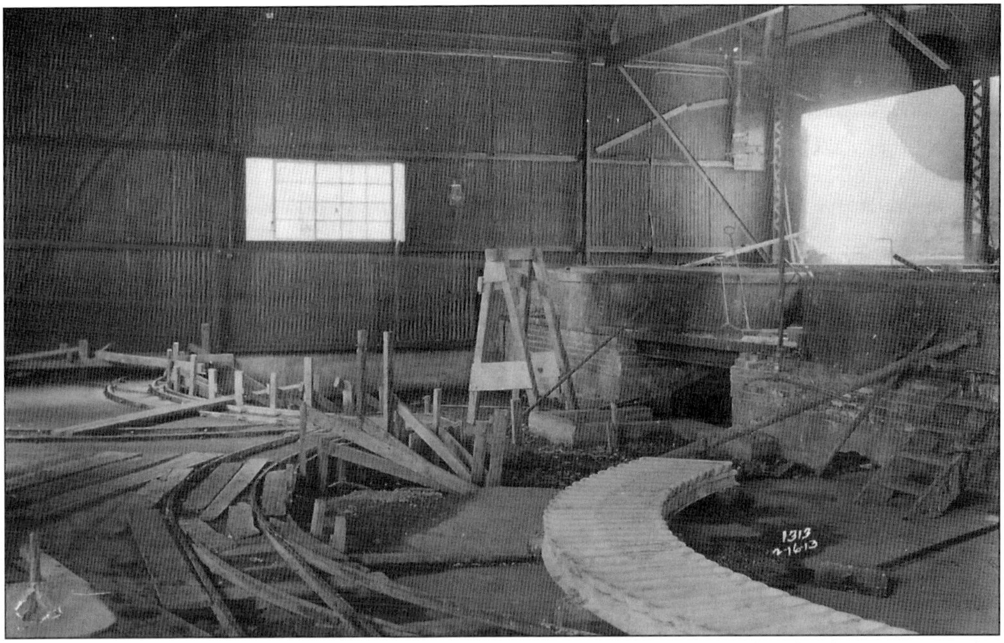

Bits of track, lumber, and various other parts wait on the floor of an unfinished structure at the International smelter. These appear to be destined for the blast furnace charge floor or the drossing plant, but it is difficult to tell at this stage. (Courtesy of the Tooele Valley Railroad Museum.)

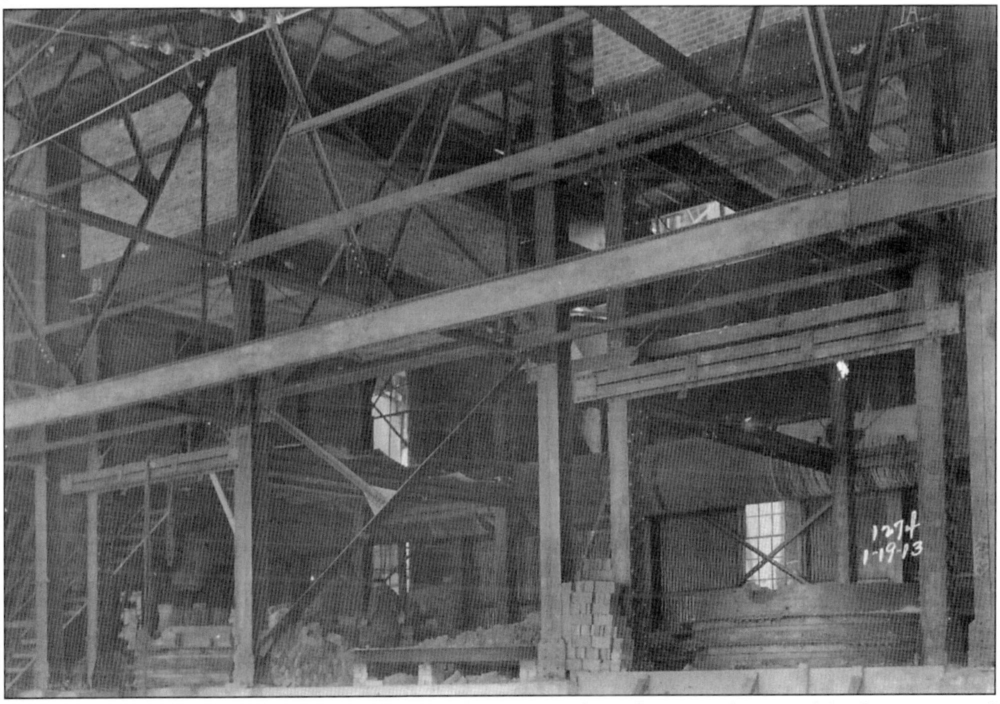

Steel supports, scaffolding, and unplaced bricks are seen here from inside one of the International smelter's structures during construction in the early 1900s. The original plan for International's combined on-site facilities, as envisioned before the lead smelter addition, required an estimated 9,900 tons of structural steel. (Courtesy of the Tooele Valley Railroad Museum.)

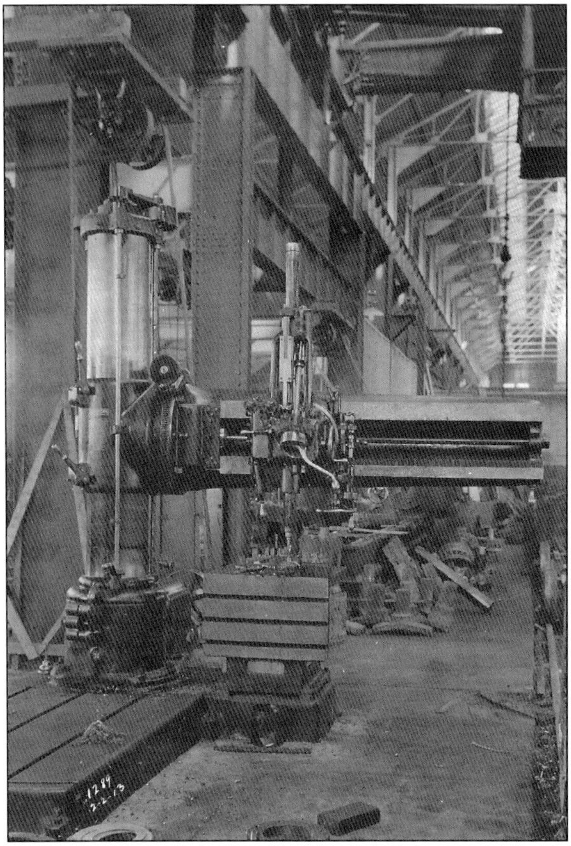

Machinery awaits assembly during construction at the International smelter. Initially, construction costs totaled $2.5 million. The lead smelter added another $500,000, bringing the smelter's total costs to $3 million in 1912. Had International built its smelter in 2012, it would have cost approximately $70 billion. (Courtesy of the Tooele Valley Railroad Museum.)

Below, assembled smelter machinery is ready for production. The International smelter remained under construction from December 1908 to January 1912, thanks to the last-minute lead smelting addition. An editorial in the *Tooele Transcript* estimated that the city's population decreased by 600 when construction workers left town with their families. (Courtesy of the Tooele Valley Railroad Museum.)

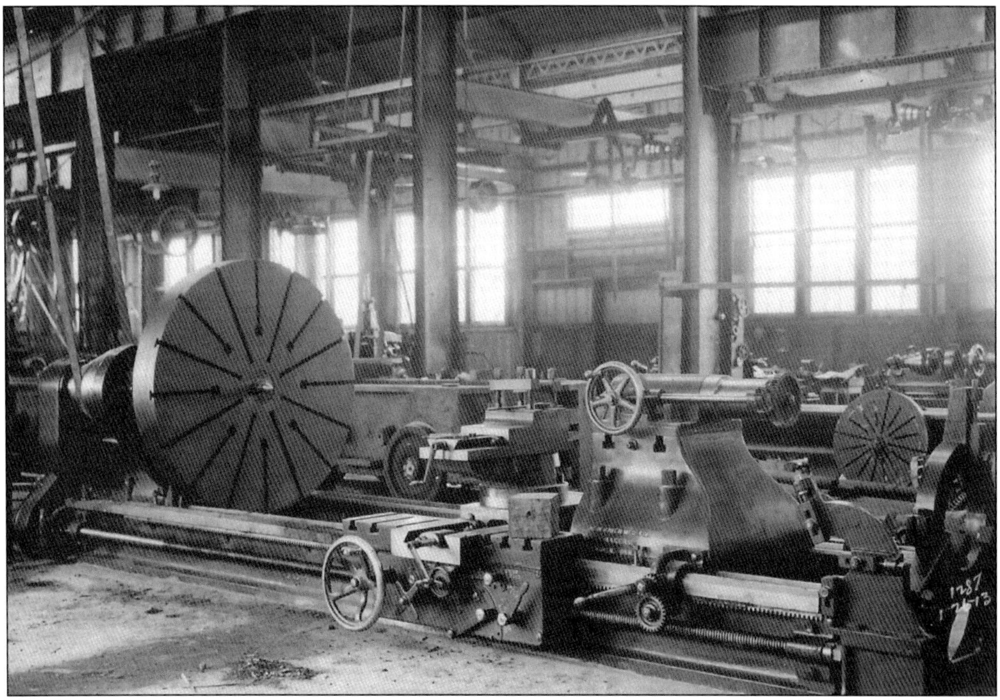

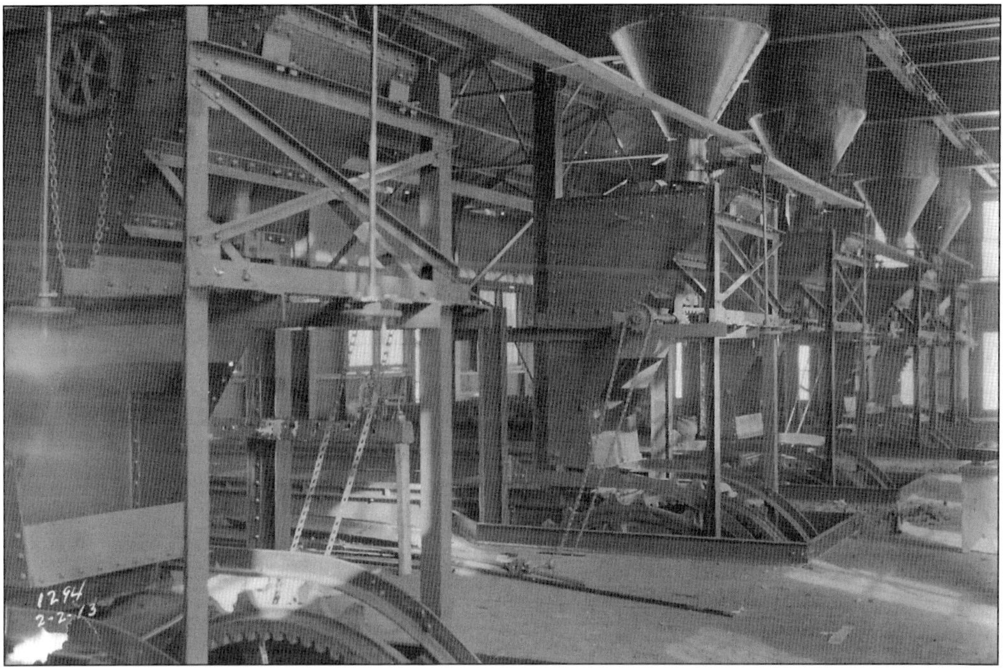

Flues like these portioned sinter, ores, fluxes, coke, and other materials by weight and deposited them in carts for transport to other on-site facilities such as the blast furnaces. The weight of these portions could be quite large; lead ingots shipped out at the end of the process, for example, weighed about four tons each. (Courtesy of the Tooele Valley Railroad Museum.)

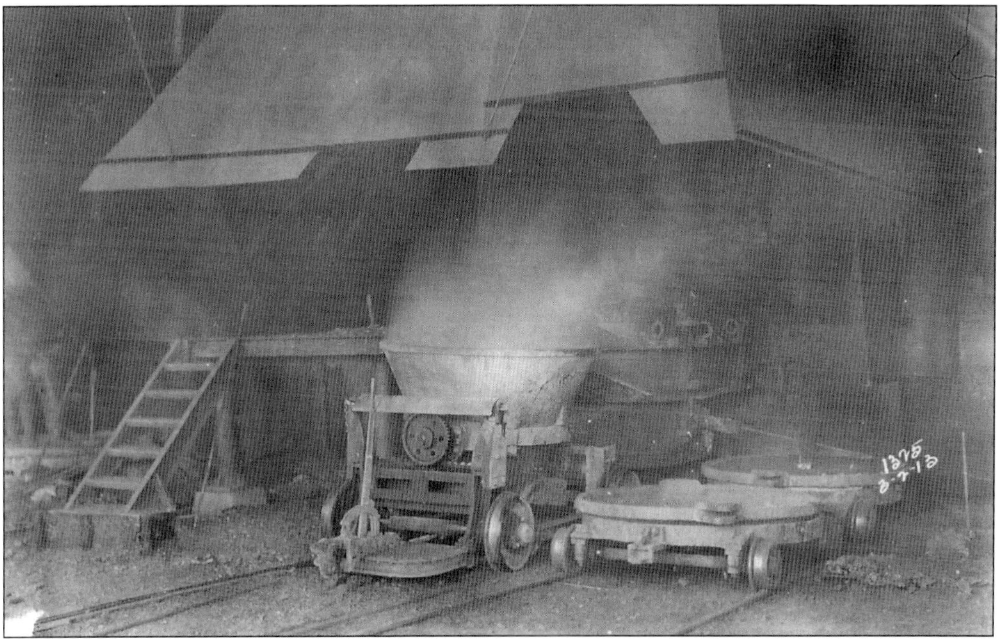

Within the smelter, carts like these collected slag in pots. International began dumping slag in 1910. Over the course of the next 60 years, this changed the face of the canyon. Later, in 1941, International constructed a slag treatment plant to extract lead and zinc that earlier workers discarded with the slag as waste product. (Courtesy of the Tooele Valley Railroad Museum.)

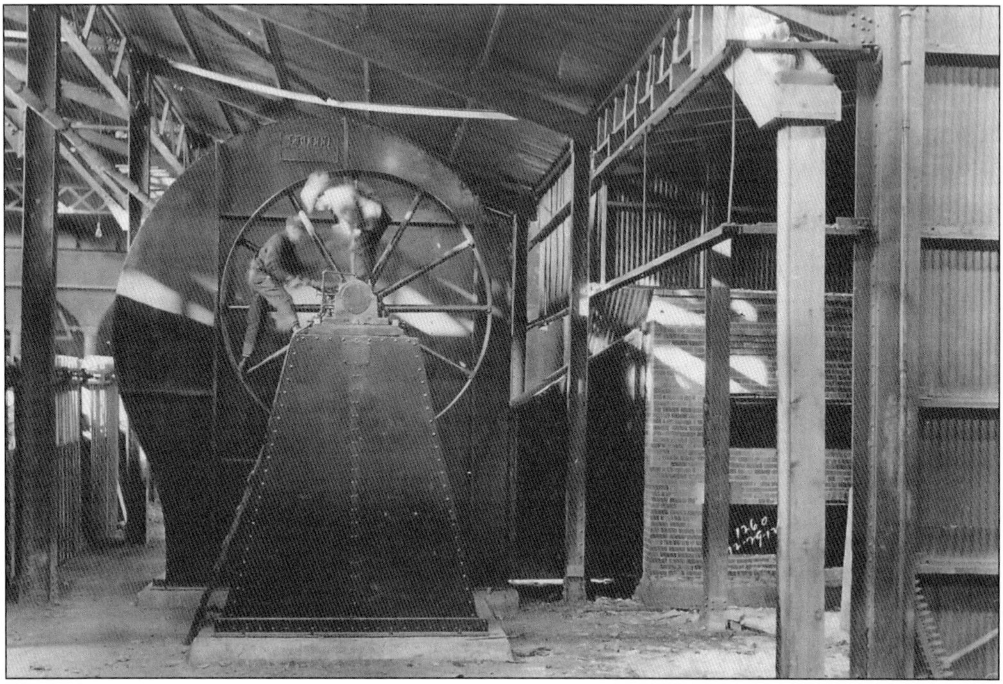

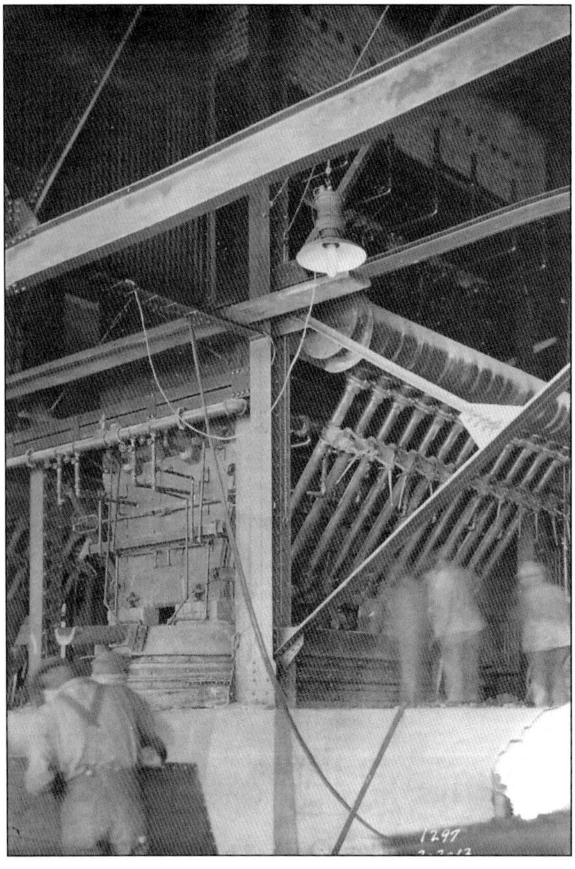

Above, International employees inspect a turbine in 1912, a year after the smelter's completion. The smelter provided work for hundreds, employing as many as 600 men during the construction phases. Many of these left Tooele when construction work ended, but the smelter and the industries it supported doubled the town's population. (Courtesy of the Tooele Valley Railroad Museum.)

Men monitor metal production in 1913, a few years after the smelter's completion. The numerous pipes feed tuyeres, nozzles that continuously inject air into a blast furnace. International produced compressed air, as well as AC and DC power, at its own on-site power plant. (Courtesy of the Tooele Valley Railroad Museum.)

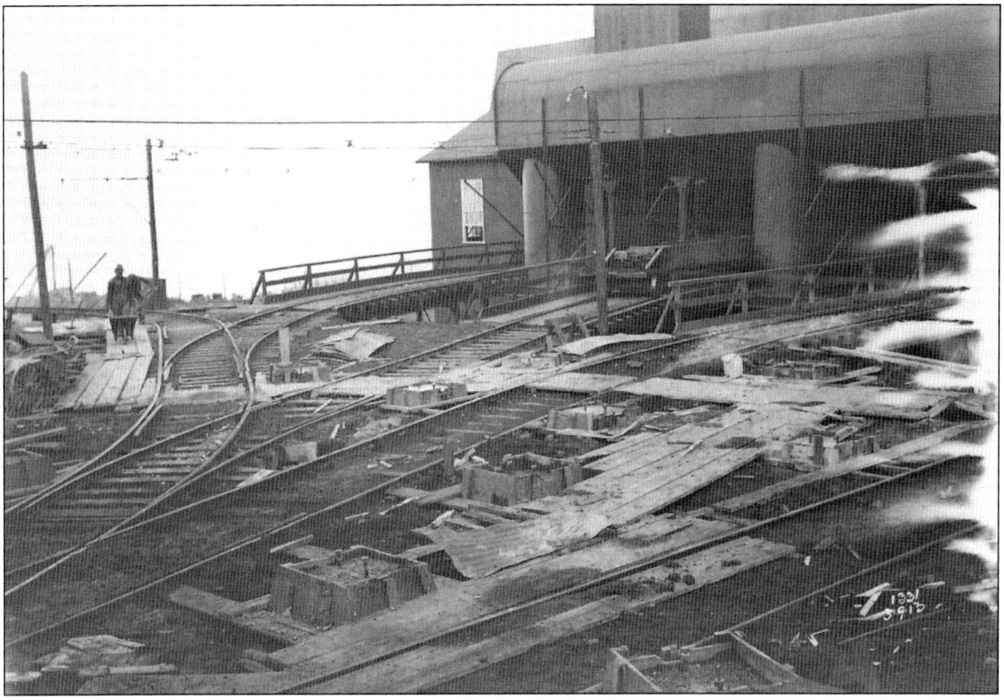

The rail yard at International Smelting not only directed shipments of ore to the proper smelting departments, it also served as the Tooele Valley Railroad's main rail yard. For many years, cars and engines not currently in use were stored at the smelter. A portion of the rail yard is seen here in 1913. (Courtesy of the Tooele Valley Railroad Museum.)

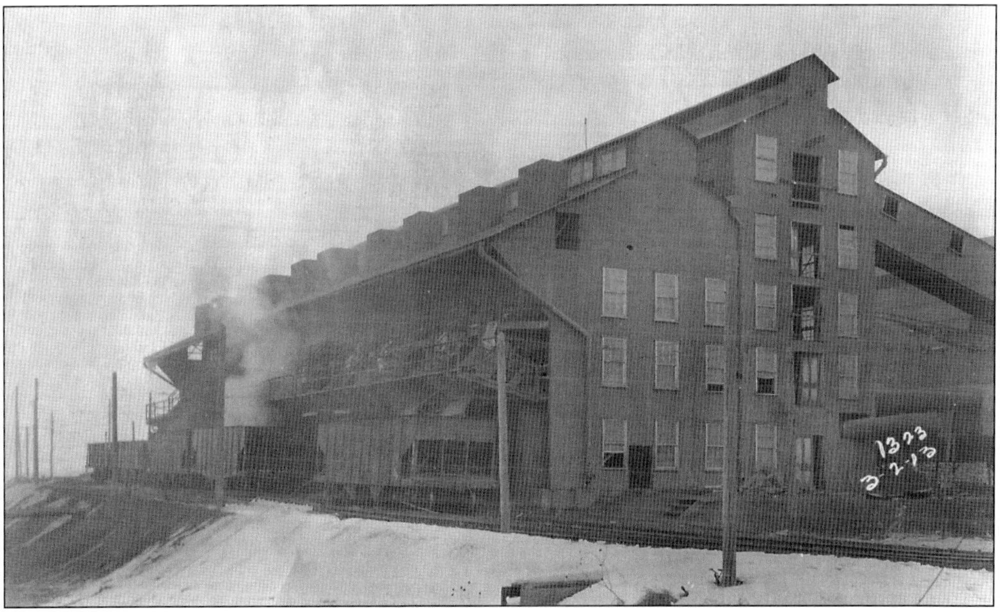

Railcars not only delivered ore to the International smelter, but also conveyed it from one building to the next. Here, cars received unfinished metals from the sintering plant, where 10 sintering machines roasted ores to remove excess sulfur. Upon leaving the sintering plant, the cars conveyed the unfinished metal to the blast furnace. (Courtesy of the Tooele Valley Railroad Museum.)

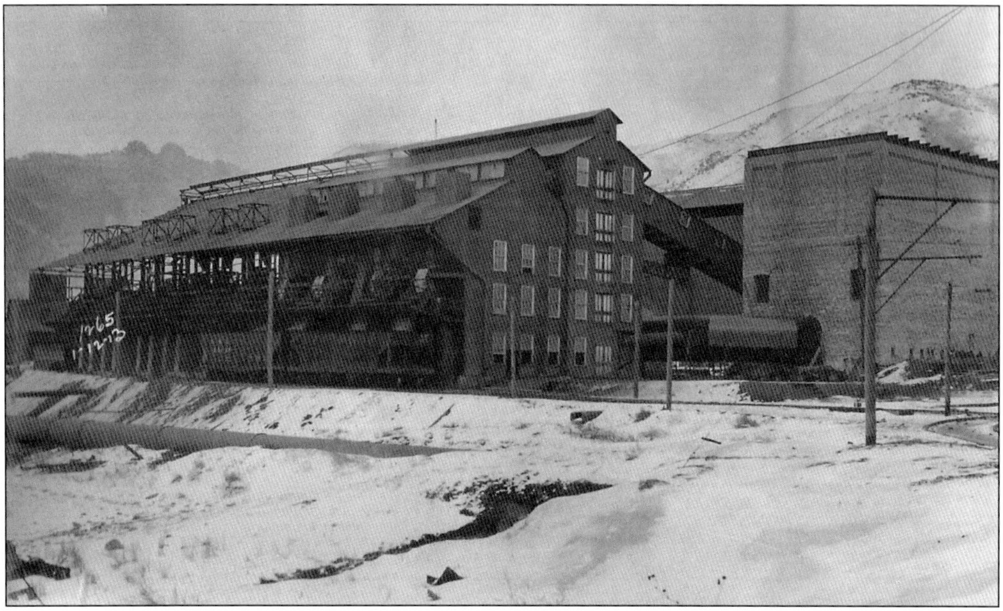

Railroad cars arrive at the unfinished International smelter sintering plant. The smelter was slated to open for operation in May 1910. The first ore arrived at the smelter in July, and the first copper metal was finished in August, though the addition of an unplanned lead smelting division extended construction through 1911. (Courtesy of the Tooele Valley Railroad Museum.)

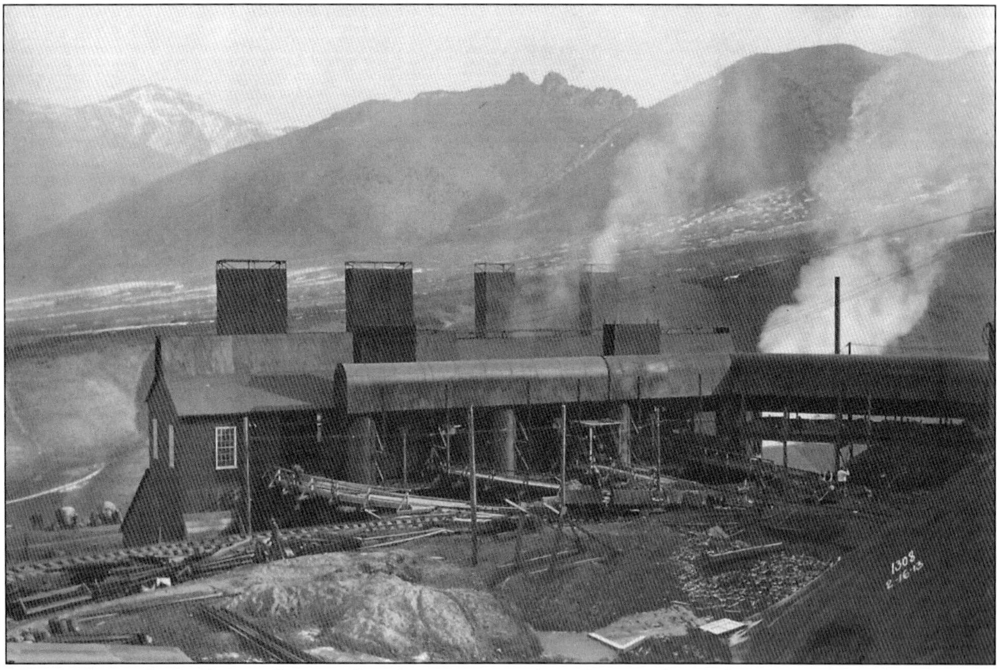

This is a view from the newly completed International smelter in the early 1900s, facing north, with snowcapped Nelson Peak in the background. The smelter occupied a 200-acre site at the mouth of Pine Canyon, and the original plans called for storage facilities, a sampling mill, reverberatory furnaces, converters, an independent power plant, and numerous other structures. (Courtesy of the Tooele Valley Railroad Museum.)

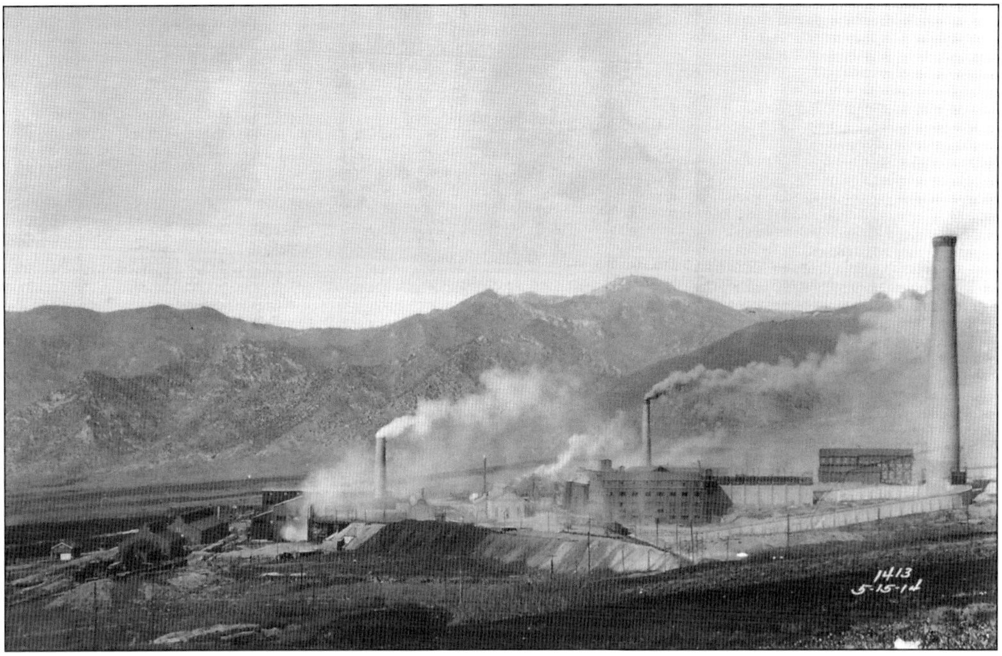

The International smelter was in full production during the summer of 1914. Smoke and fumes from the smelter were no less a nuisance in Tooele than in Salt Lake City. Locals referred to the smelter as Old Smoky because of the smog that would gather at Pine Canyon each morning. Years later, the mysterious death of several horses was linked to the pollution. (Courtesy of the Tooele Valley Railroad Museum.)

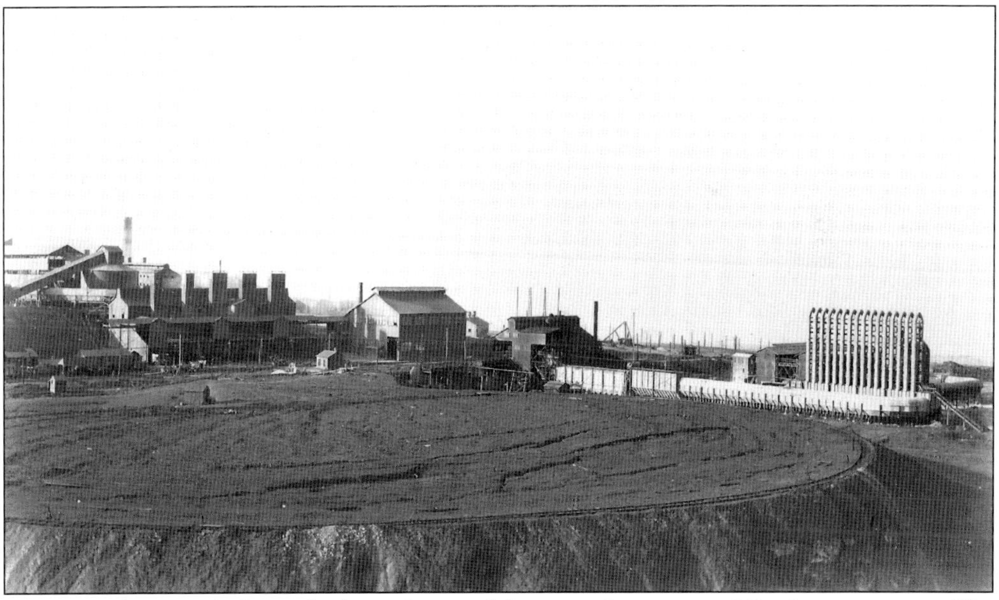

This 1971 photograph shows the future layout of the entire International Smelting operation. The original copper plant is off to the left, with facilities for processing lead and zinc at center. Though International did not anticipate lead and zinc production when the company first incorporated in the early 1900s, they later became the smelter's primary products. (Courtesy of the Tooele Valley Railroad Museum.)

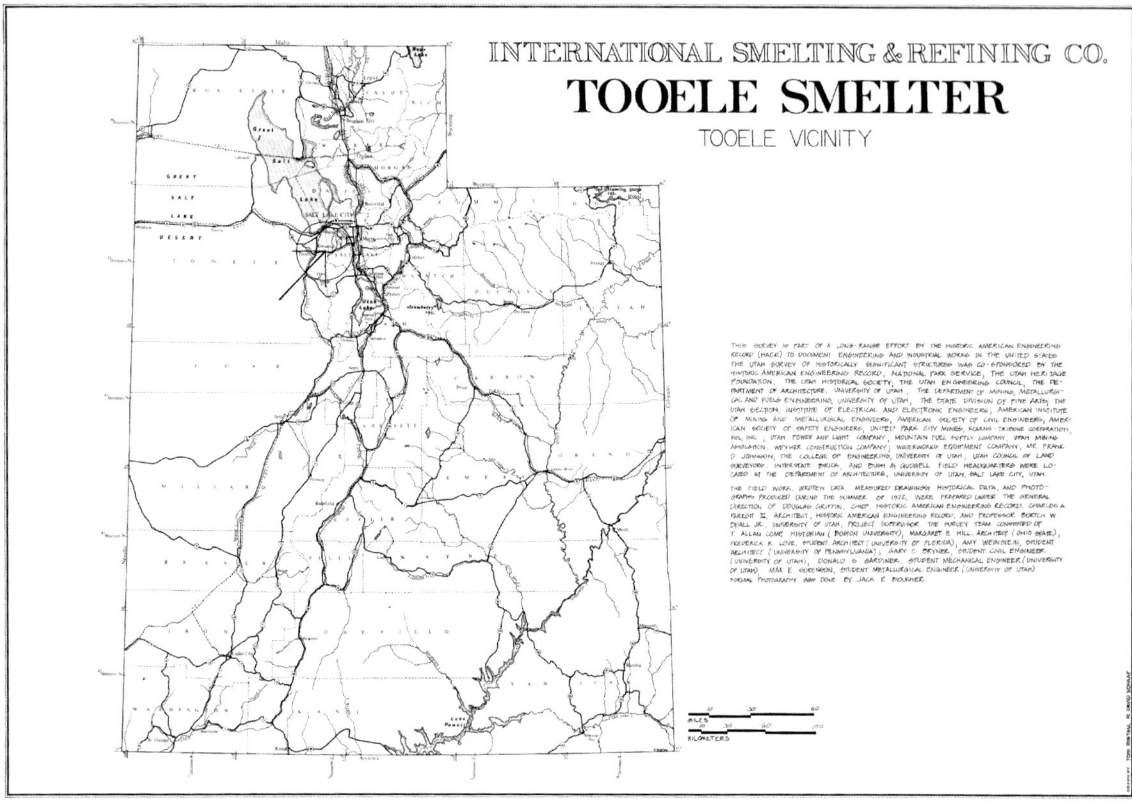

This map shows the International smelter's location in the state of Utah. (Courtesy of the Library of Congress.)

This unidentified International Smelting building is possibly the company's power plant, with a brick smokestack in the background. The smelter had several brick stacks, the largest of which was 350 feet tall and 25 feet in diameter. Construction crews finished the Big Stack, as it was called, on February 27, 1910. (Courtesy of the Tooele Valley Railroad Museum.)

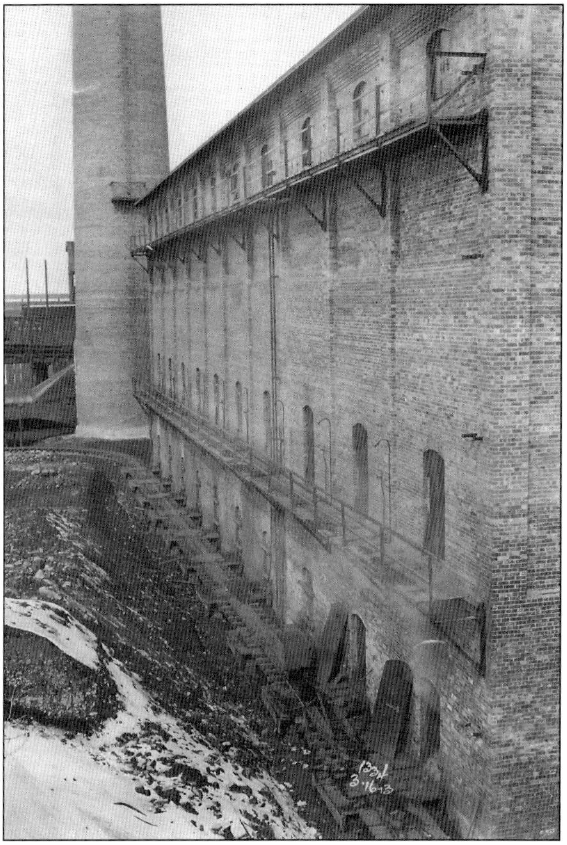

An unfinished brick structure at the smelter site is seen below, with frames for additional buildings in the background and unused bricks in the foreground. Few on-site structures were built of brick, but International purchased them by the millions. The main stack alone required more than 1.75 million individual bricks. (Courtesy of the Tooele Valley Railroad Museum.)

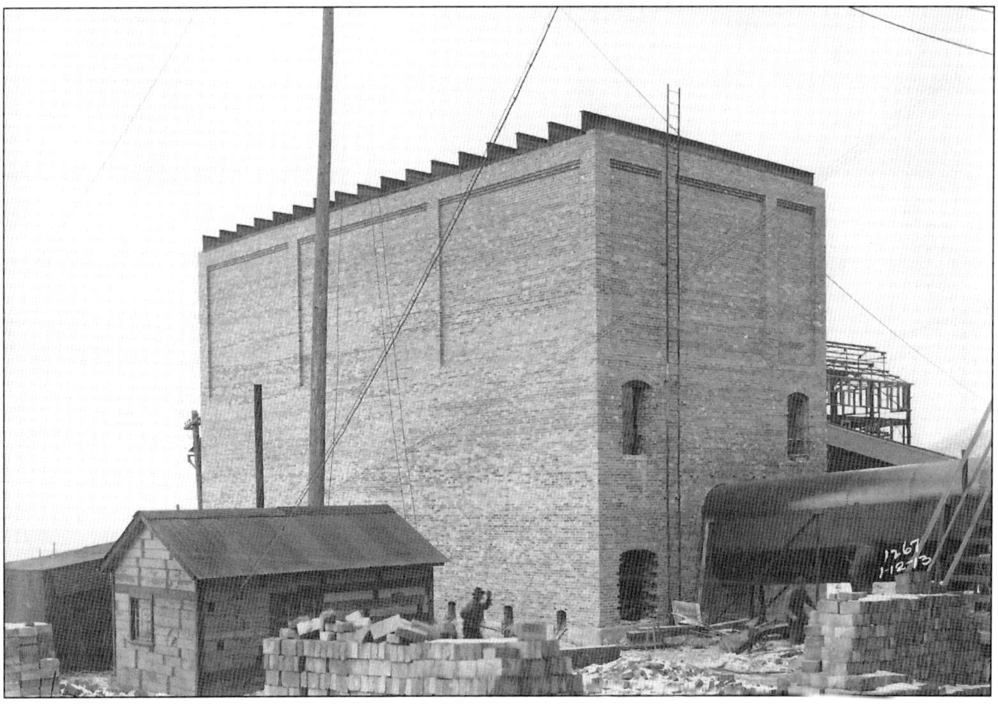

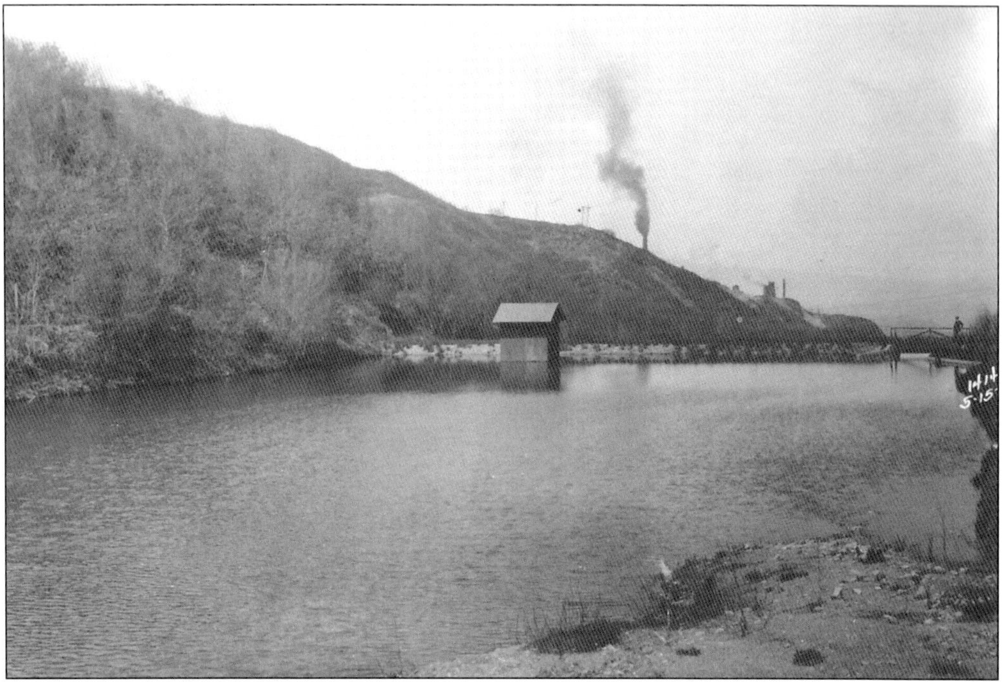

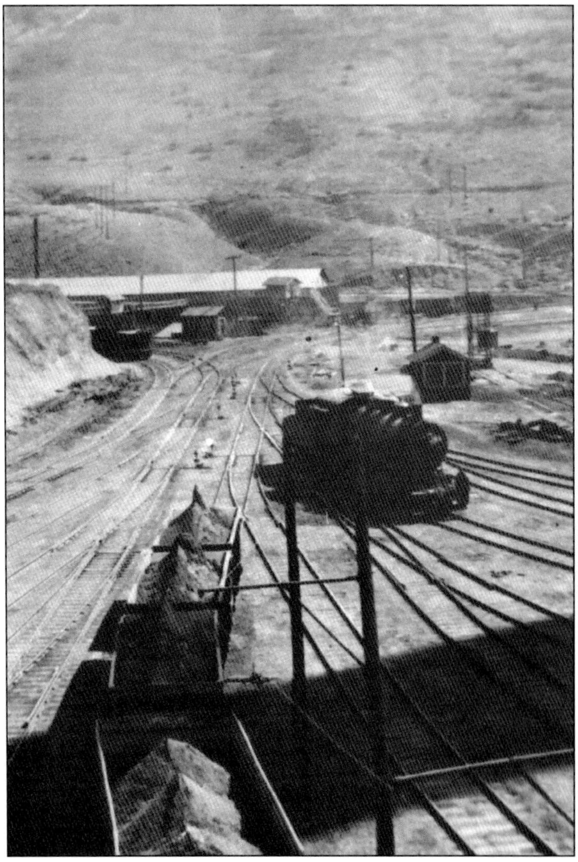

This dam, seen here in the early 1900s, provided International's water supply. Smoke from the newly operational smelter is clearly visible in the background. The dam no longer exists. Today, most runoff is captured before it reaches the reservoir. (Courtesy of the Tooele Valley Railroad Museum.)

Ore arrives at the International smelter's rail yard. The railroad brought carloads of ore from mines in Utah, Idaho, and Nevada on a daily basis during the smelter's heyday, but ore could arrive at the smelter via other means as well. (Courtesy of the Tooele Valley Railroad Museum.)

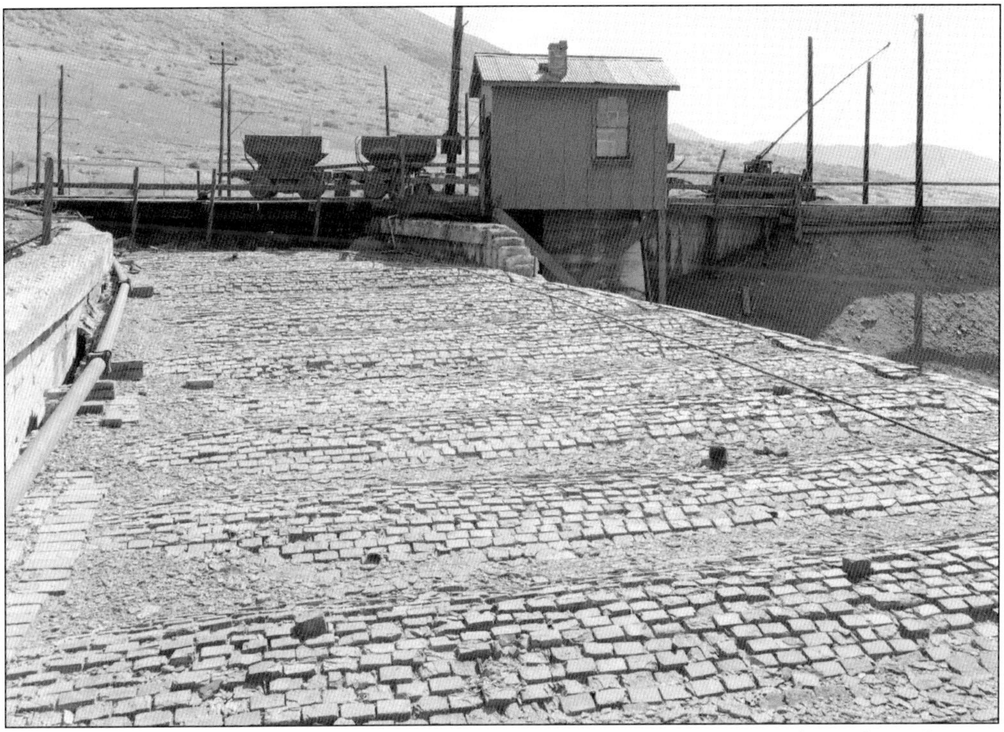

Trenton Iron Works constructed a 20,000-foot aerial tram that connected Bingham Canyon mines with the smelter in Tooele. Large buckets delivered the ore, several hundred pounds at a time. Each bucket was spaced 200 feet from the next and traveled at a rate of 600 feet per minute. Later, ore also arrived at the smelter through various tunnels dug through the Oquirrh Mountains to meet and drain mine shafts. (Both courtesy of the Library of Congress.)

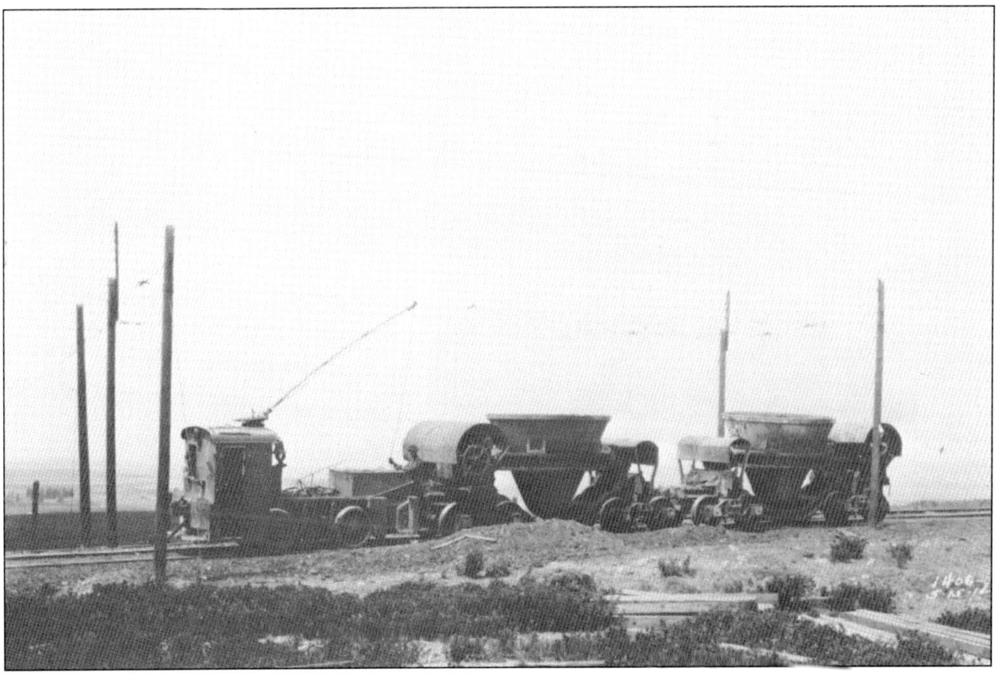

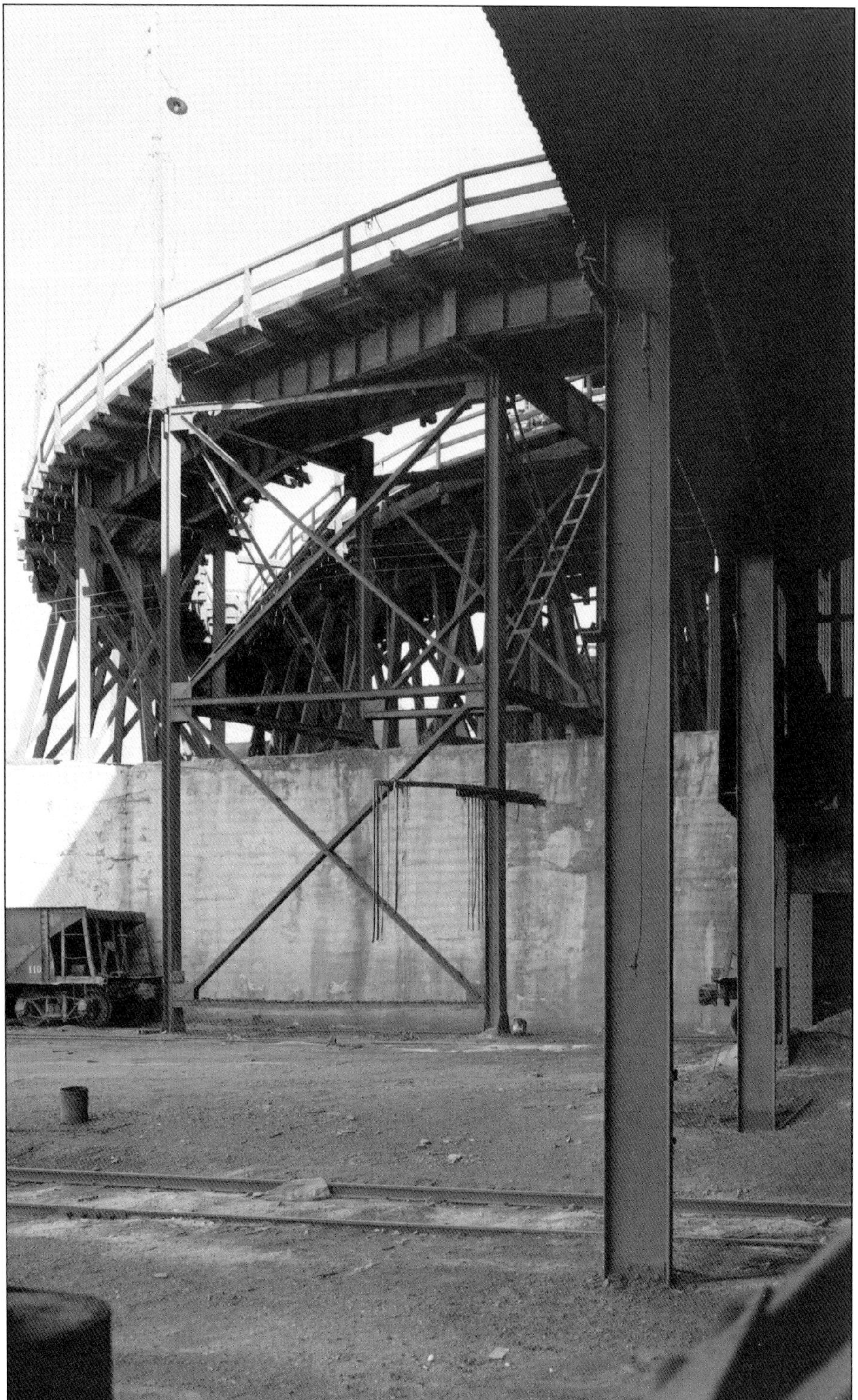

The elevated tracks at the International smelter are seen here in 1972. (Library of Congress.)

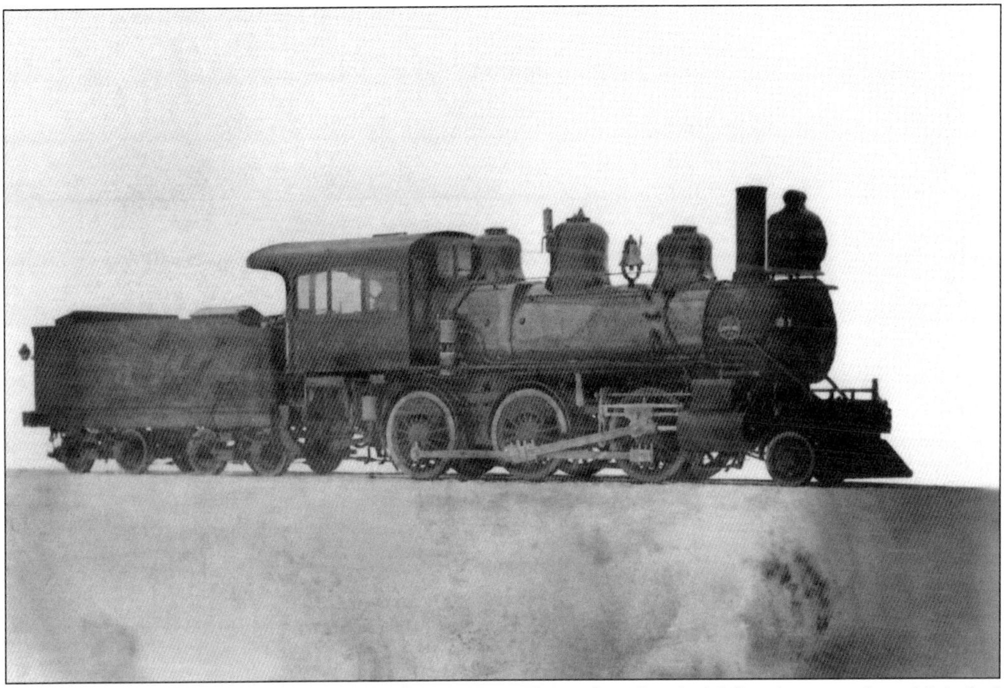

This early photograph of an unmarked engine working the Tooele Valley line was hand-labeled "Tooele Valley Railroad Engine No. 2." It is not one of the four well-known steam engines the railroad company used extensively until the 1950s. However, it is possible that this engine No. 2 may have predated those four, the first of which was purchased by the company in 1912. (Courtesy of the Tooele Valley Railroad Museum.)

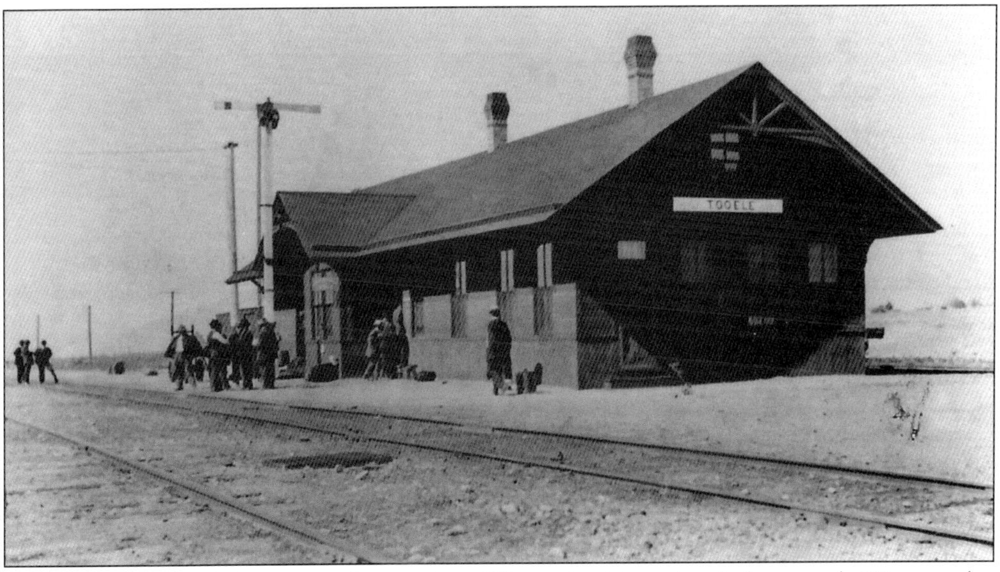

Passengers mingle while waiting for a train at Warner in this undated photograph. Warner, also called the Tooele station, marked the western end of the Tooele Valley Railroad's line. The railroad met lines from the Union Pacific, the Rio Grande, and the Western Pacific here. Until the 1940s, Tooele residents could take passenger trains to Salt Lake City from this station. (Courtesy of the Tooele Valley Railroad Museum.)

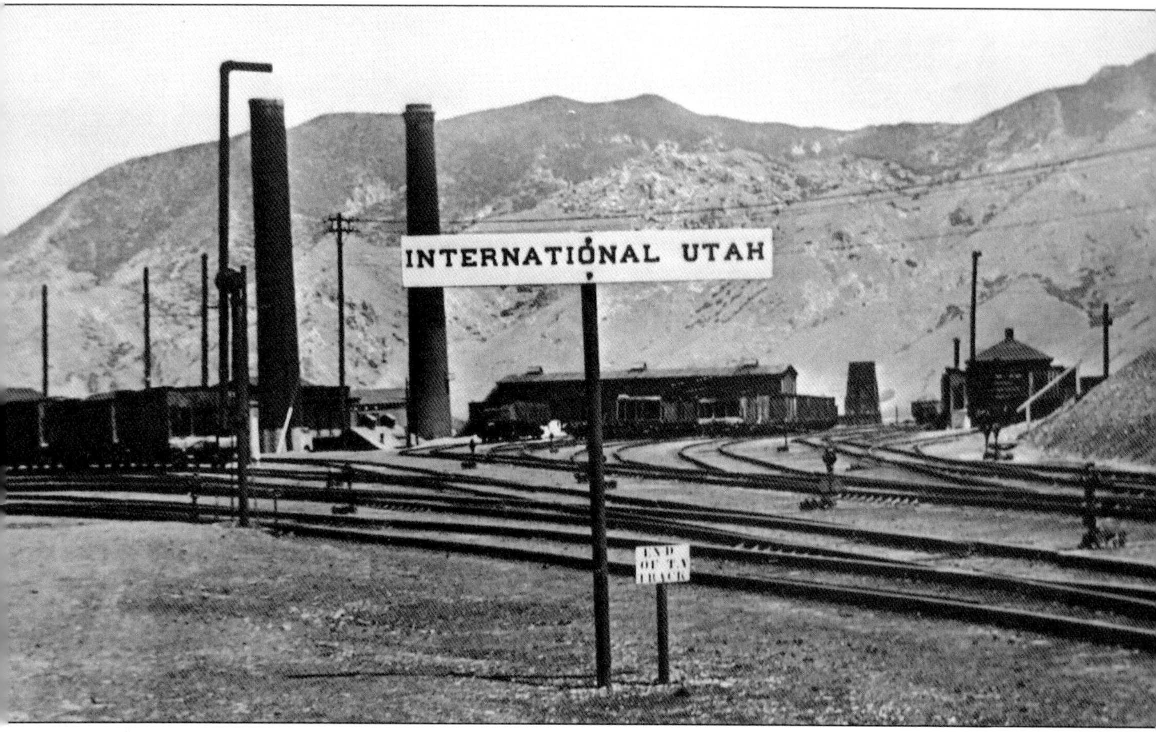

This sign greeted passengers and freight alike when they first arrived at the smelter via the Tooele Valley Railroad. International built its smelter outside Tooele city limits. In fact, the closest town was a tiny settlement called Lincoln. International solved this problem of location by referring to the smelter as though it were a city unto itself. (Courtesy of the Tooele Valley Railroad Museum.)

Two

Boon and Boom Times 1911–1928

After two years of unprecedented growth, bad fortune returned to this newly reinvented smelter town. Toward the end of 1910, ore supplies from the Bingham Canyon copper mines dropped off unexpectedly. International began to pursue independent operations after months of running below capacity and, on March 1, 1911, announced a $500,000 expansion of the Pine Canyon smelter that would allow it to process both copper and lead. However, this expansion was not expected to dramatically increase the number of individuals employed by International.

The railroad, likewise, failed to live up to the community's expectations. In early 1911, a small issue arose between city government and the Tooele Valley Railway's managers. City leaders had expected that the railroad would be electrified after the first few years of operation. Executives from the railroad, International, and Utah Consolidated, on the other hand, saw no reason to transition away from steam power. As the dispute came to an ugly head, E.P. Mathewson threatened to have the railroad tracks removed and the railway rerouted around Tooele if city government would not permit the railroad to operate steam engines.

Despite these setbacks, competitors took note of International's early success, particularly as it began to attract independent smelting contracts from mines beyond the Oquirrhs. Agents from Anaconda Copper, which had recently acquired the American smelter in Salt lake City, spread rumors of a possible buyout in local newspapers. "A move in a bigger game than the world appreciates is on," the *Tooele Times* cautioned.

But International would at last hit its pace as a custom smelter within the decade. The glory years of the 1920s saw International processing copper and lead ores from Bingham, Park City, Tintic, Bauer, and even Idaho. With success at the smelter came success on the railroad. As many as 85 to 90 railcars filled with ore could arrive on any given day. The Tooele Valley Railroad greeted these new arrivals at the Warner junction and then escorted them six miles east to International.

Passenger services also steadily increased in popularity. Tickets had originally cost 20¢ but later decreased to 5¢ per passenger. One fare could take individuals up to work at the smelter or out west to Warner, where an additional $1 could purchase passage to Salt Lake City on the Union Pacific. Tooele rode the roaring tide of the 1920s alongside the rest of the West.

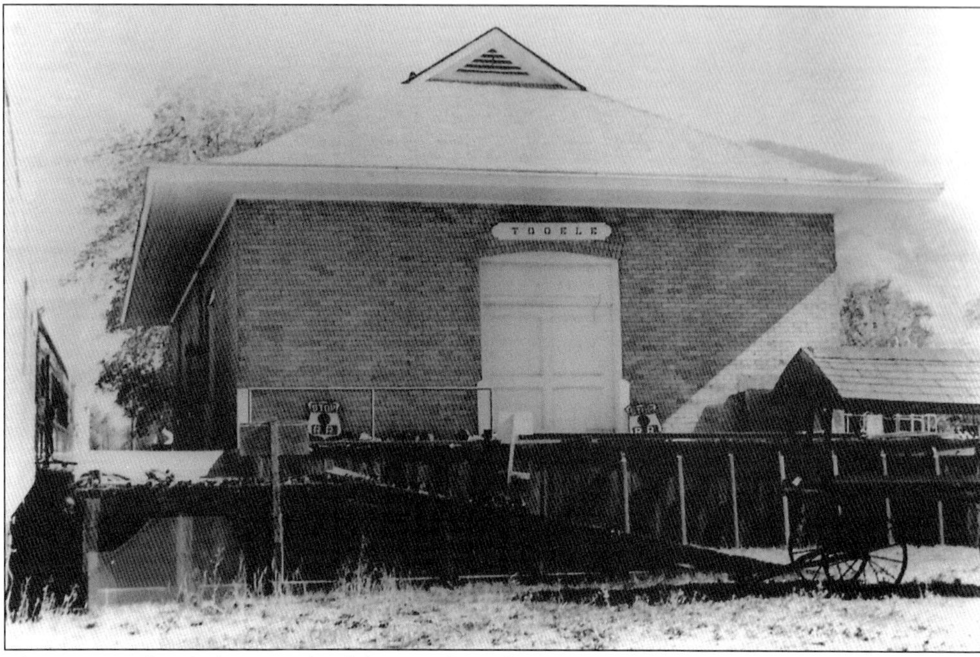

This is an undated photograph of the Tooele Valley Railroad depot at 35 North Broadway. This building functioned as the railroad's main passenger station and company headquarters. Passengers could depart from this station en route to either Salt Lake City, via the junction at Warner, or the International smelter. Freight shipped to Tooele City proper unloaded here. (Courtesy of the Tooele Valley Railroad Museum.)

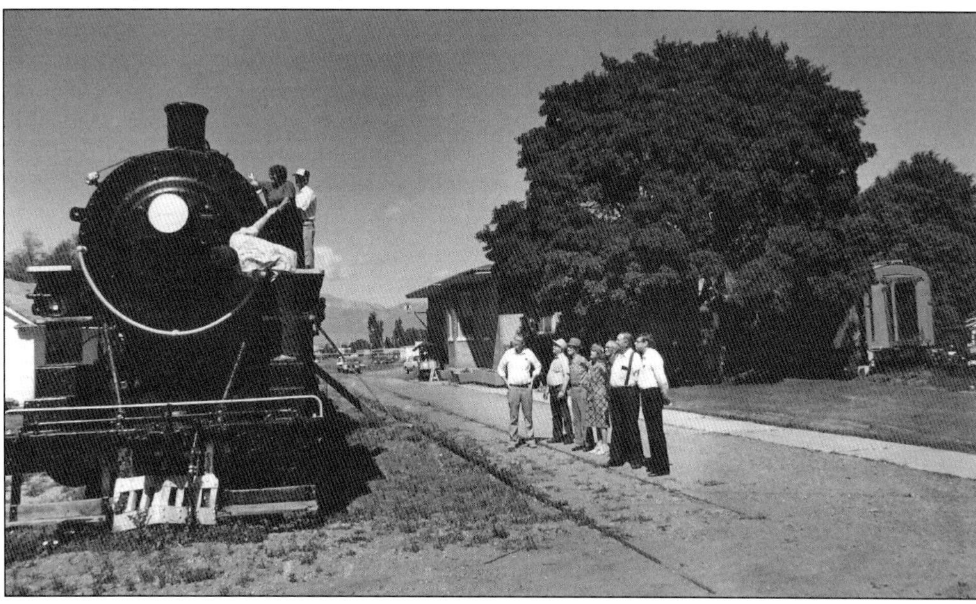

The Tooele Valley Railroad depot is seen here in its modern arrangement, with the engine out front and several freight and passenger cars parked behind the station. Historically, trains came around to a platform on the back side of the station to unload freight and passengers. The front side of the station, with the bay window, faces Vine Street. Broadway is on the right. (Courtesy of the Tooele Valley Railroad Museum.)

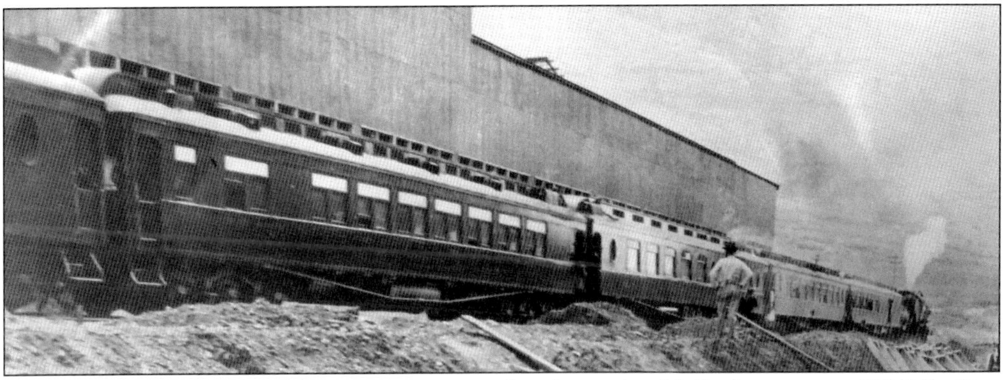

The Tooele Valley Railroad departs International with a carload full of tourists on Old Folks Day in 1910. Local residents were fond of community-wide celebrations like Old Folks Day, which celebrated Tooele's seniors. The railroad became a prominent part of the tradition, offering free outings on the holiday. In this case, seniors rode the train for a tour of the new International smelter. (Courtesy of the Tooele Valley Railroad Museum.)

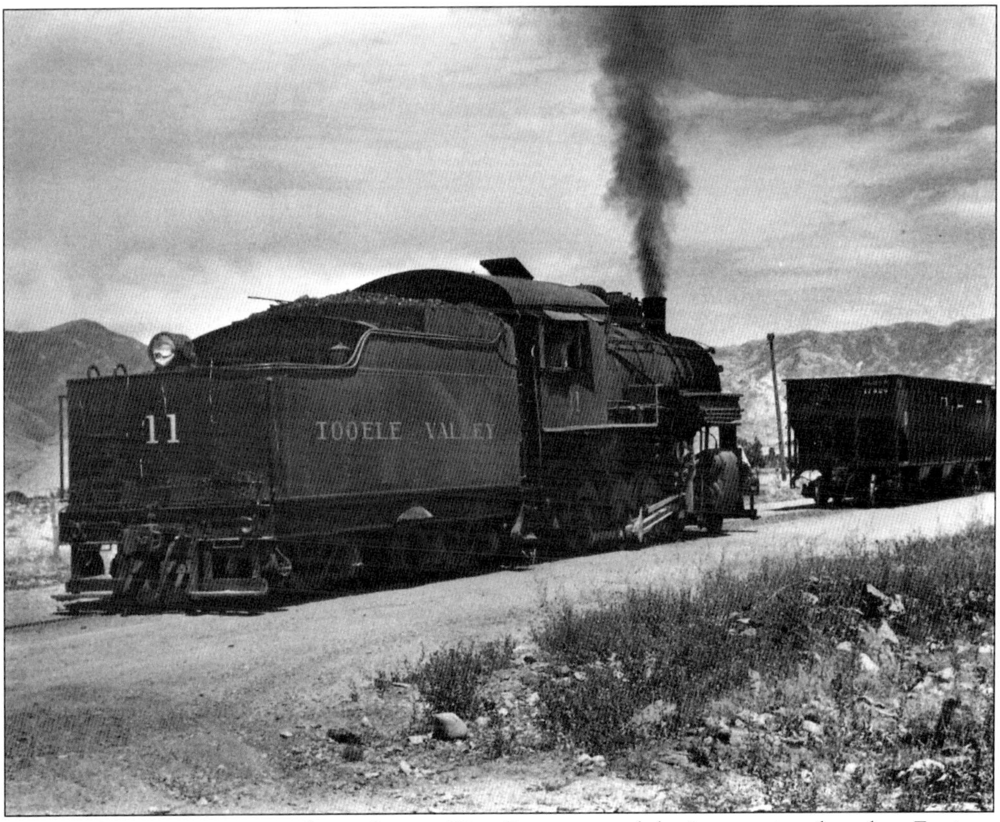

Engine No. 11 prepares to push a railcar up Vine Street toward the International smelter. Engines on the Tooele Valley Railroad almost always pushed loads up a relatively steep grade of about 2.4 percent, because company executives worried that cars could break loose if pulled up the hill. The right-of-way on Vine Street, a busy road that bisected the town, further concerned railroad administrators. (Courtesy of the Tooele Valley Railroad Museum.)

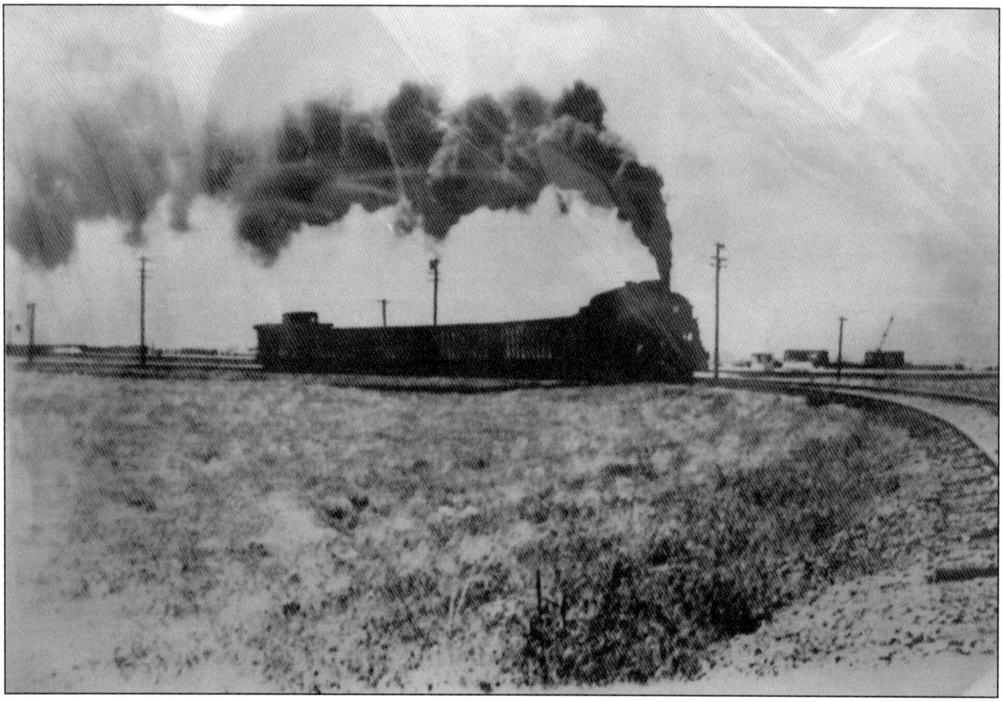

A full load approaches the International smelter, coming around the final bend, which locals referred to as the Big Curve. This tight corner not only caused a notorious racket every time a train passed, but also limited the size of the Tooele Valley's locomotives. (Courtesy of the Tooele Valley Railroad Museum.)

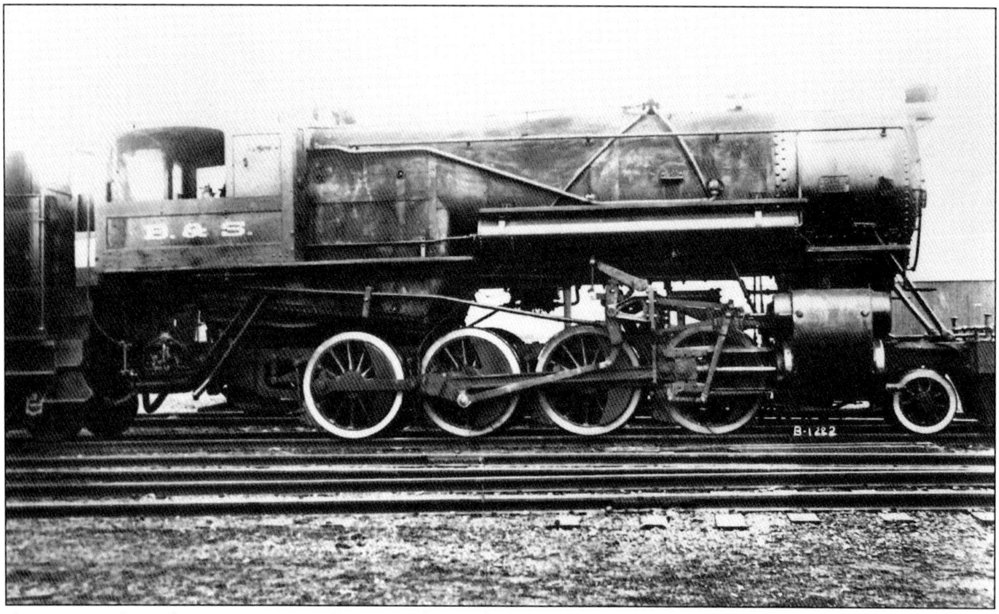

An unnumbered engine is seen here working the Tooele Valley line in the early 1900s, probably before the railroad purchased its own engines. The railroad later purchased two engines from the Buffalo & Susquehanna Railroad, but this does not appear to be either. (Courtesy of the Tooele Valley Railroad Museum.)

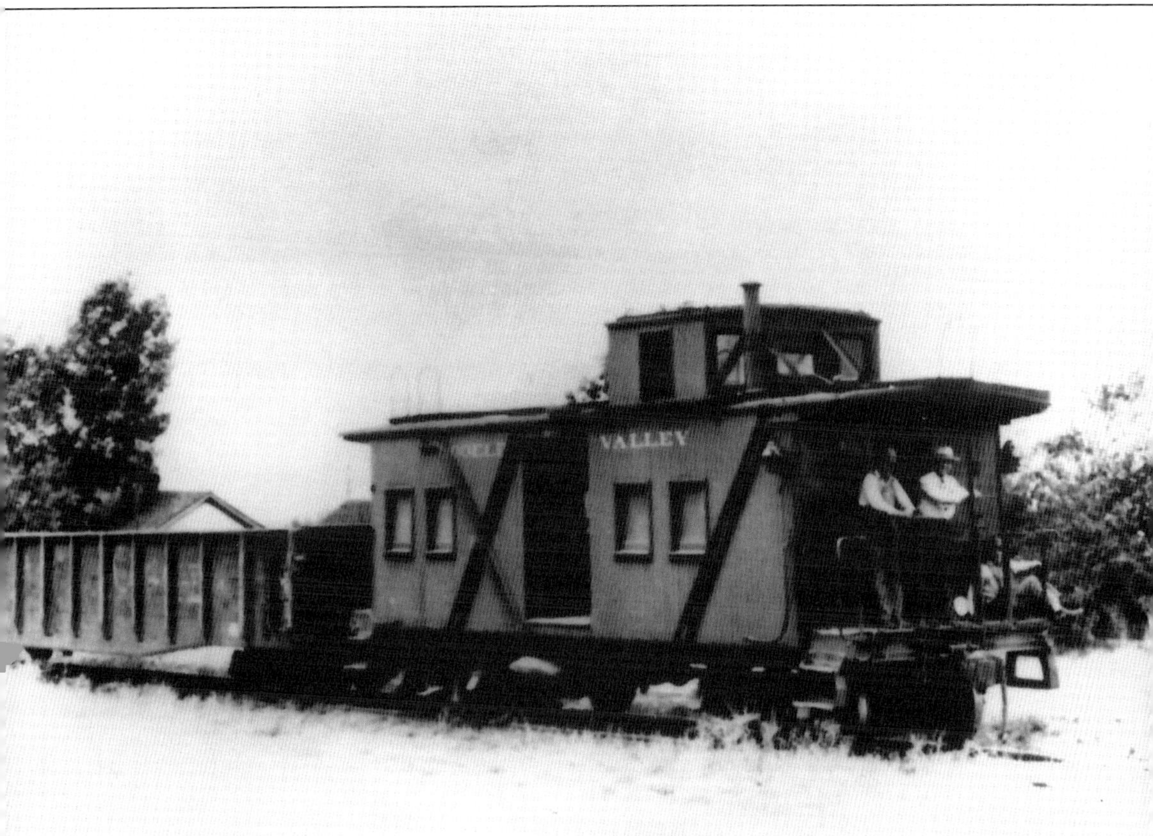

This early photograph shows one of the Tooele Valley's iconic cabooses. Because the caboose always preceded the train, Tooele Valley Railroad administrators had the caboose equipped with a horn and headlights. The railroad acquired this particular caboose, No. 3, on October 25, 1937, and it remained in the railroad's possession until the line closed in the 1980s. (Courtesy of the Tooele Valley Railroad Museum.)

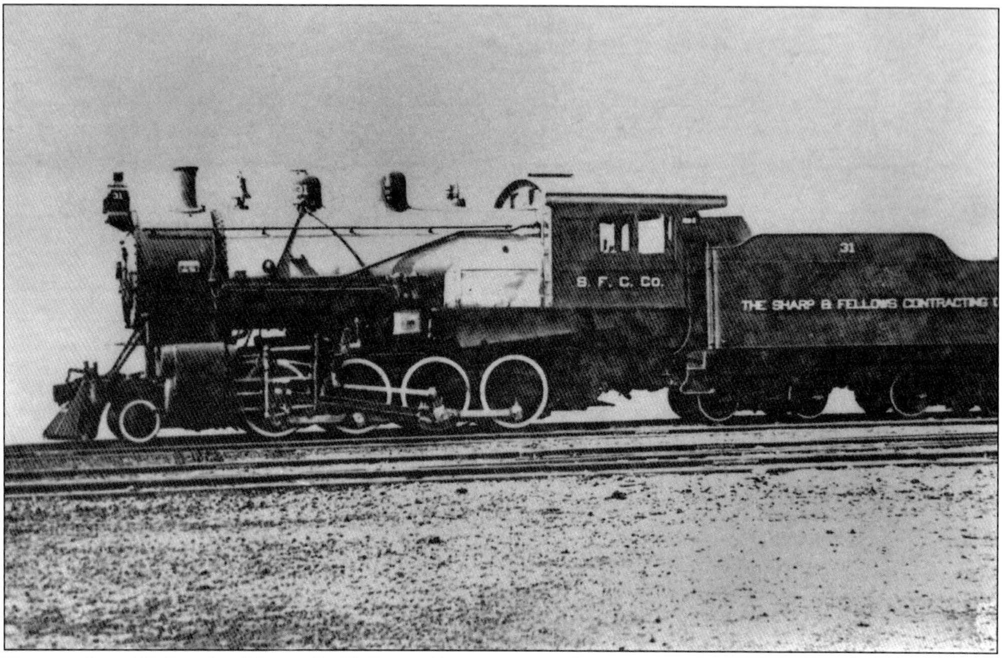

Engine No. 31 for the Sharp & Fellows Contracting Company is seen here while visiting the Tooele Valley Railroad. Most likely, the engine was leased from Sharp and Fellows while the Tooele line and the smelter were under construction. However, the photograph is undated, and the Tooele Valley was known to lease additional engines from time to time. (Courtesy of the Tooele Valley Railroad Museum.)

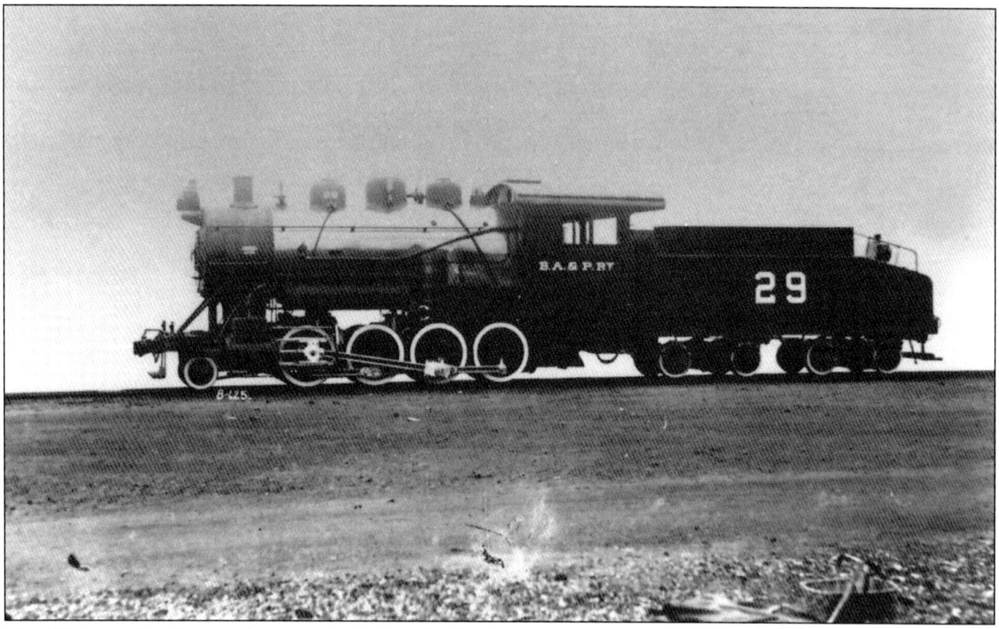

No. 29 from the Butte, Anaconda & Pacific Railway is seen here shortly after it arrived in Tooele. The Tooele Valley purchased the engine on November 18, 1925, and later renumbered it No. 9. It remained in Tooele until the railroad sold it for scrap in 1950. (Courtesy of the Tooele Valley Railroad Museum.)

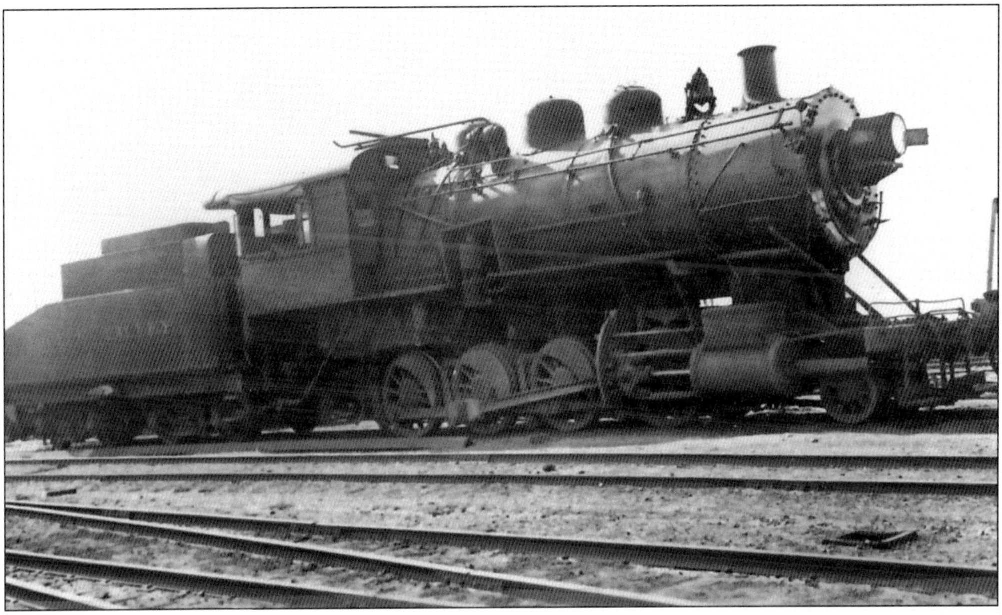

Tooele Valley engine No. 9 is seen here after its new paint job made it an official member of Tooele's railroad family. The slope-back tender on this engine and on No. 10 made for increased visibility while backing up. This made switching up at the smelter easier. (Courtesy of the Tooele Valley Railroad Museum.)

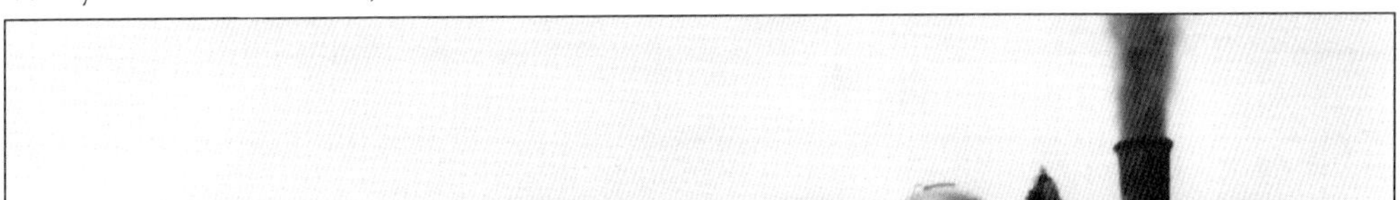

Another unmarked engine is seen here on the Tooele Valley line. It is unclear exactly what engines the Tooele Valley Railway owned prior to 1912. The railway also rented a number of engines after the boiler on engine No. 11 was condemned in 1963. The resulting delays prompted railroad administration to purchase a second diesel, engine No. 104. (Courtesy of the Tooele Valley Railroad Museum.)

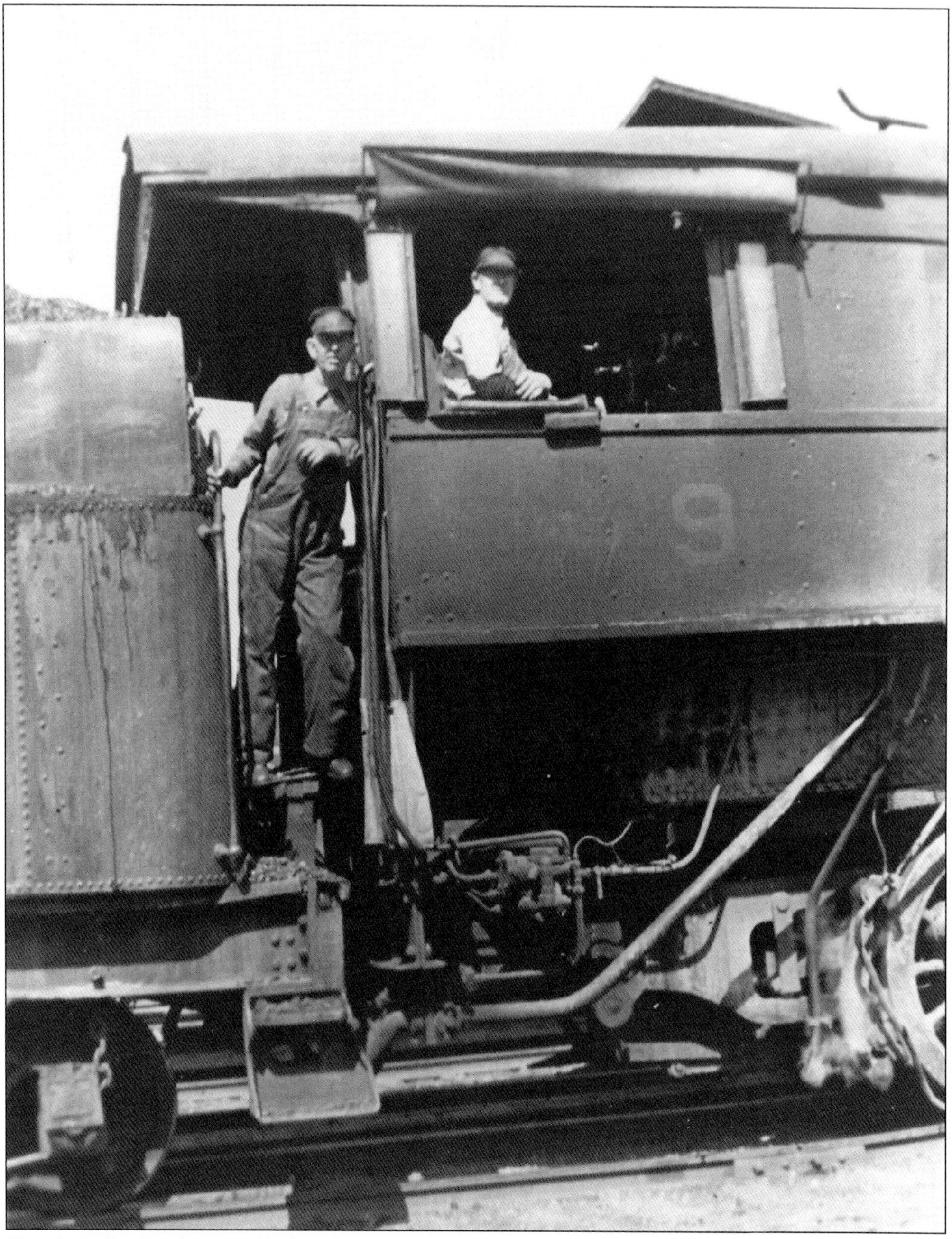

Tooele Valley Railway staff take a break from work to pose for this close-up photograph of engine No. 9. The American Locomotive Company built the No. 9 in 1910 as a 2-8-0 with 21-inch-by-28-inch cylinders, 52-inch drivers, and Stephenson valve gear. (Courtesy of the Tooele Valley Railroad Museum.)

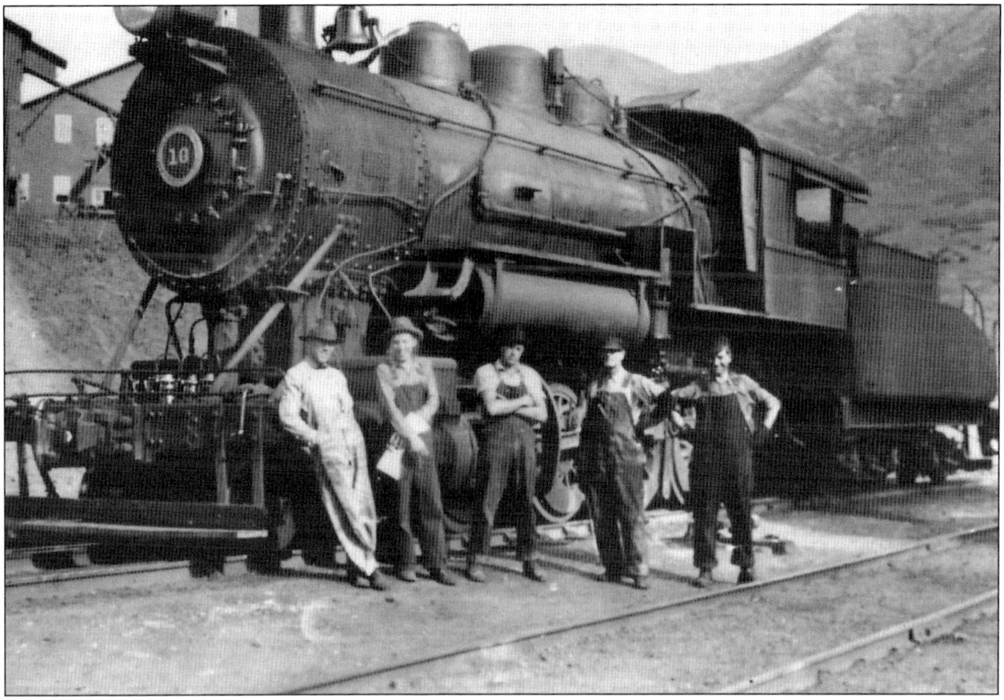

Men pose for a photograph in front of Tooele Valley Railway engine No. 10 near the International smelter. The No. 10, similar to the No. 9, was a 2-8-0 built in 1907 with 21-inch-by-28-inch cylinders, 52-inch drivers, and Stephenson valve gear. (Courtesy of the Tooele Valley Railroad Museum.)

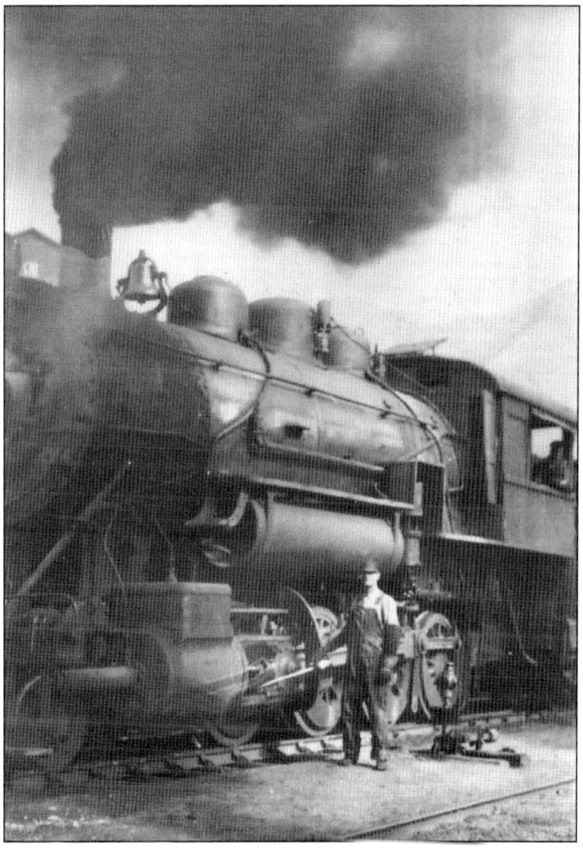

Engine No. 10 is seen here again near the International smelter. The Tooele Valley Railroad also acquired this engine from the Butte, Anaconda & Pacific Railway in April 1916. It remained in operation in Tooele until April 1955, when the railroad sold it for scrap. (Courtesy of the Tooele Valley Railroad Museum.)

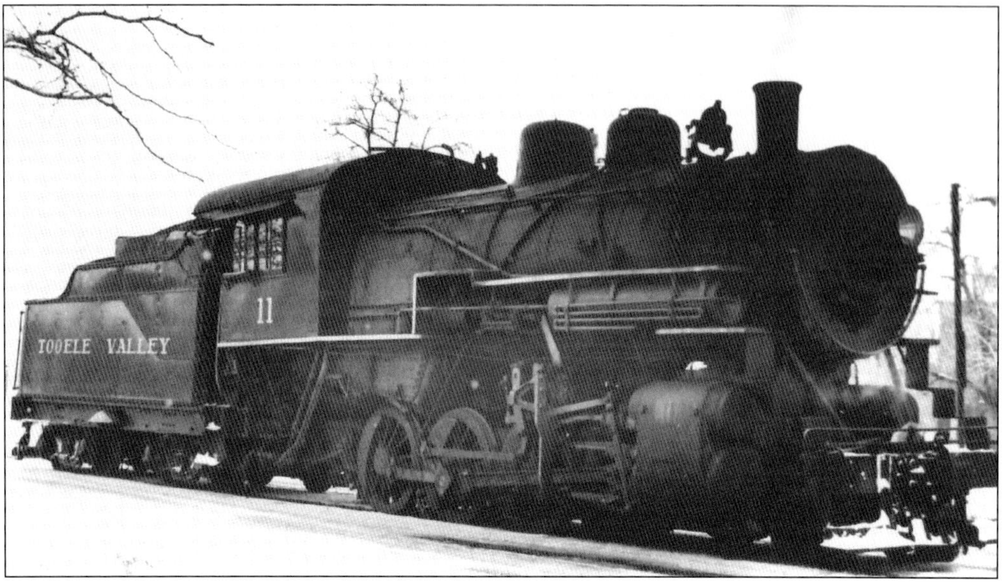

The Tooele Valley Railway's most famous engine was No. 11, which came to Tooele from New York in 1912 and continued operating in the valley until its final run in 1963. The railroad used this engine on a standby-only basis after 1955, but sporadic use until the early 1960s made this engine the final steam locomotive in common carrier service in Utah. (Courtesy of the Tooele Valley Railroad Museum.)

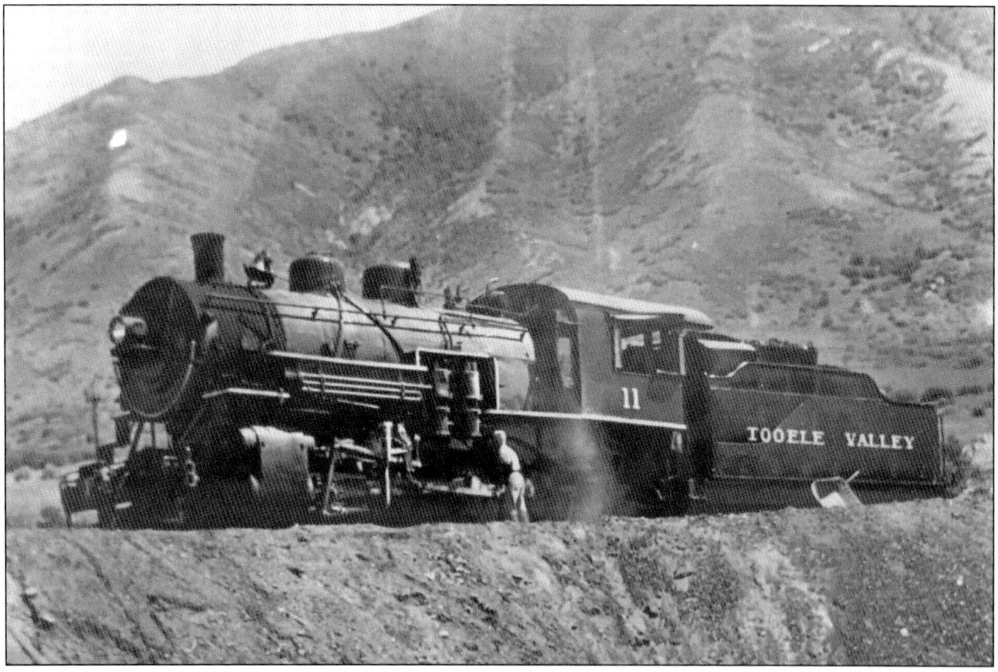

Engine No. 11 is seen here in Pine Canyon near the International smelter site. The American Locomotive Company built this engine in April 1910 for the Buffalo & Susquehanna Railroad. It proved more popular with the Tooele Valley Railway than engines No. 9 and No. 10 because the builder had outfitted it with more efficient Walscharets valve gear. (Courtesy of the Tooele Valley Railroad Museum.)

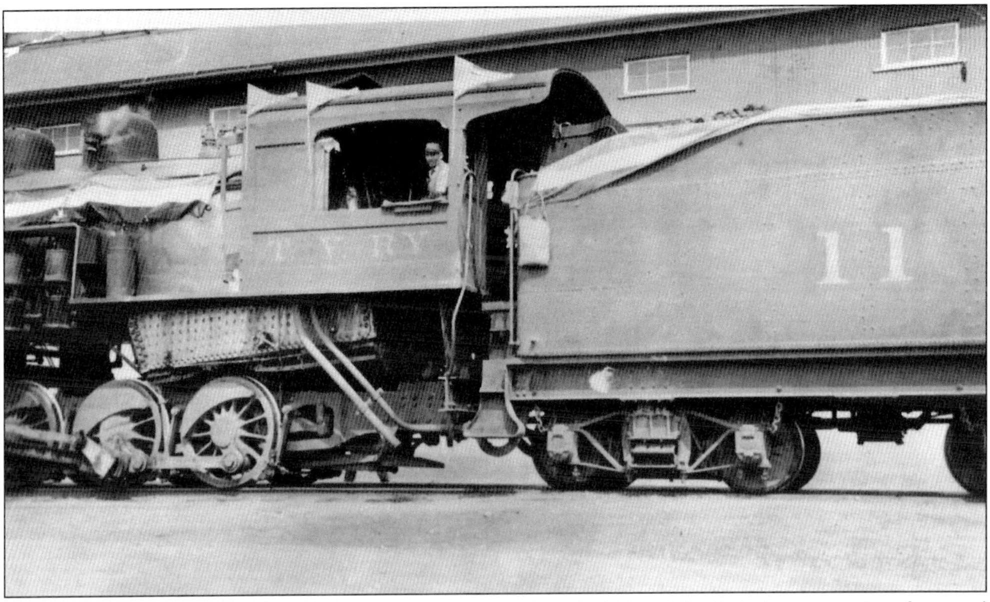

This close-up of engine No. 11 shows it dressed up for a holiday. The 2-8-0 type engine featured 21-inch-by-28-inch cylinders and 51-inch drivers. When new, the engine was known to push six or even seven loaded cars up the railroad's steep grade on its own, though that number dwindled to four in later years. (Courtesy of the Tooele Valley Railroad Museum.)

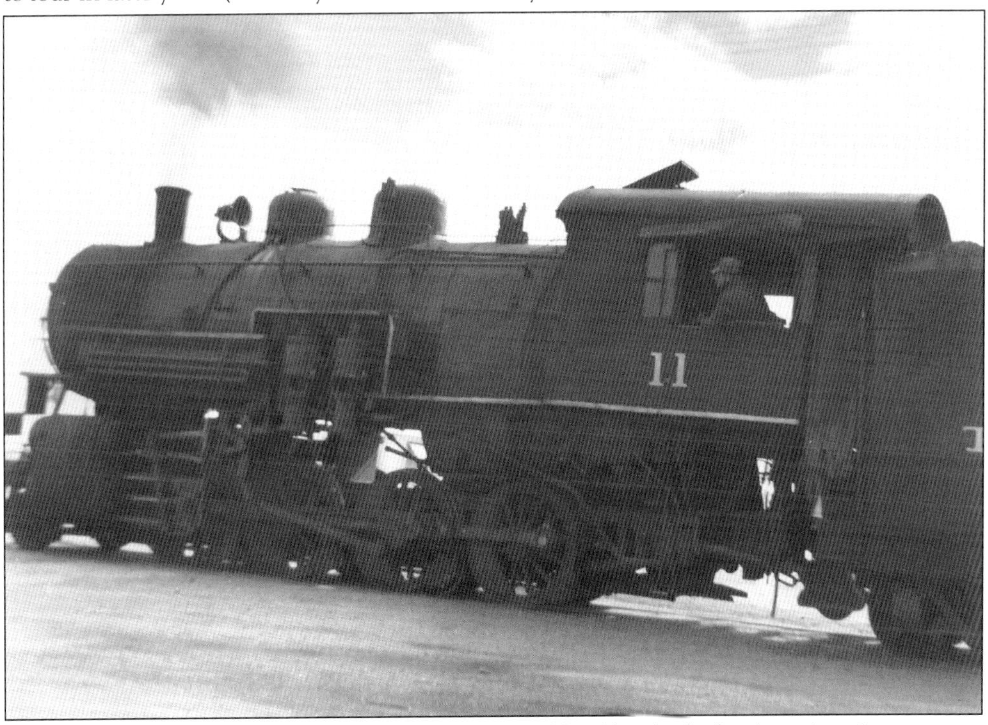

The No. 11 was nearly identical to its sister engine, No. 12, which the American Locomotive Company also built for the Buffalo & Susquehanna Railroad in 1910. Engine No. 11 remained in service longer than its sibling, but the No. 12 was the railroad's favorite. It was said that the engine rode smoother than the No. 11. (Courtesy of the Tooele Valley Railroad Museum.)

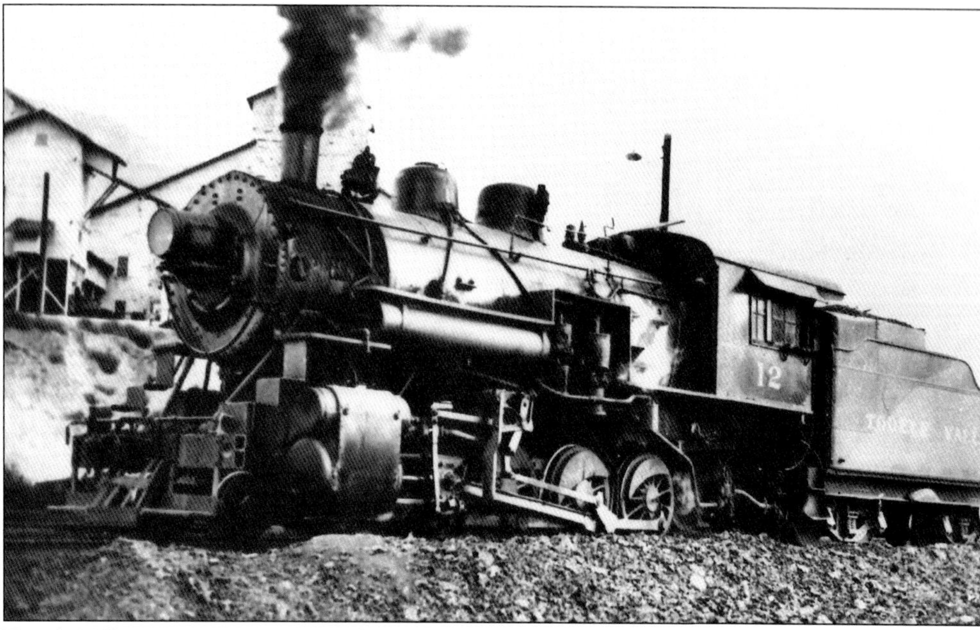

Tooele Valley engine No. 12 is seen here near the International smelter. The engine was purchased alongside its sibling in April 1910 and remained on the roster through May 1956, a year after the railroad scrapped its other steam engines in favor of diesels. (Courtesy of the Tooele Valley Railroad Museum.)

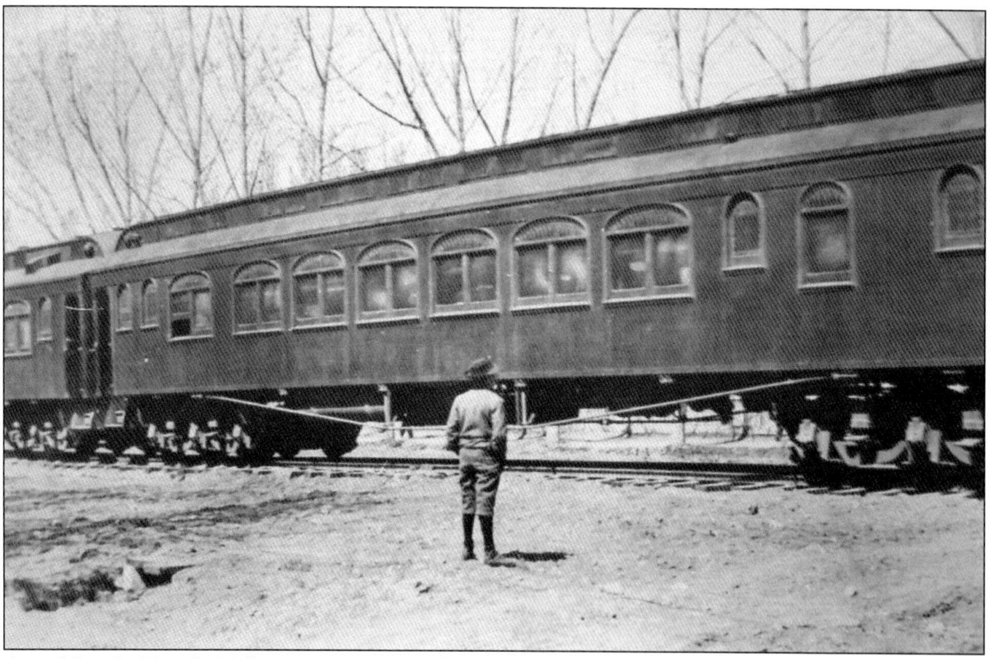

An old-style Tooele Valley passenger coach is seen here passing through the more rural side of town on the west side of Main Street. Passenger coaches like these remained in service on the railroad until company officials acquired new coaches in the 1940s, around the same time the railroad restricted passenger services to International employees. (Courtesy of the Tooele Valley Railroad Museum.)

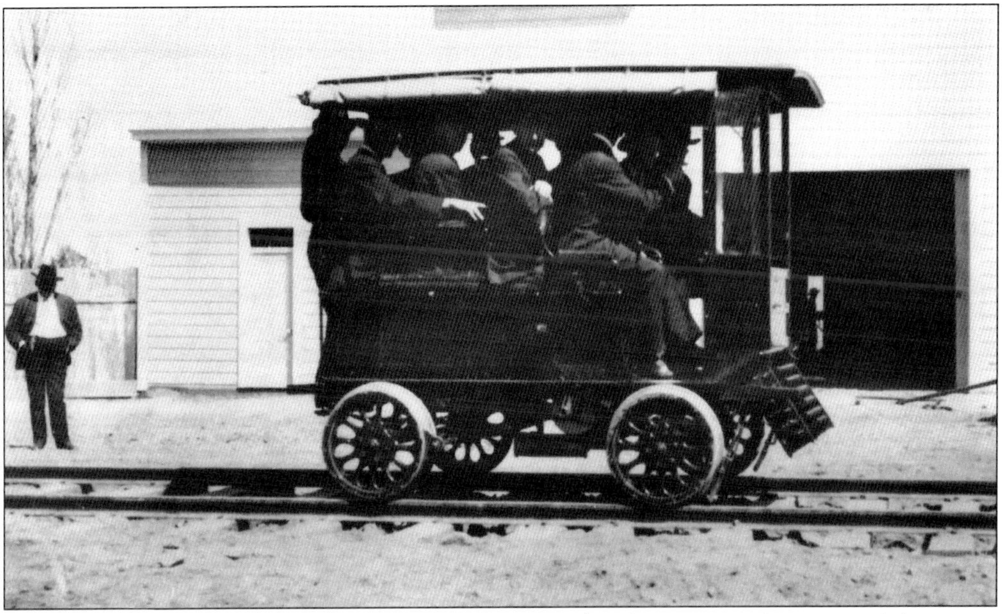

This is a homemade, rail-bound buggy built from spare railroad car parts and an automobile engine. Little cars like these were common on the Tooele Valley line, especially during the railroad's early years, when they were used to transport company officials and other VIPs from place to place. (Courtesy of the Tooele Valley Railroad Museum.)

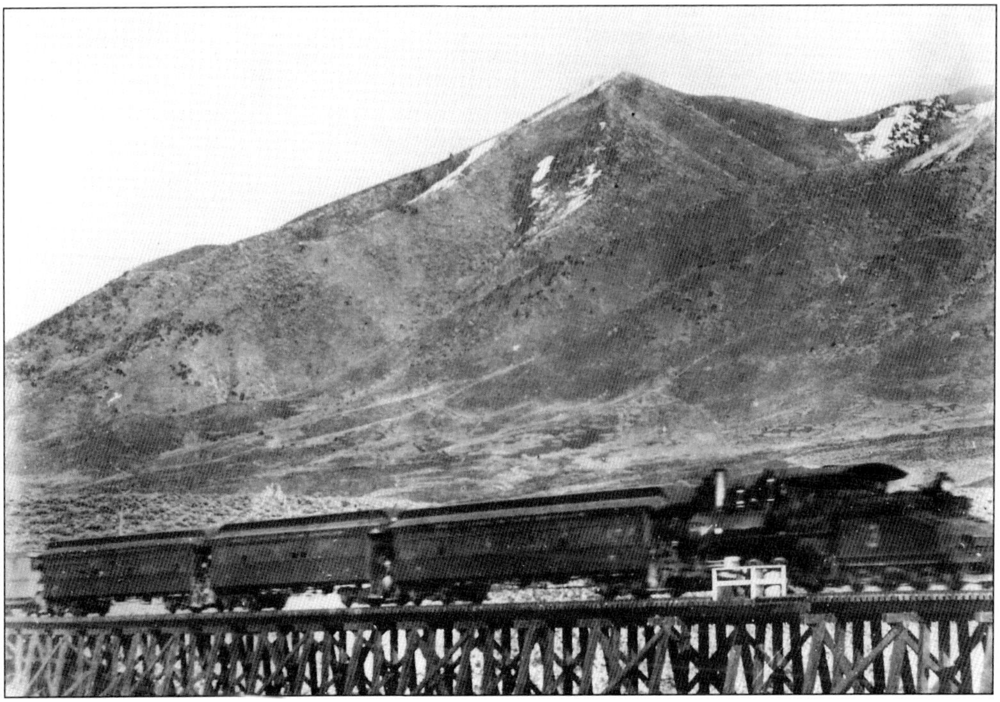

A train of passenger coaches crosses the Middle Canyon trestle on its way back to the International smelter. The engine appears to be Tooele Valley's No. 3, one of the railroad's first engines. No. 3 was an 0-6-0 that the railroad sold in May 1929. (Courtesy of the Tooele Valley Railroad Museum.)

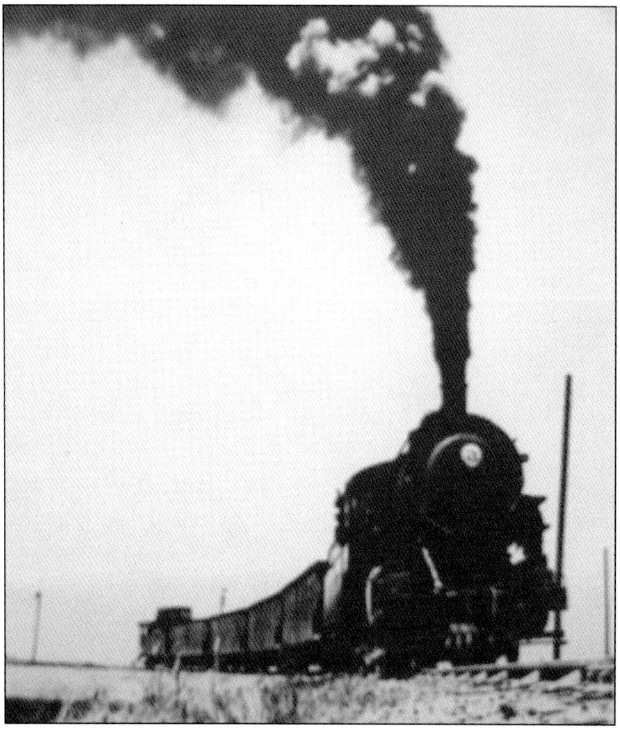

A train conveys cars filled with raw ore around the Big Curve toward International. Tooele Valley trains structured their schedules around passenger services until the mid-1940s. Trains running in the early morning or late evening, popular times for passenger service, often carried only passengers. Ore and freight trains such as this one waited until midday to run. (Courtesy of the Tooele Valley Railroad Museum.)

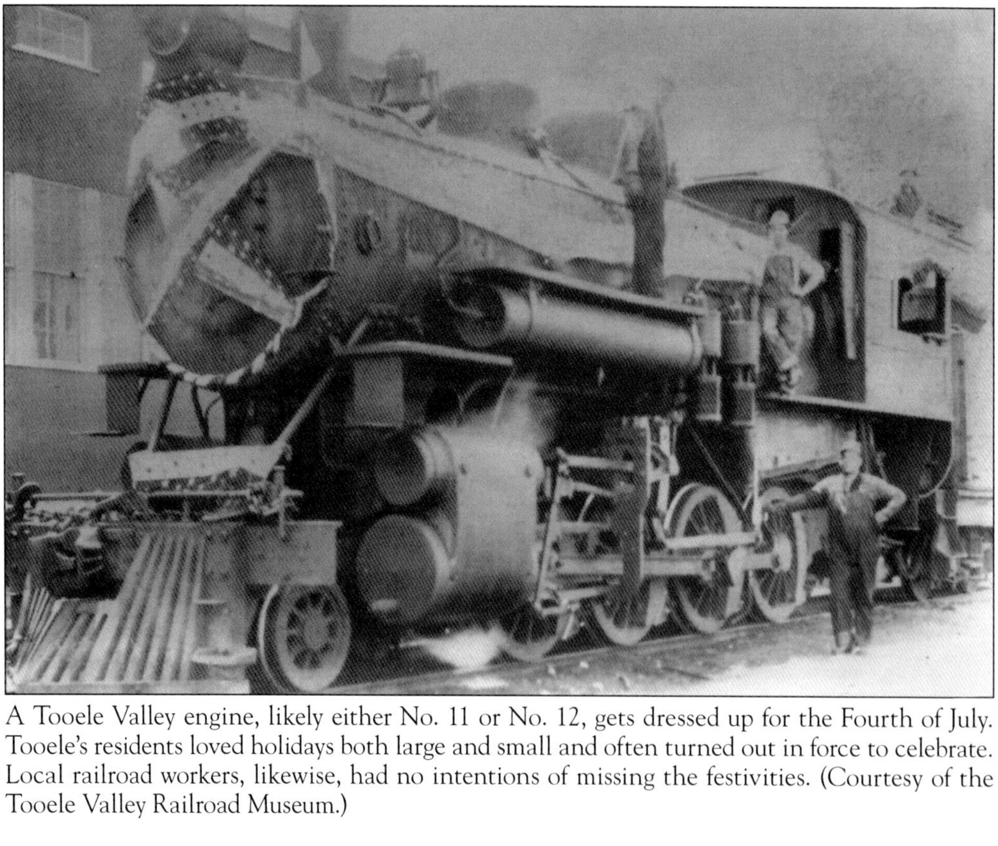

A Tooele Valley engine, likely either No. 11 or No. 12, gets dressed up for the Fourth of July. Tooele's residents loved holidays both large and small and often turned out in force to celebrate. Local railroad workers, likewise, had no intentions of missing the festivities. (Courtesy of the Tooele Valley Railroad Museum.)

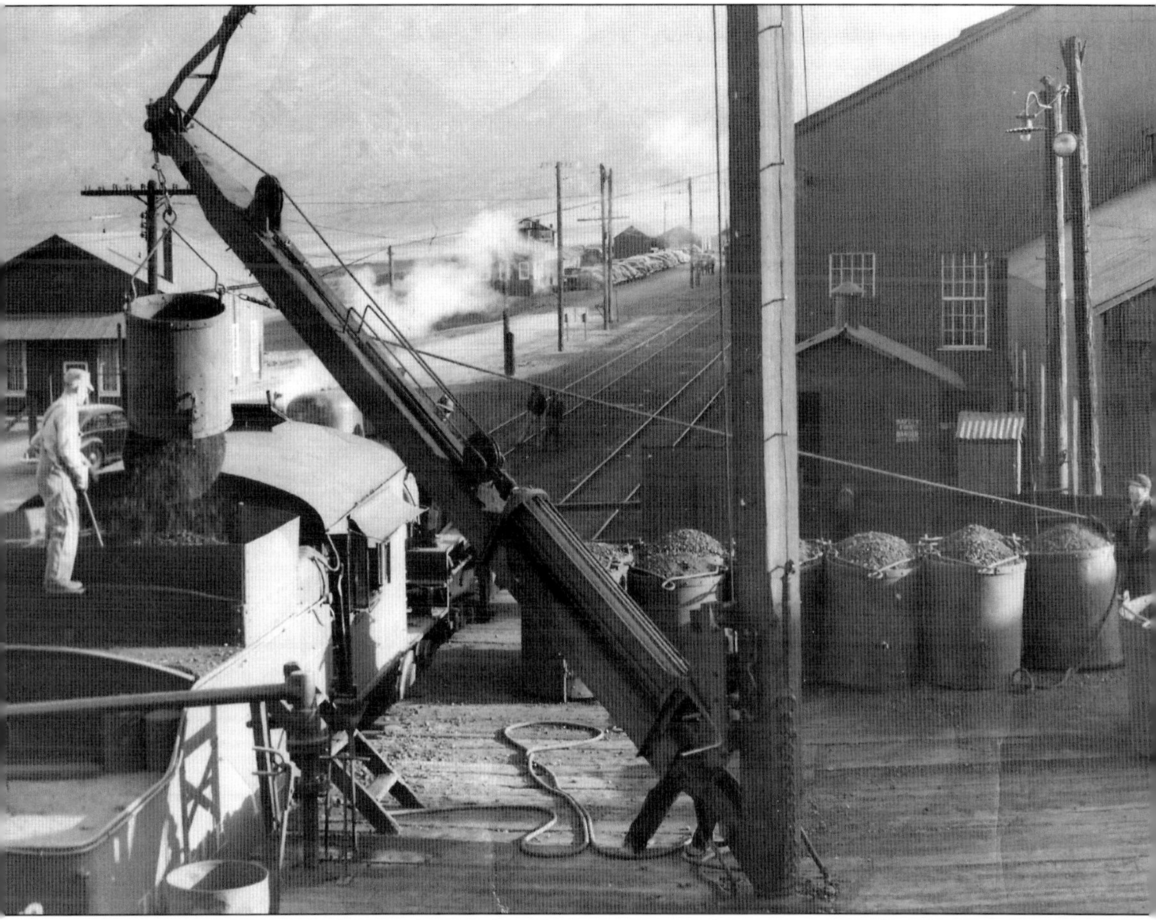

Railroad workers load coal into the tender of an engine in the International rail yard. Most maintenance, storage, and reloading for the Tooele Valley Railway took place at International, where the railroad's three-stall engine house, boiler shop, and coal dock were all located. (Courtesy of the Tooele Valley Railroad Museum.)

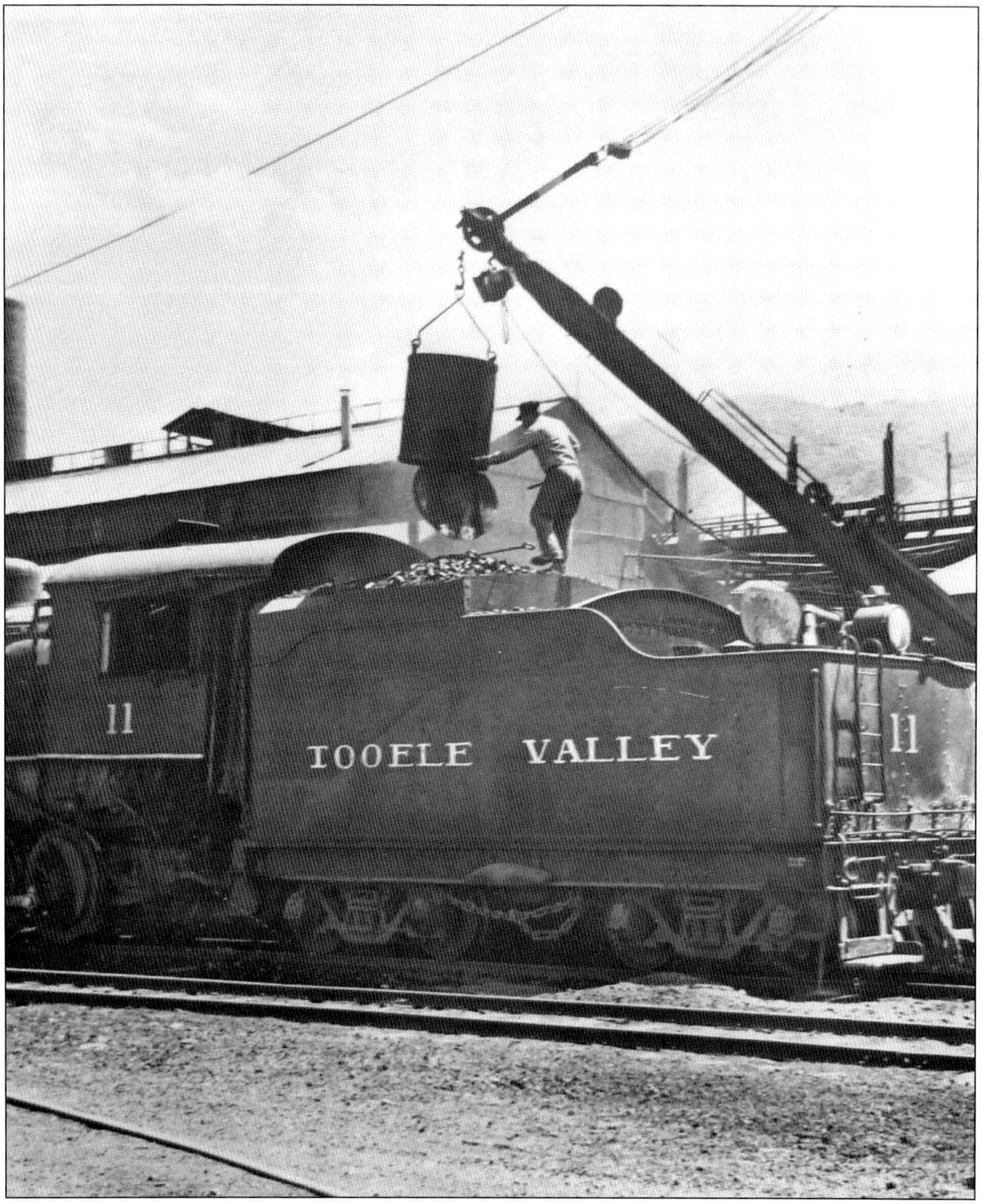

Engine No. 11 stops at the International rail yard to refill its coal supply. The railroad valued this engine and its sibling, No. 12, for their fuel efficiency, especially because the slope-back tenders the Tooele Valley preferred decreased the engine's coal capacity without significantly reducing the engine's size. (Courtesy of the Tooele Valley Railroad Museum.)

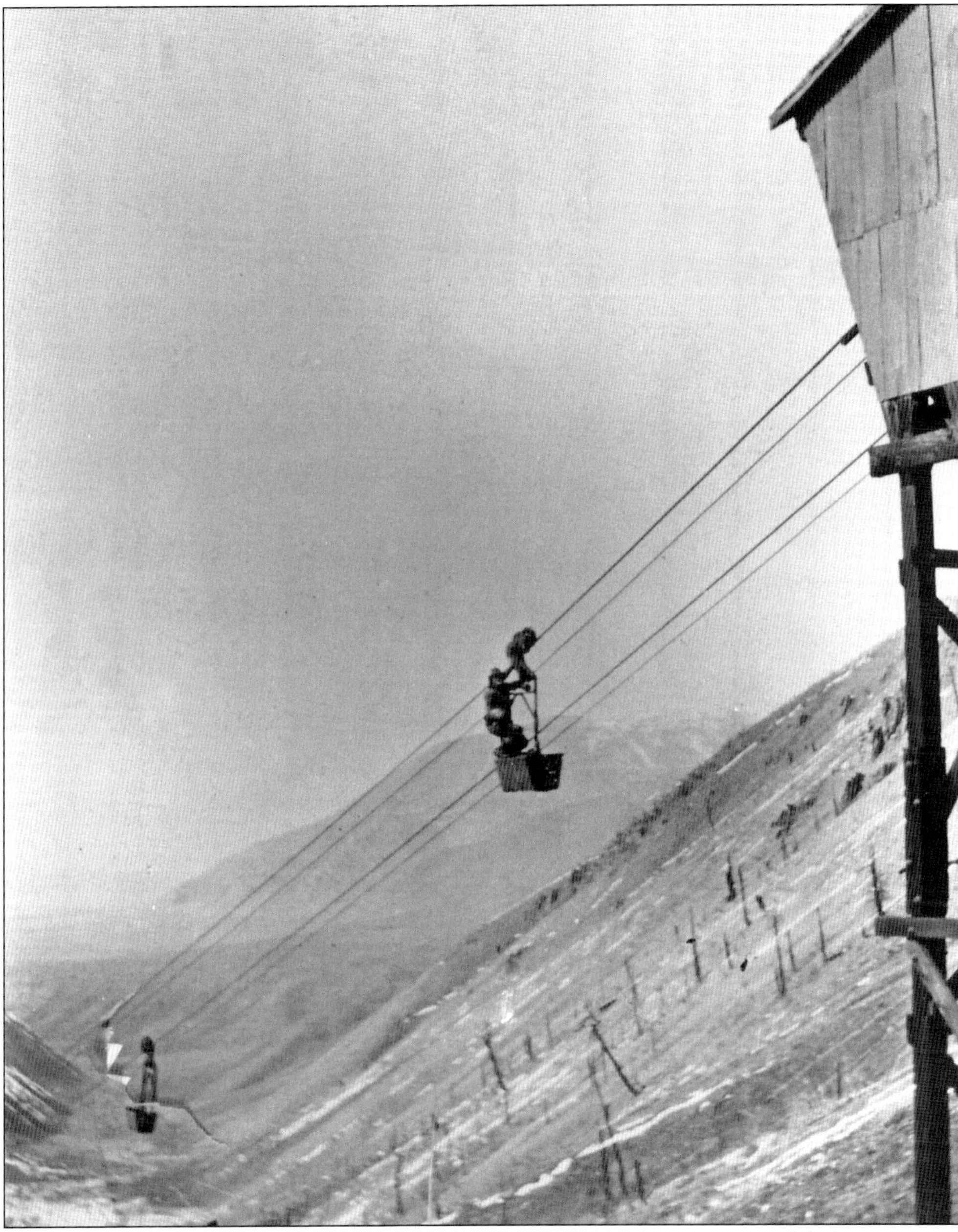

An unidentified man rides the aerial tram between the Bingham Canyon mines and the International smelter. This practice was not uncommon, though hitchhikers were advised to grasp either side of the bucket with one hand. Occasionally, were the bucket not fastened securely, the bottom could come loose, potentially dumping a load—or a passenger—on the rocky slopes below. Frank Dunlavy, who worked in the smelter's labs for more than 40 years, recounted some of his memories in *Mining, Smelting and Railroading in Tooele County*. He recalled the bucket in front of him coming loose and dumping a load during his first trip over the tram, giving him quite a scare. His subsequent trips over the tram proved uneventful, and he soon became accustomed to riding the tram over the mountain to visit various mines. (Courtesy of the Tooele Valley Railroad Museum.)

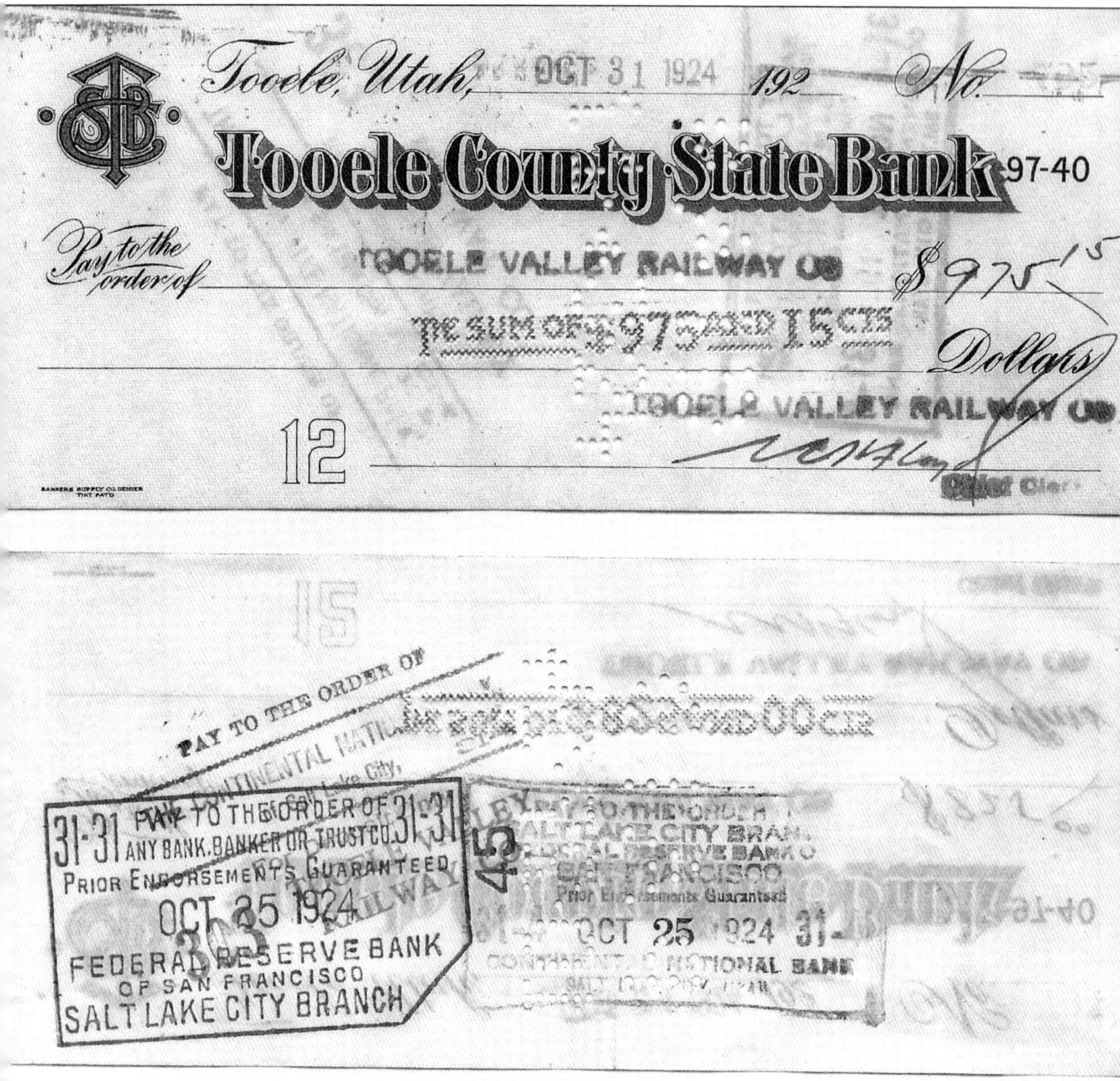

These checks were issued to the Tooele Valley Railway Company and dated October 31, 1924. The railroad company was very successful in the mid-1920s; 85 to 90 cars of ore could arrive at Warner on any given day, and demand for passenger service could fill an entire train of coaches each morning. (Courtesy of the Tooele Valley Railroad Museum.)

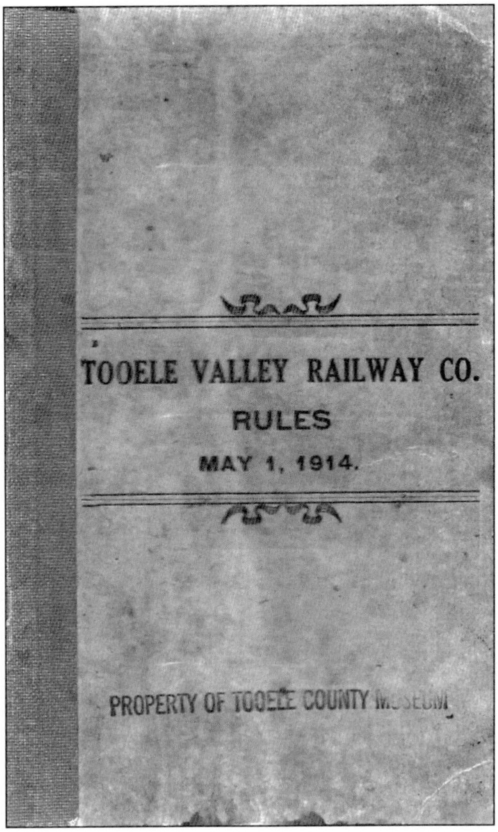

The page below, from the 1914 railroad employee guide (right), illustrates lamp signals used by Tooele Valley employees at the time. The book covered a number of other topics as well and discussed each train's schedule at length. Handbooks such as this were distributed among the railroad's 70 or so employees whenever company policies required updating. The railroad's strict adherence to its own internal policies likely deserves partial credit for the company's clean safety record. The number of major accidents on the line can be counted on a single hand, and most were related to weather or teenage mischief rather than employee negligence. (Both courtesy of the Tooele Valley Railroad Museum.)

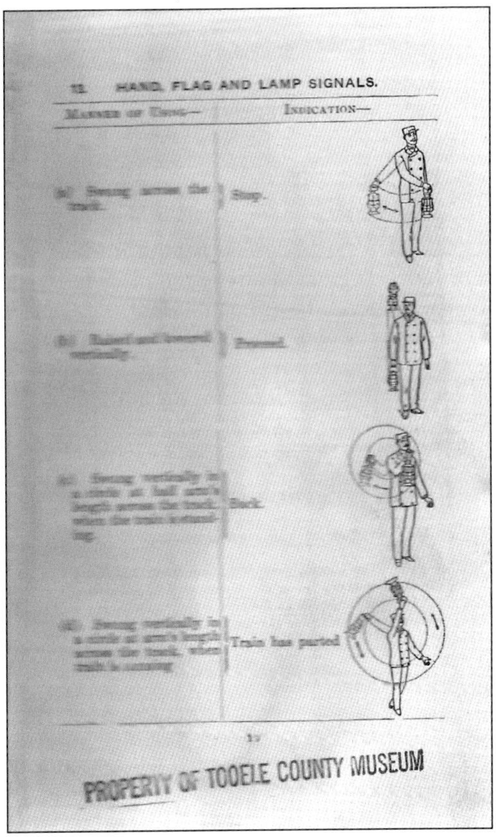

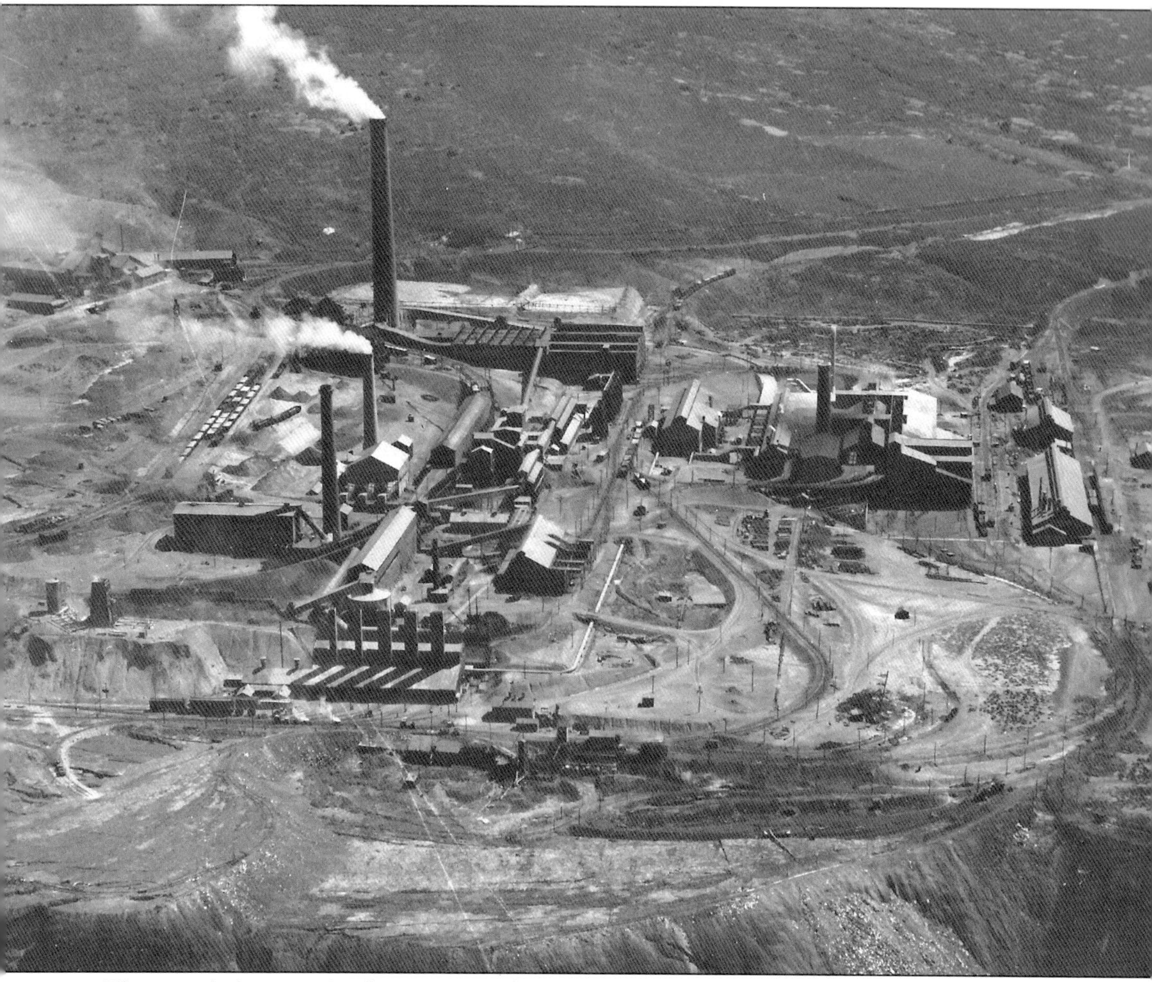

This aerial photograph of International was commissioned by the company itself in 1927. The smelter's original facilities for copper production are mostly concentrated near the top of the photograph, near the 350-foot-tall main smokestack. Administrative and maintenance buildings are concentrated on the right, and the lead addition is visible at the bottom. (Courtesy of the Tooele Valley Railroad Museum.)

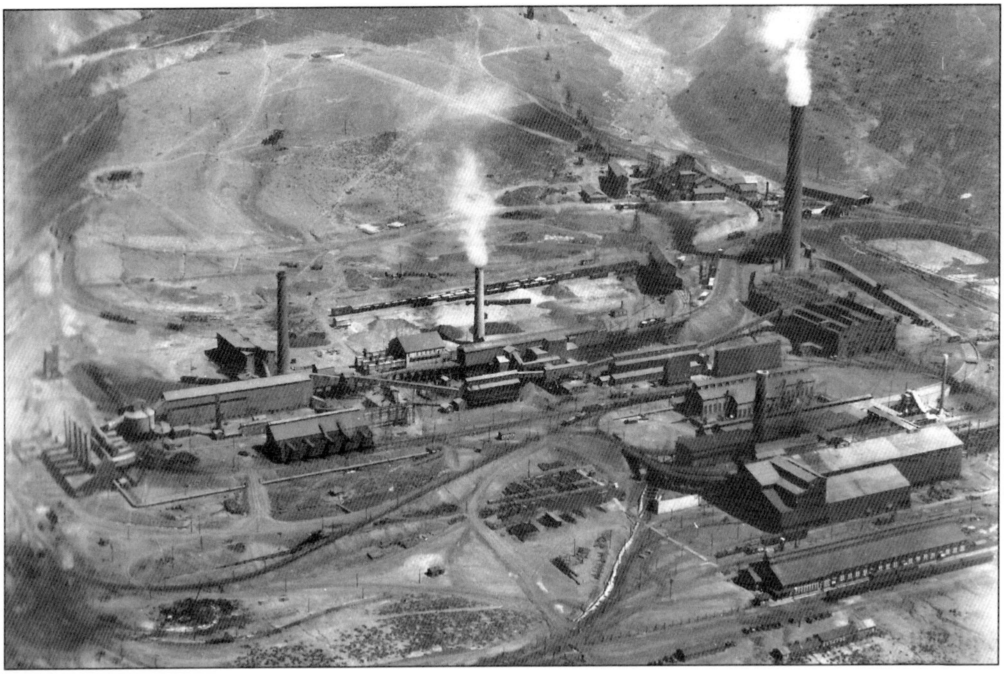

This east-facing aerial view shows the International smelter in 1927. Note the smelter-side terminal of the aerial tram, visible at the top. The lead sintering plant is nearly cut off on the far left and the company power plant is between the rail yard and the McDougall Roaster, below the main stack. (Courtesy of the Tooele Valley Railroad Museum.)

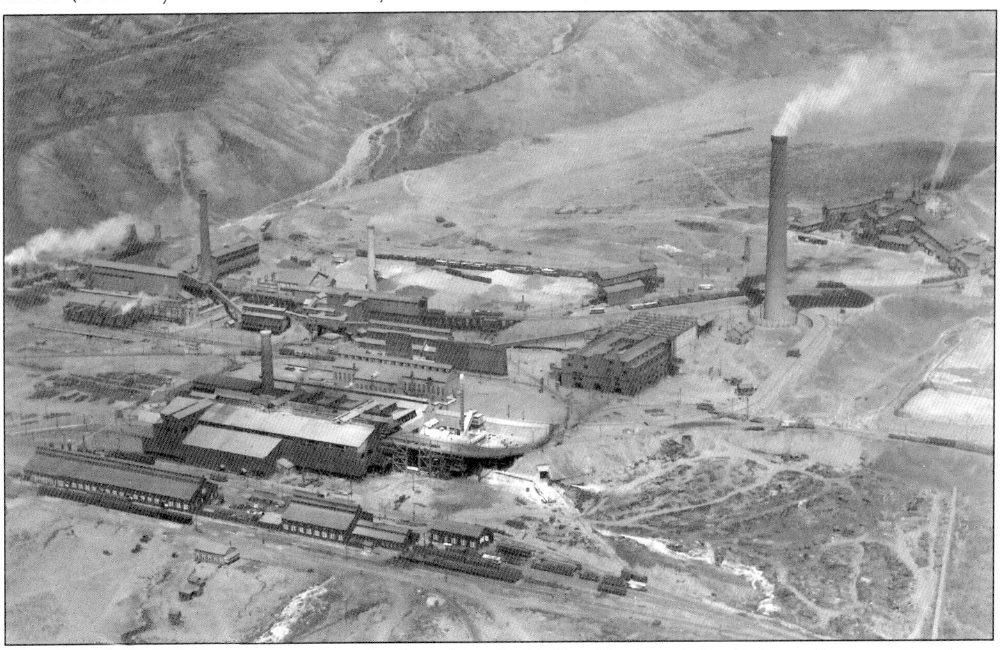

Tracks leading to the rail yard and other Tooele Valley Railroad facilities at International are clearly visible in the bottom left of this northeast-facing aerial photograph. From this angle, the company power plant is clearly centered amid the smelter's various other facilities. (Courtesy of the Tooele Valley Railroad Museum.)

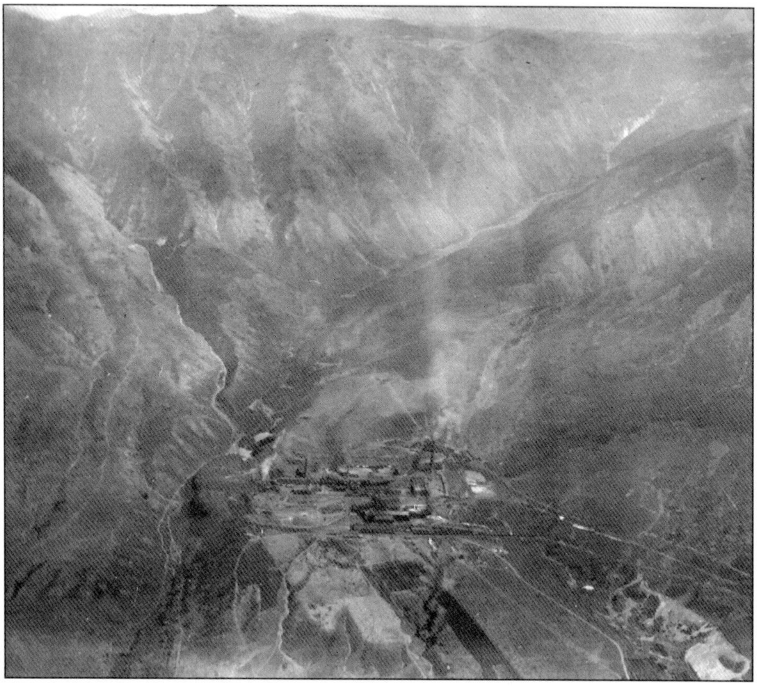

This 1927 aerial photograph of International and Pine Canyon shows the location of the smelter relative to the canyon. Bingham, though not visible, is located just opposite Pine Canyon, on the east side of the Oquirrh Mountains. Roads and railway lines departing the smelter at the bottom of the photograph run southwest toward Tooele City. (Courtesy of the Tooele Valley Railroad Museum.)

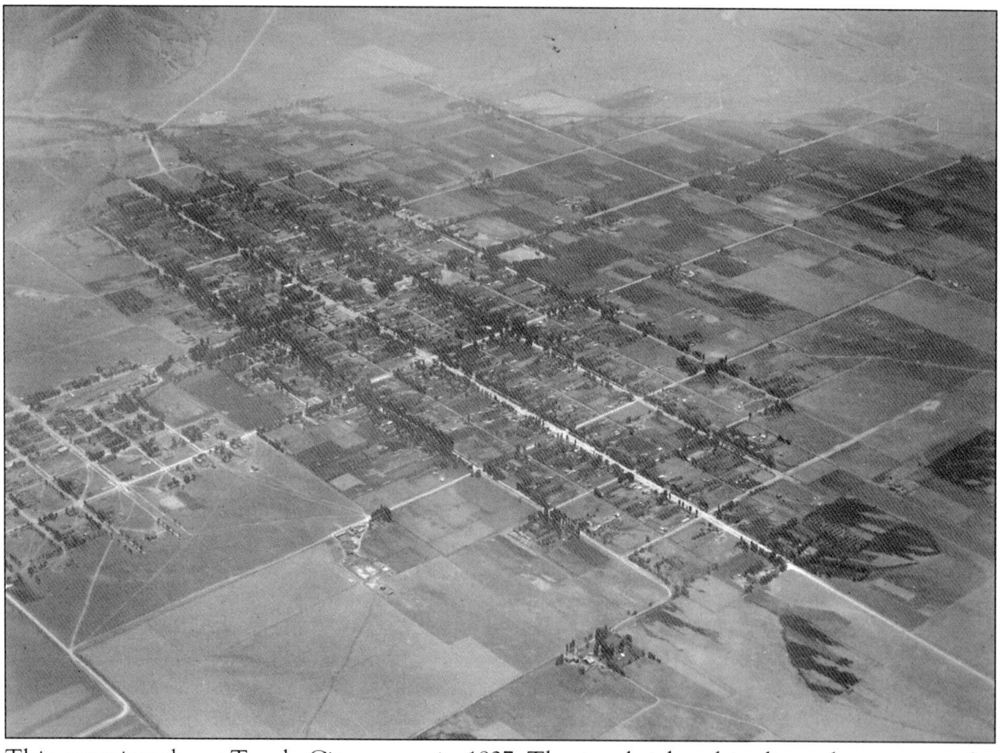

This overview shows Tooele City proper in 1927. The two bright white lines that meet at the center of town are Main and Vine Streets. Main Street runs north to south, from the bottom right corner to the top left. Vine Street runs east to west, from the bottom left to the top right. (Courtesy of the Tooele Valley Railroad Museum.)

Three

Depression and Unity 1929–1941

The rapid pace of industrialization in Tooele—and throughout the world—derailed the following decade, in the early 1930s. Tooele and its railroad successfully rode out the Depression, but the spectacular growth seen during the first 10 years of International smelter operations stagnated.

Facing the possibility of decreased hours and wages, International smelter workers banded together to found their first official labor union in 1933. Three years later, the union accomplished its first strike at International, on October 13, 1936.

In 1937, a new company entered the scene with a proposal that Tooele, desperate to renew the glory and growth of the 1920s, could not refuse. James Elton, the general manager of International Smelting and Refining, envisioned Tooele as a world leader in mining and smelting technology. In relatively short order, he united his remaining competitors under one ambitious umbrella company. Utah Consolidated and its mines in Bingham and Carr Fork, the Utah-Apex mine, the Utah-Delaware mine, and the Utah Metals mine all came under the control of a new company, headed by Elton himself, called the National Tunnel and Mines Company.

The centerpiece of Elton's grand vision was a 4.5-mile tunnel beneath the Oquirrh Mountains. It was intended to increase the productivity of the Apex and Delaware copper mines by alleviating a severe drainage problem and to more efficiently ship ores from the mines in Bingham to International. The other end of the tunnel would be serviced by a new 2.33-mile branch of the Tooele Valley Railroad. The project would bring much-needed irrigation water to Tooele's farmers and, more importantly, employment and immigration. Locals greeted Elton's proposal with a citywide celebration on June 15, 1937. Tunnel Day, as the street carnival was called by the local Lion's Club that organized it, was declared a local holiday.

Three months after Elton announced the imminent completion of his tunnel project, the drilling crew hit an underground fissure filled with quicksand. Progress was delayed, expenses accrued, and by the time the tunnel was formally opened on August 21, 1941, it had cost the National Tunnel and Mines Company $1.5 million.

However, the community remained optimistic about the tunnel's potential. On September 5, 1941, the Tooele Valley Railway announced plans to discontinue passenger services, which executives believed would interfere with increased freight traffic from the tunnel.

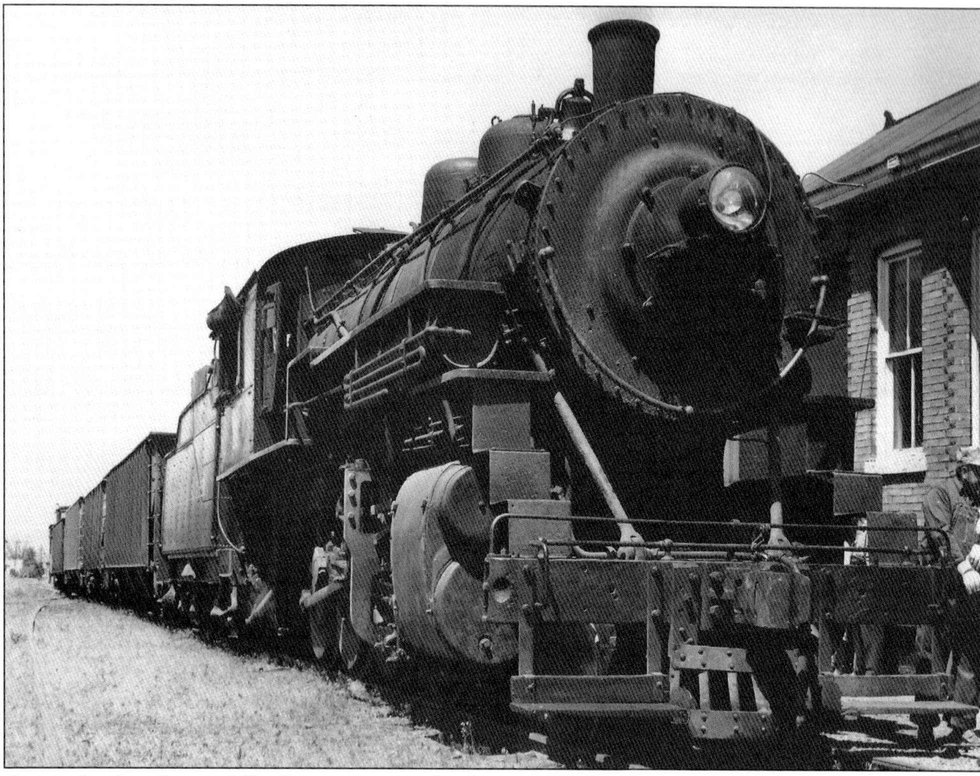

A trainload with cars full of ore arrives at the downtown Tooele station on Broadway. The station was well equipped, with a scale and baggage room inside for weighing and handling shipments, as well as a boxcar-level platform surrounding three sides of the building's exterior for unloading. (Courtesy of the Tooele Valley Railroad Museum.)

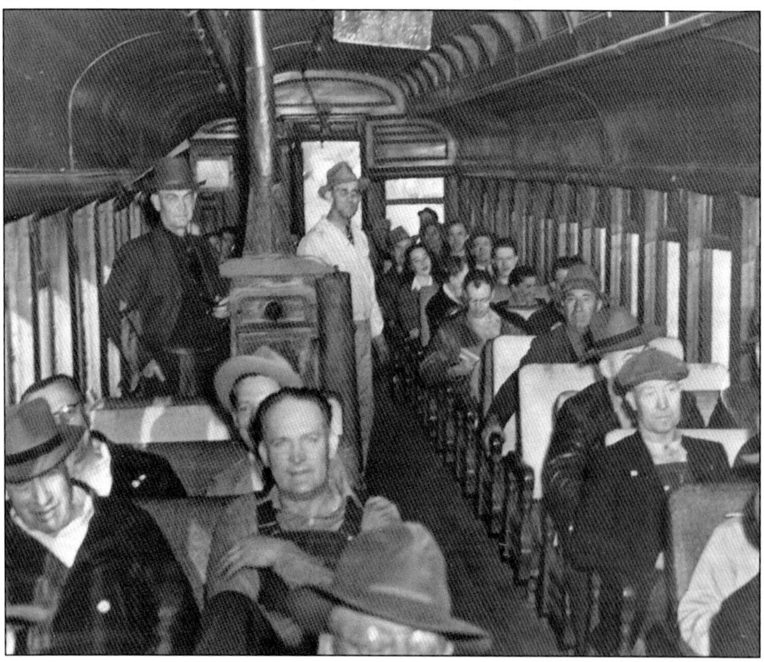

Passengers board a train at the International smelter after a day's work in this 1930s photograph. Those looking for work were more likely to find available shifts on the swing shift, from 4:00 p.m. to 12:00 a.m., or on the graveyard shift, from 12:00 a.m. to 8:00 a.m. (Courtesy of the Tooele Valley Railroad Museum.)

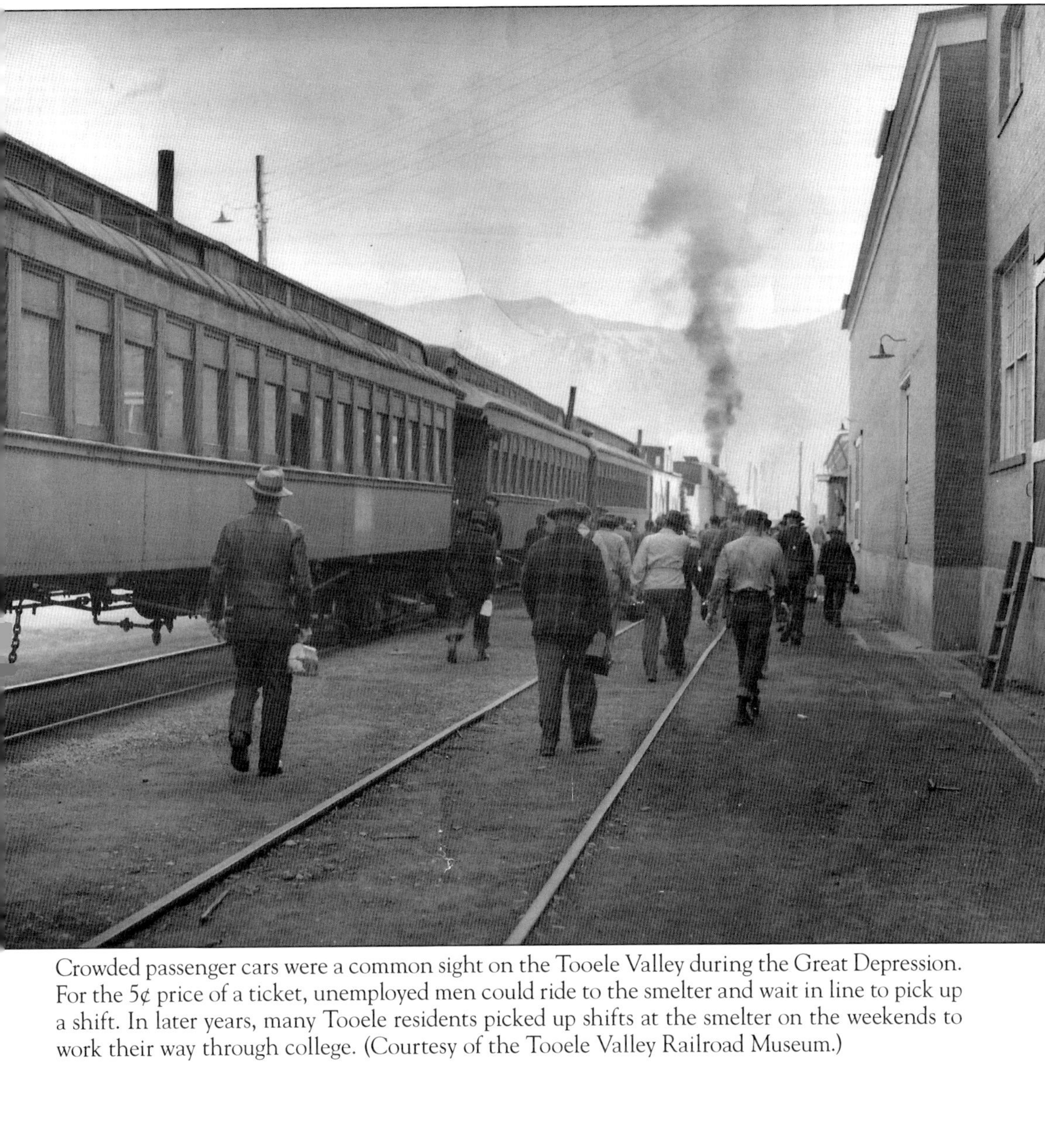

Crowded passenger cars were a common sight on the Tooele Valley during the Great Depression. For the 5¢ price of a ticket, unemployed men could ride to the smelter and wait in line to pick up a shift. In later years, many Tooele residents picked up shifts at the smelter on the weekends to work their way through college. (Courtesy of the Tooele Valley Railroad Museum.)

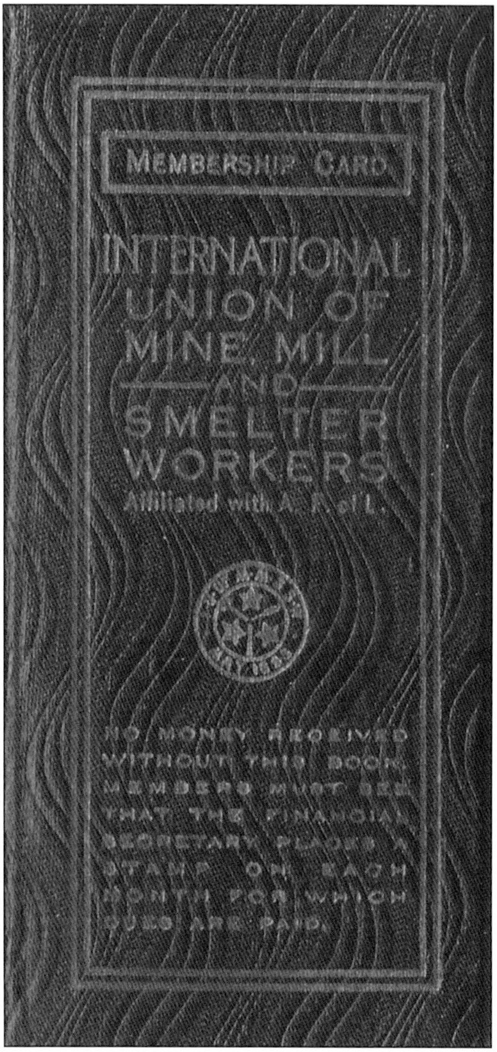

These cards belonged to a member of the International Union of Mine, Mill and Smelter Workers. Tooele's chapter, Union No. 55, formed in July 1933. The union provided smelter workers and their families various social activities throughout the year and organized a number of strikes at International. For the most part, however, it was a rather quiet organization. In 1947, the union received $14,000 to reimburse it for unused contributions to the larger organization's strike fund. This money was used to pay workers in the event of a strike, but Tooele's members contributed far more than they actually needed. The chapter later put the funds toward building a new lodge on Vine Street. (Both courtesy of the Tooele Valley Railroad Museum.)

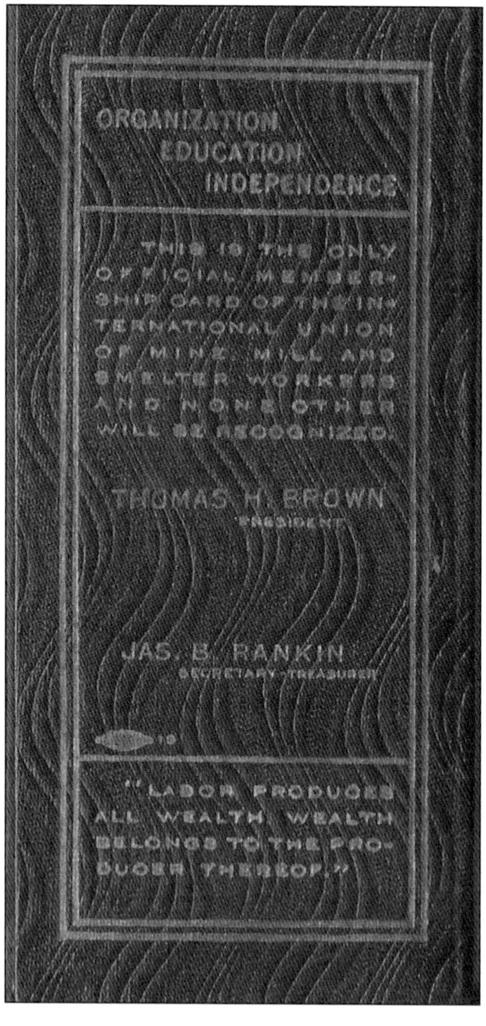

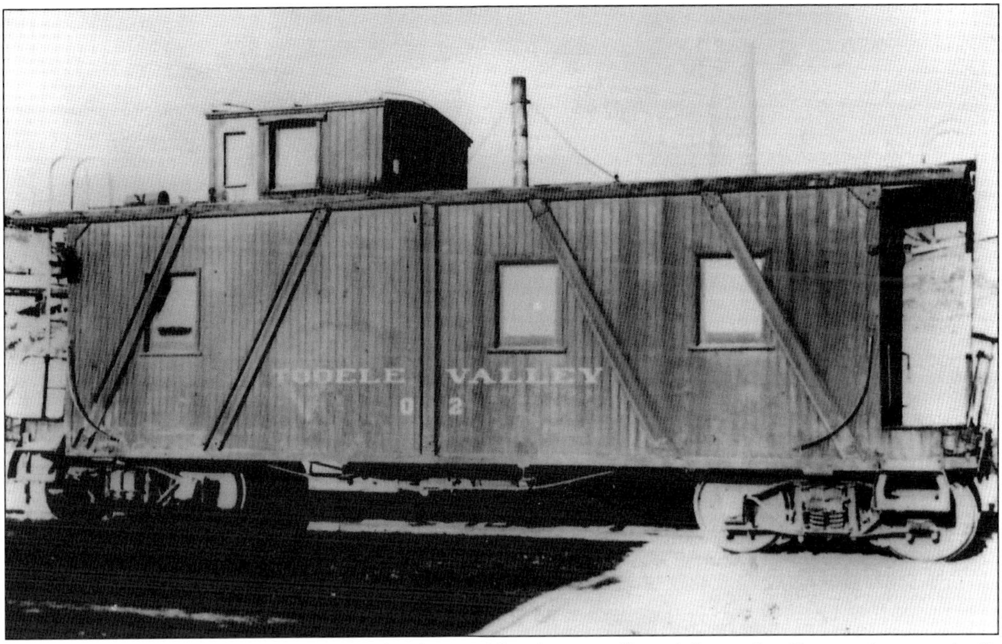

The Tooele Valley Railway acquired caboose No. 2 secondhand from the Butte, Anaconda & Pacific Railroad in 1925 to replace the railroad's first caboose, which was scrapped and converted into a flatcar soon after. No. 2 was retired and scrapped in 1957. (Courtesy of the Tooele Valley Railroad Museum.)

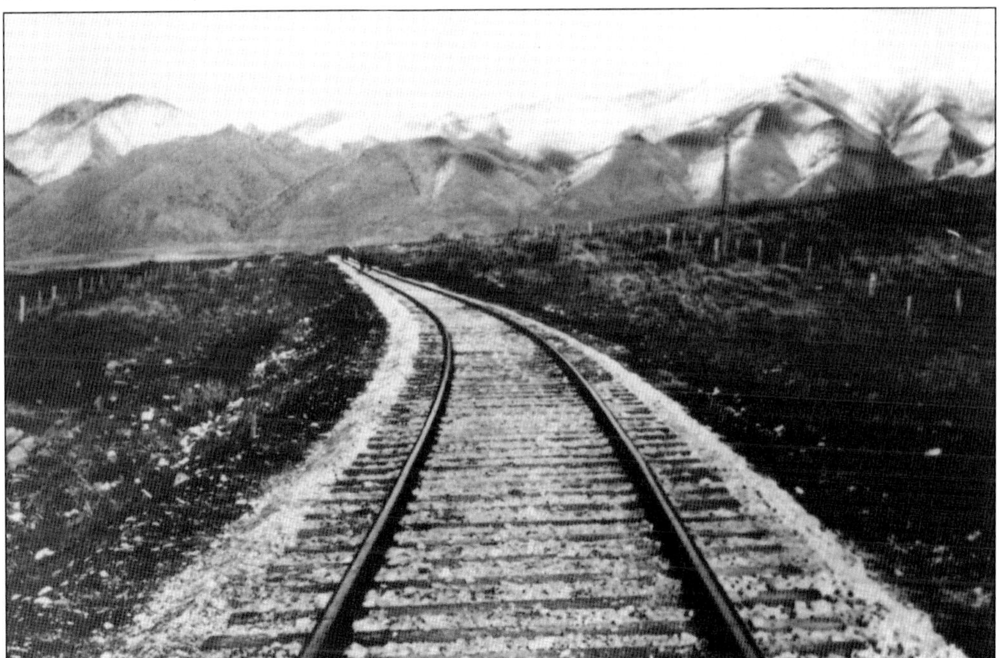

This photograph shows the Tooele Valley tracks on the west side of town, near Warner, with no train in sight. In the far distance, a number of people walk the rails. Overall, the railroad had a clean safety record, but the 1930s and 1940s were not good decades for accidents. (Courtesy of the Tooele Valley Railroad Museum.)

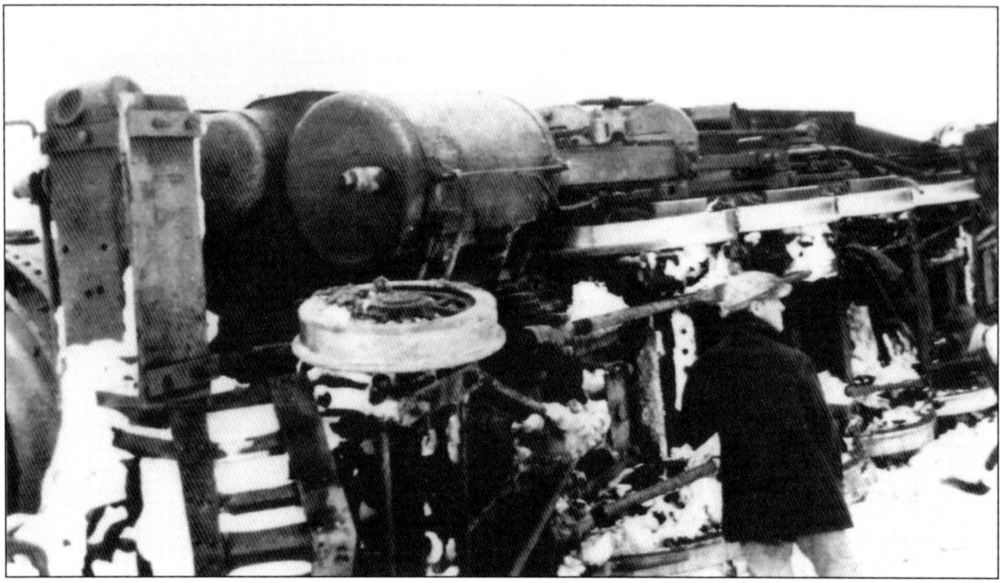

The Tooele Valley Railway's most infamous accident occurred on January 24, 1933, and was widely attributed to the winter's harsh weather. That year, motorists took to driving their vehicles on the tracks in the middle of Vine Street to avoid the snowbanks building up on either side of the street. Compacted snow froze onto the tracks themselves, clogging the rails' flangeway. When a westbound train hit a patch of ice at the edge of town, near Coleman Street, engine No. 12 derailed and flipped onto its side, taking several railcars with it. (Both courtesy of the Tooele Valley Railroad Museum.)

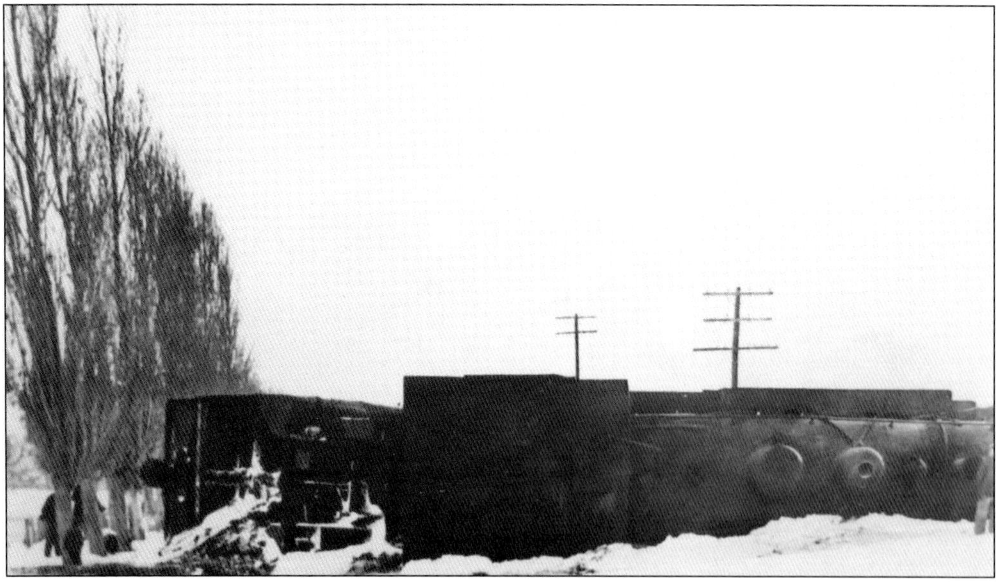

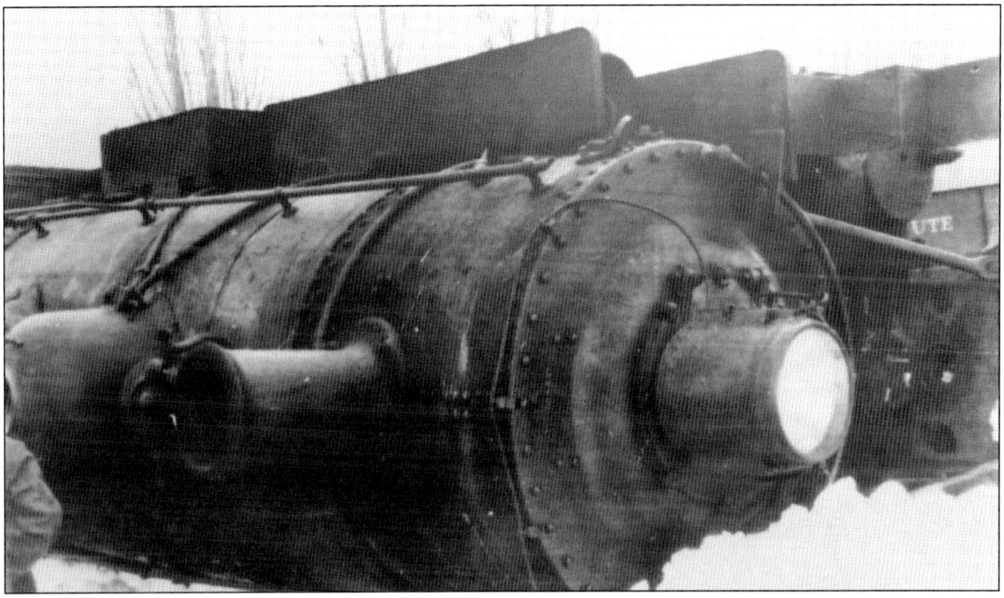

Despite the evident severity of the accident, engine No. 12 sustained little damage. The locomotive was repaired in-house at a cost of about $600 and soon returned to service on the Tooele Valley line. One of the train's section hands suffered a dislocated vertebra as a result of the wreck, but everyone else on board escaped with minor cuts and bruises. (Courtesy of the Tooele Valley Railroad Museum.)

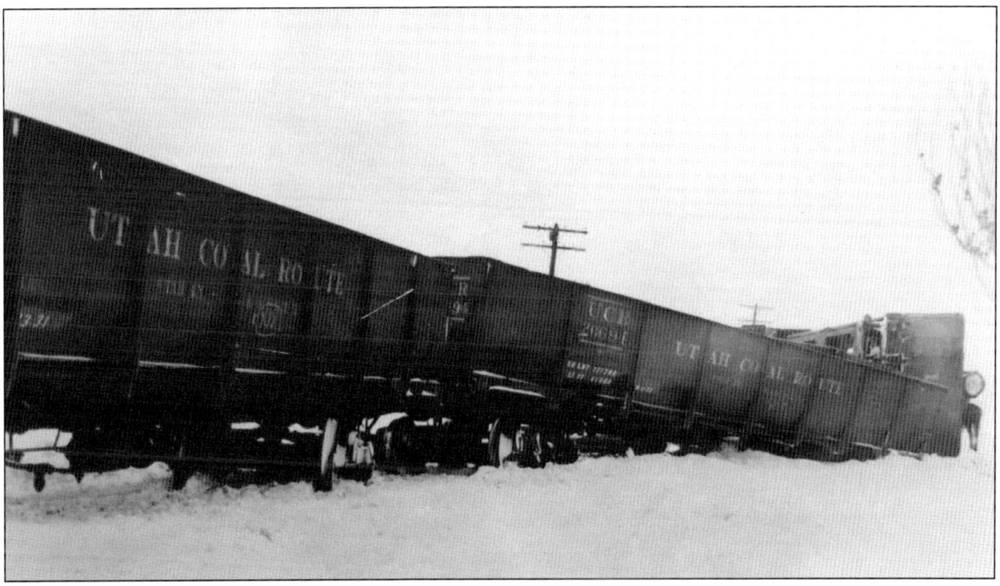

The tipping engine took the first two of the train's cars with it when it derailed. The train's engineer, fireman, and brakeman quickly bailed out of the cab and ran for cover, fearing an explosion from the potentially damaged boiler. When they returned, they realized the damage was not as severe as they had thought. (Courtesy of the Tooele Valley Railroad Museum.)

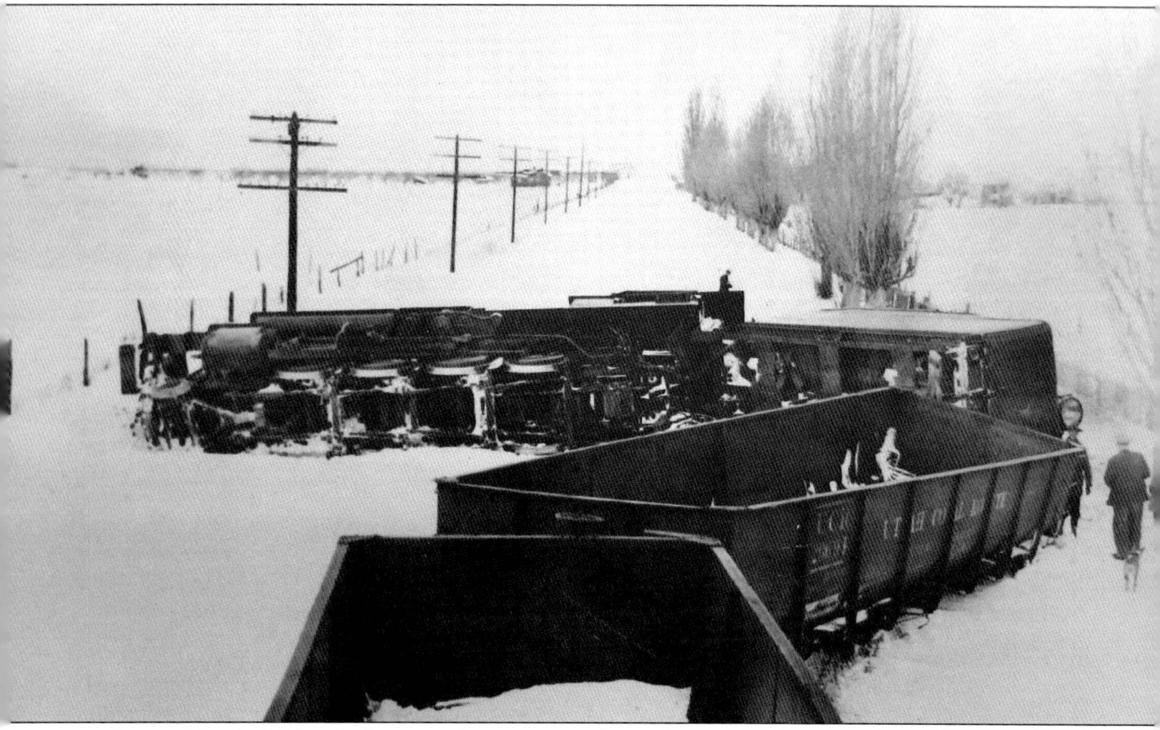

As the Tooele Valley Railway's only major accident, the scene soon drew a small crowd of local spectators. The January 24, 1933, incident is the only derailment recorded on the railroad besides a few minor derailments that occurred at or near the International smelter rail yard. (Courtesy of the Tooele Valley Railroad Museum.)

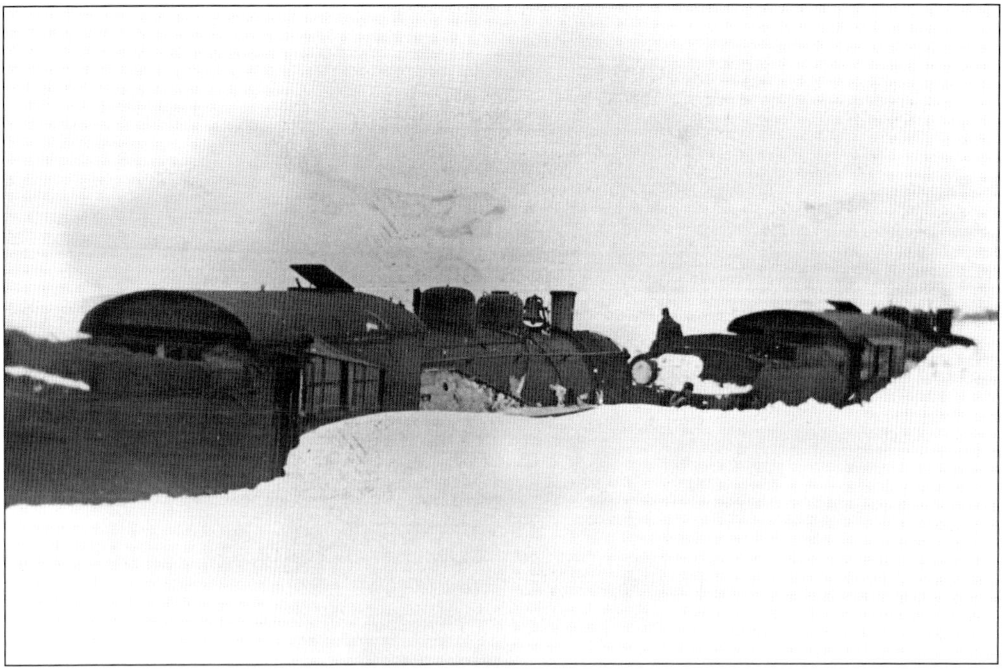

Despite the city's high elevation, Tooele's climate is so dry that it does not typically see large quantities of snow—typically. In 1937, however, the area experienced a series of famous blizzards that dumped feet of snow on the city. Snowdrifts near the smelter at the mouth of Pine Canyon effectively buried trains. (Courtesy of the Tooele Valley Railroad Museum.)

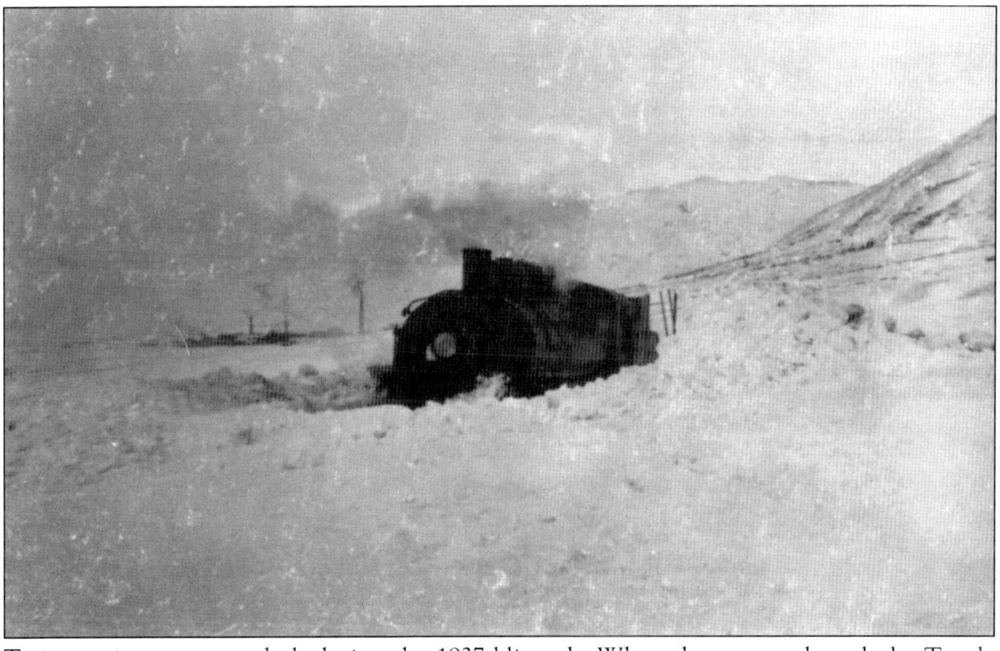

Train service came to a halt during the 1937 blizzards. When the storms cleared, the Tooele Valley Railway discovered its trains snowed in at the smelter. The company summoned swarms of workers and began to shovel a path to town for the trains. (Courtesy of the Tooele Valley Railroad Museum.)

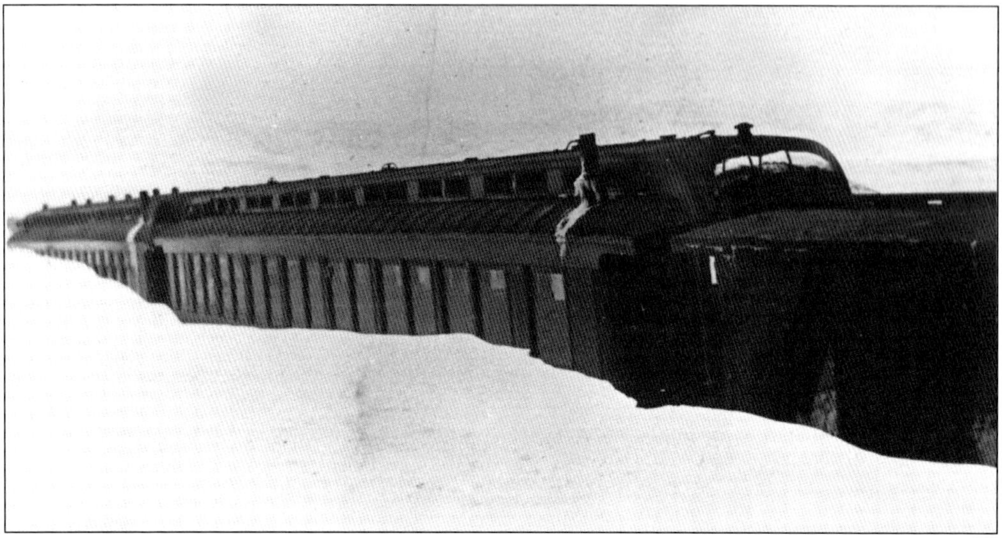

Passenger coaches buried in feet of snow illustrate the depth of the snowdrifts, which in some areas could have covered the railcars entirely. This train is empty and making little progress toward town while it waits for railroad staff to clear the tracks ahead. (Courtesy of the Tooele Valley Railroad Museum.)

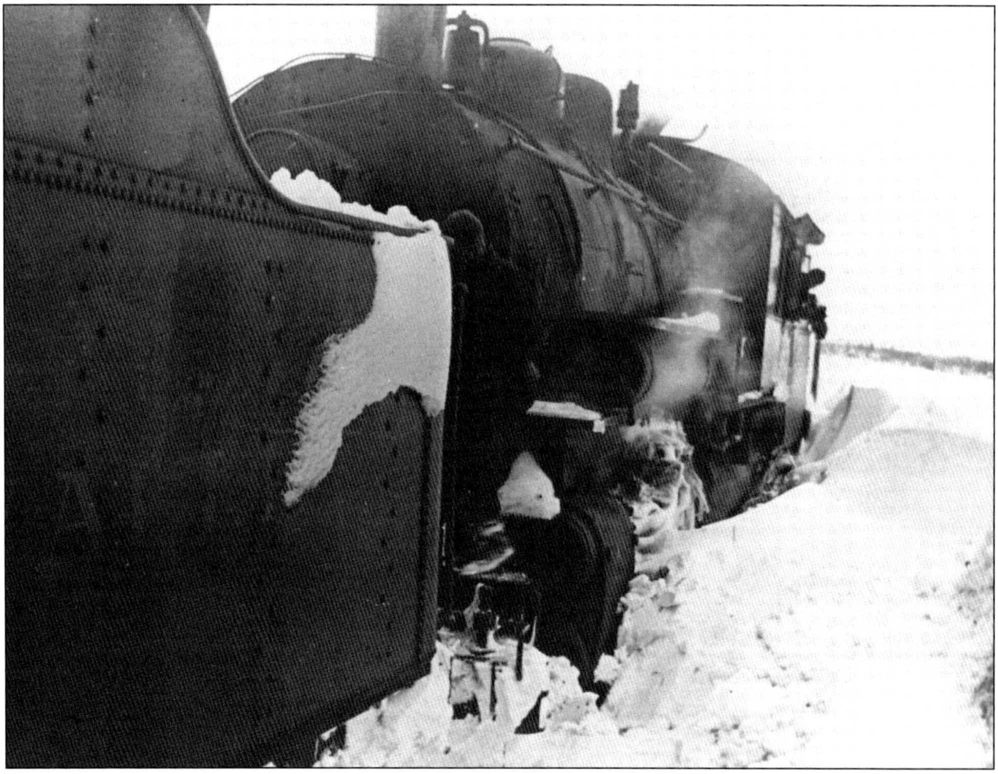

This view was taken from the side of the engine of a returning train, with the city of Tooele barely visible in the distance. Limited service continued while crews struggled to keep the tracks clear. One train remained stuck for about five days while workers dug it out. (Courtesy of the Tooele Valley Railroad Museum.)

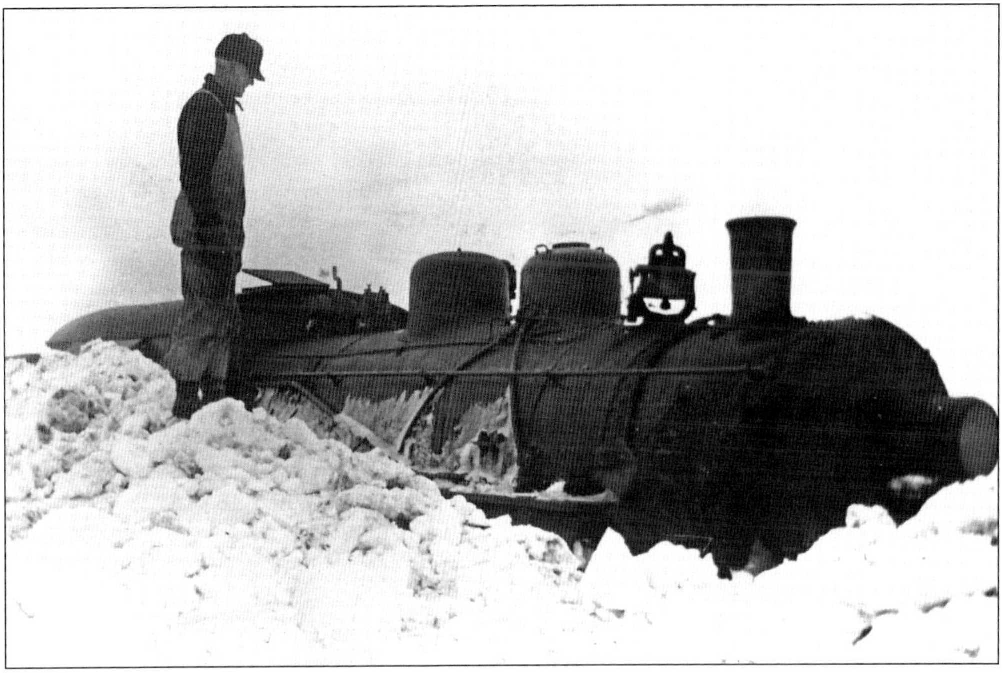

A railroad employee looks down at his engine from atop a pile of snow that could very nearly bury the entire train. This train had come to a complete standstill while it waited for a snow removal crew comprised of the Tooele Valley Railway's regular staff to clear a path back to town for it. (Courtesy of the Tooele Valley Railroad Museum.)

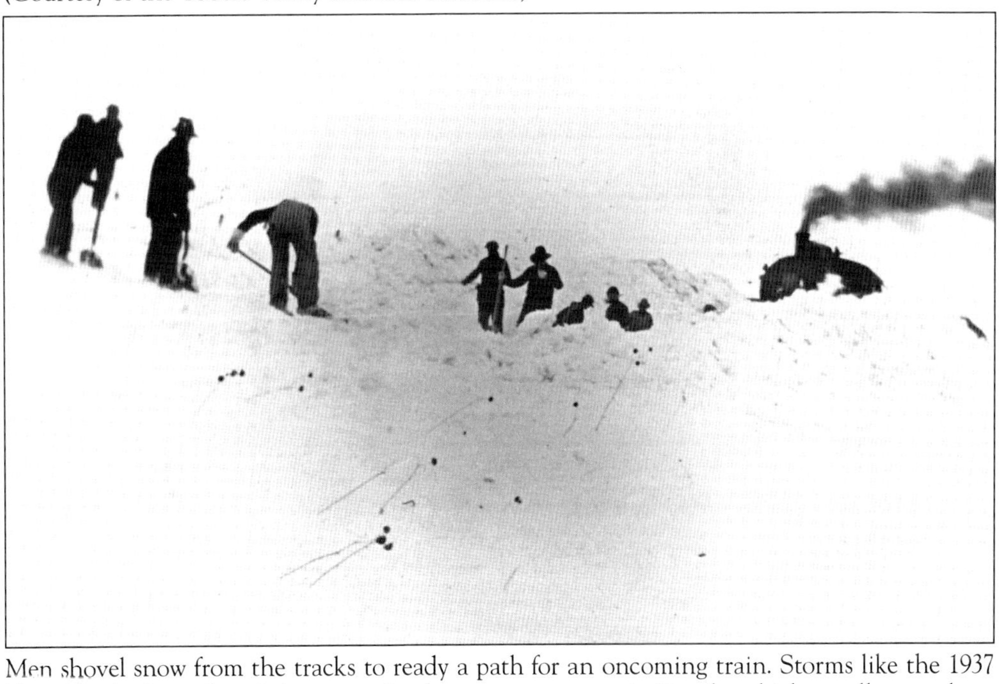

Men shovel snow from the tracks to ready a path for an oncoming train. Storms like the 1937 blizzard, which produced these snowbanks, are uncommon in Tooele, which usually sees about 17.57 inches of precipitation in an average year. Snow depths rarely exceed three inches. (Courtesy of the Tooele Valley Railroad Museum.)

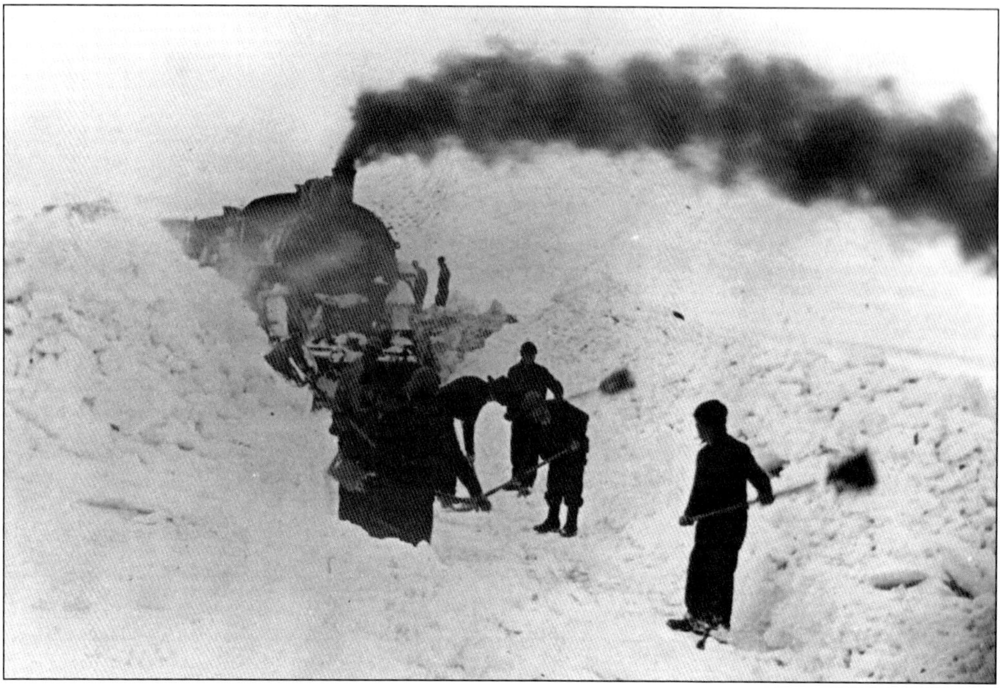

Railroad employees shovel snow off the tracks (above) for an approaching train and then scramble to the side (below) to clear the road. It is telling that the railroad's most notable incidents almost always involved snow. There are some exceptions, however. Most locals who were alive at the time recount an incident in the 1940s when a young man died after he fell in front of an oncoming train. Evidently, the youth was trying to hitch a ride on the side of a railcar, a stunt that was popular with some of his peers, when he slipped under the train's wheels. (Both courtesy of the Tooele Valle Railroad Museum.)

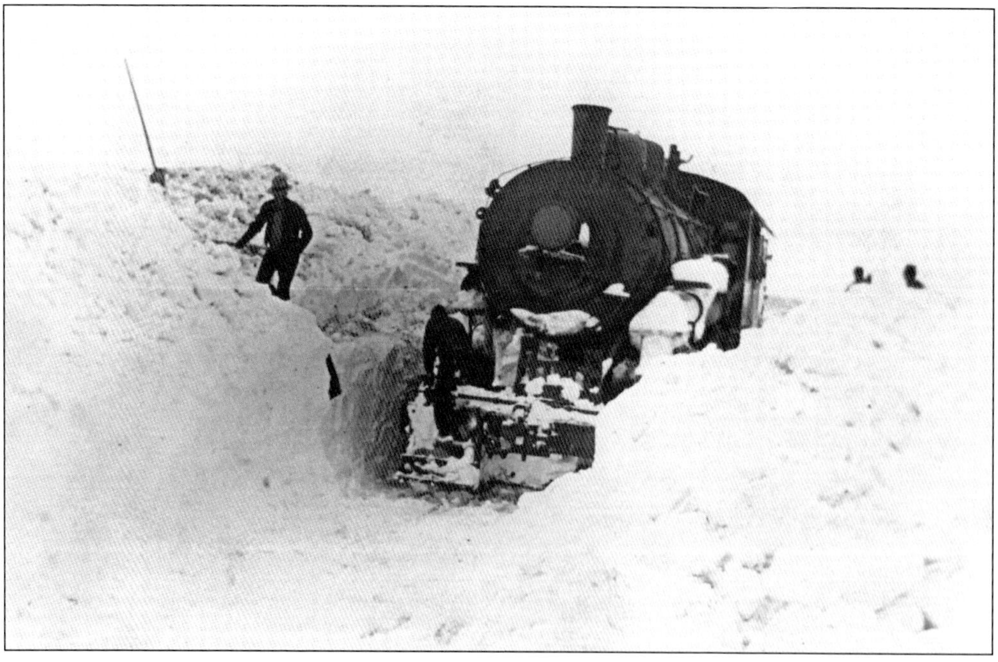

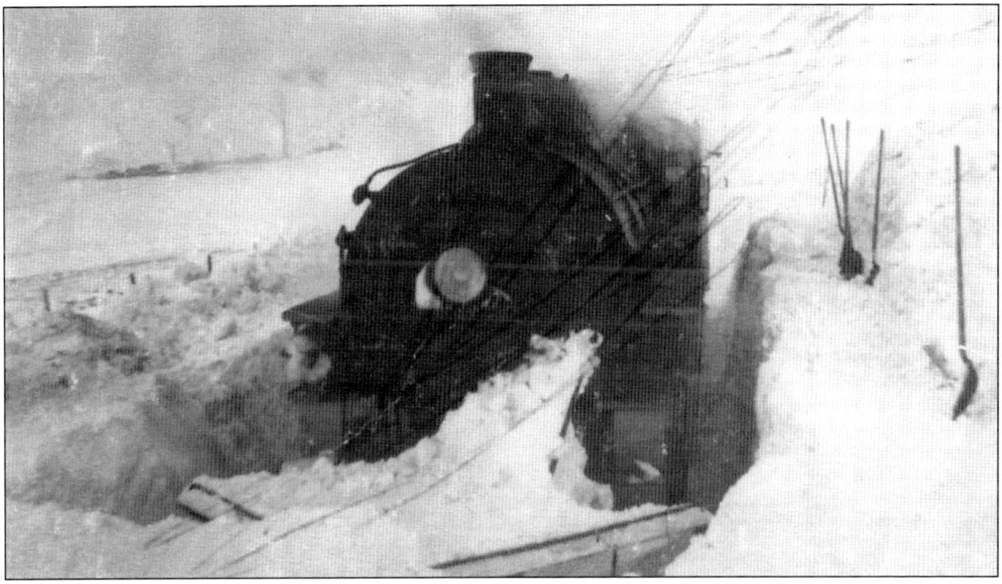

An engine attempts to force its way through a growing snowbank during the winter of 1937. The railroad's snow removal crews have shovels on standby just in case. The International smelter is barely visible at the mouth of Pine Canyon, just over the engine's shoulder. (Courtesy of the Tooele Valley Railroad Museum.)

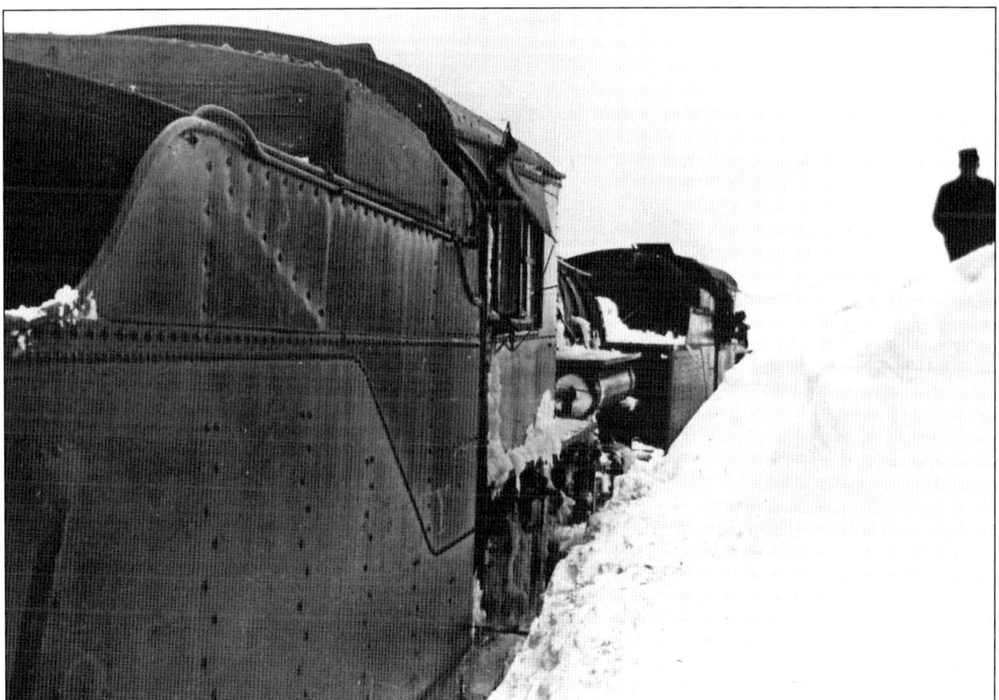

Multiple engines lead a train on its way to the International smelter. Despite the railroad's small size, trains with multiple engines were not uncommon, particularly when a large shipment of ore arrived. In this case, the use of multiple engines did not make plowing through these snowbanks any easier. (Courtesy of the Tooele Valley Railroad Museum.)

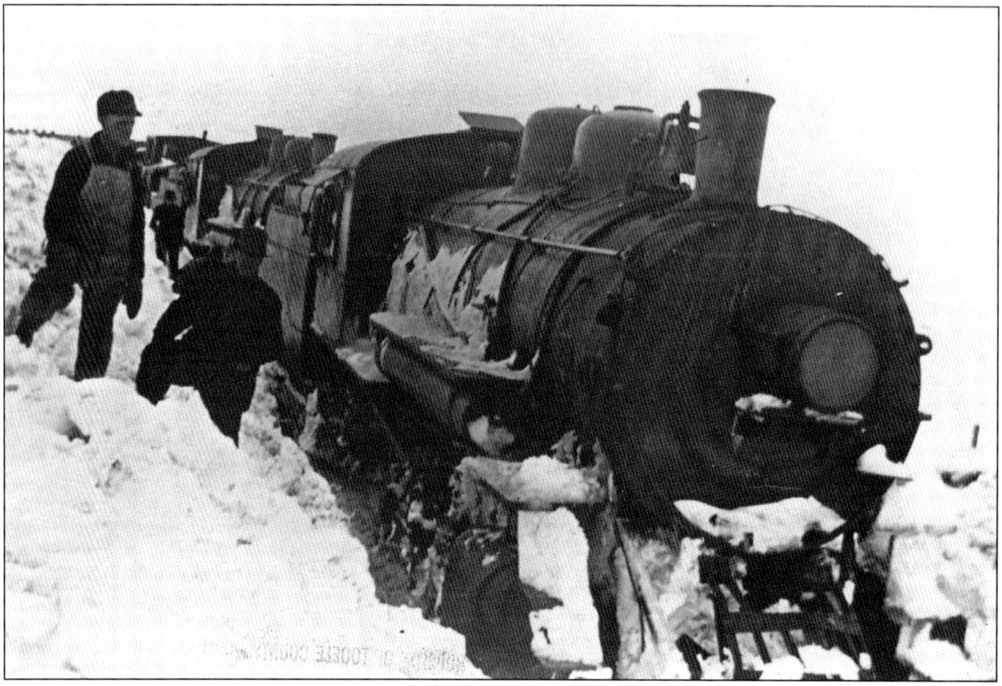

Tooele Valley Railway employees step outside the engine's cab for a photograph, posing on top of an impressive snowbank beside their train. The photograph is proof that no matter what year it is, people never grow too old to enjoy a good snow day. (Courtesy of the Tooele Valley Railroad Museum.)

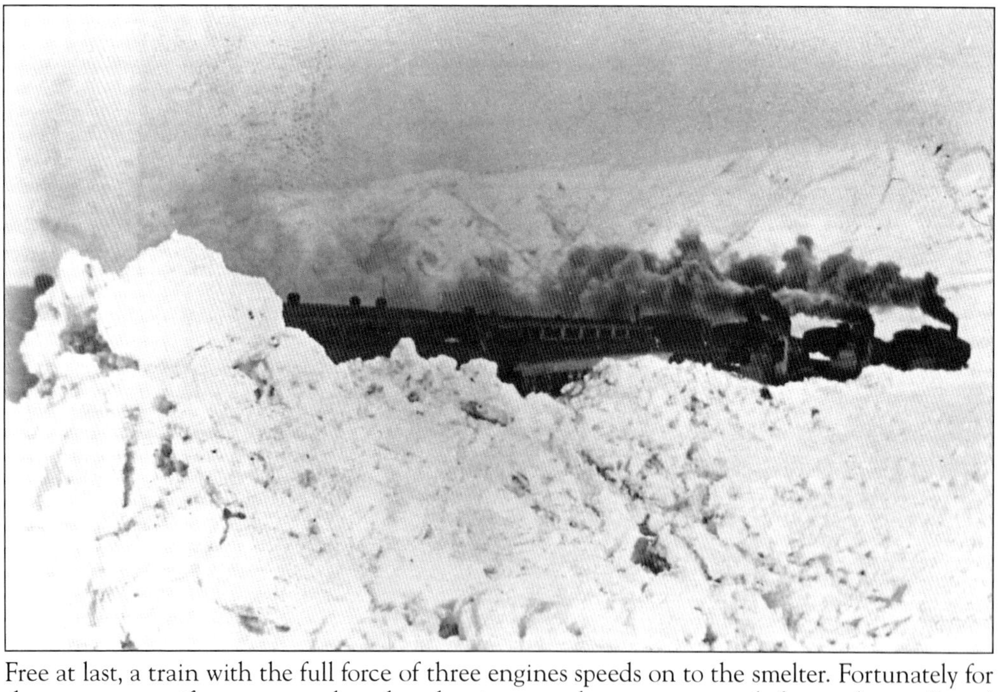

Free at last, a train with the full force of three engines speeds on to the smelter. Fortunately for the passengers—if any were on board at the time—each passenger coach featured a small coal stove to warm the car and those inside. (Courtesy of the Tooele Valley Railroad Museum.)

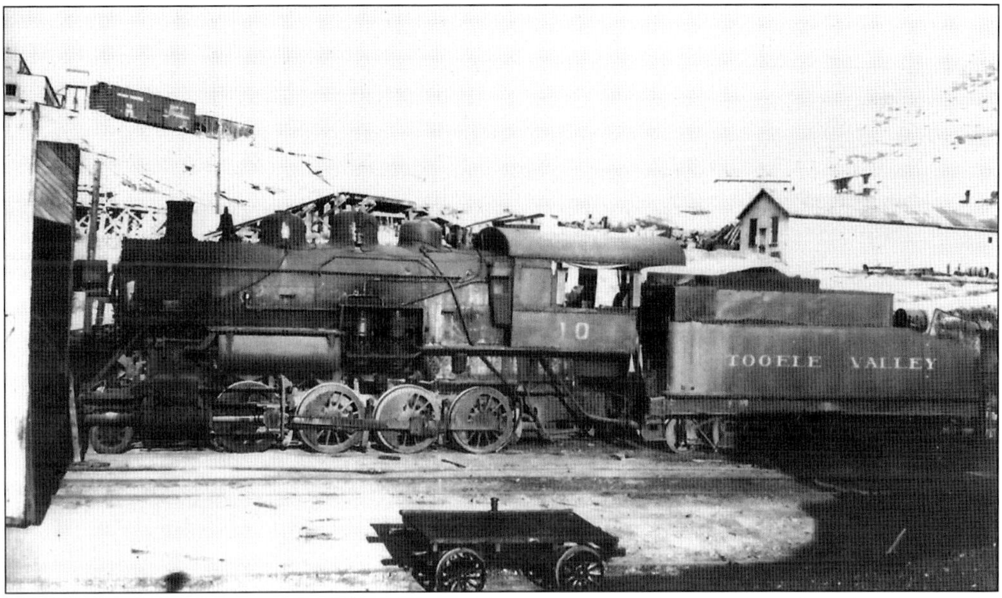

Tooele Valley engine No. 10 is seen here in the International smelter's rail yard in 1939. The engines required regular maintenance and repairs, which the company did in-house. Regular maintenance and light repairs took place in the engine house; for more extensive repairs, engines were sent to the boiler shop. (Courtesy of the Tooele Valley Railroad Museum.)

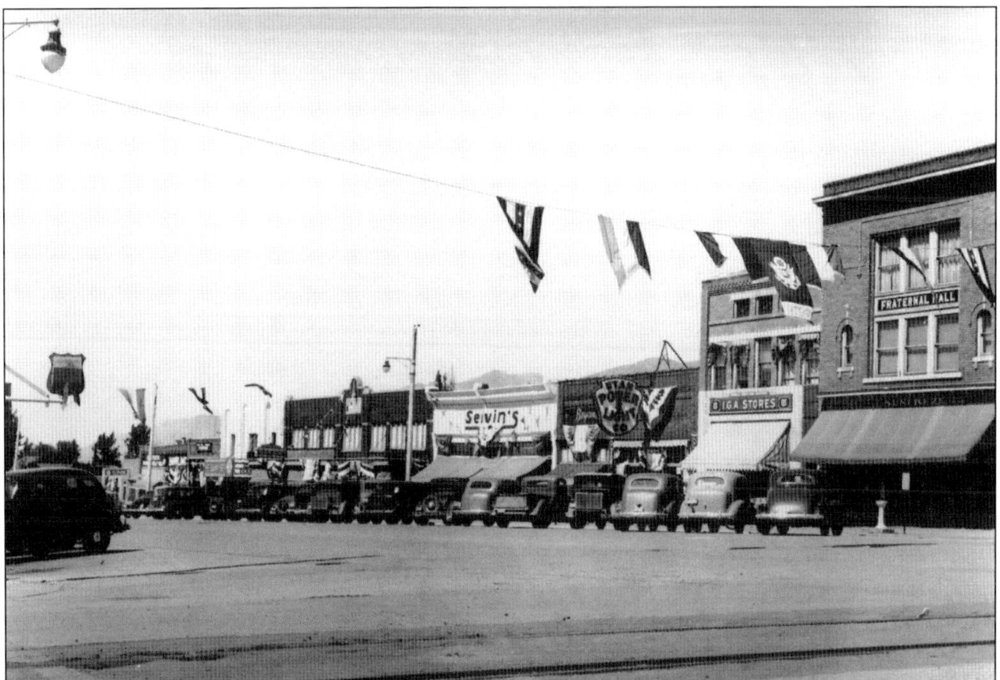

Downtown Tooele is dressed up for a holiday in 1939. Tracks, part of the Tooele Valley line, are clearly visible in the foreground. The photographer is standing at the intersection of Vine and Main Streets facing the north side of Main. The Oquirrh Mountains are just visible behind a row of businesses. (Courtesy of the Utah State Historical Society.)

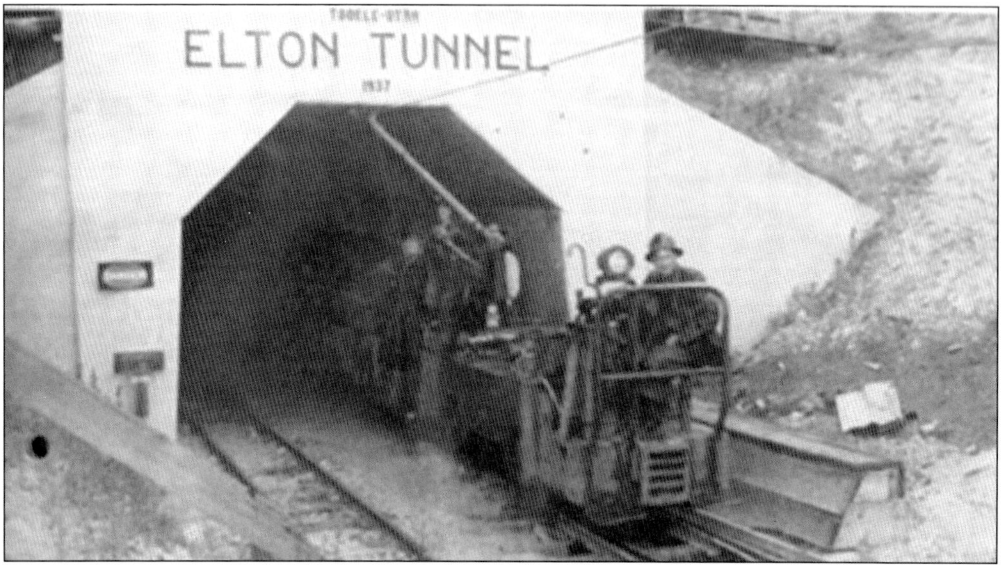

Construction workers pose at the mouth of the Elton Tunnel just before the project's completion in 1941. The Tooele Valley Railway built a 2.33-mile branch line to service the tunnel after Elton announced the project and began excavation in 1937. (Courtesy of the Tooele Valley Railroad Museum.)

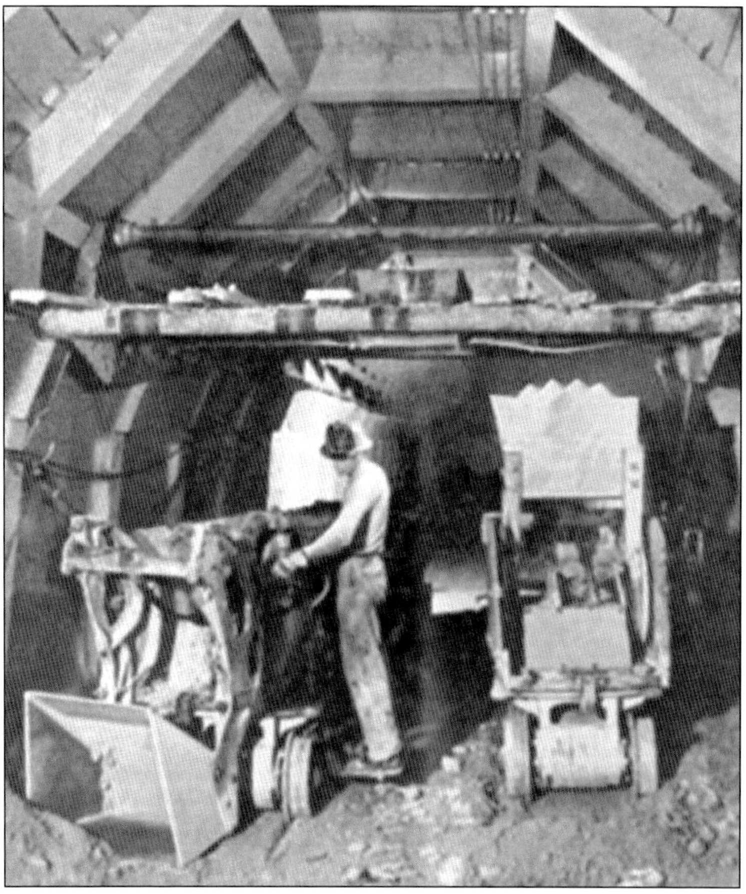

Excavators are at work within the Elton Tunnel in 1941, the year the tunnel officially opened. At the opening ceremony, James Elton predicted that his tunnel would bring $2 million worth of new homes to the valley, increasing Tooele's population by 40,000. His dreams for the tunnel, which closed in 1947, never came to fruition. (Courtesy of the Tooele Valley Railroad Museum.)

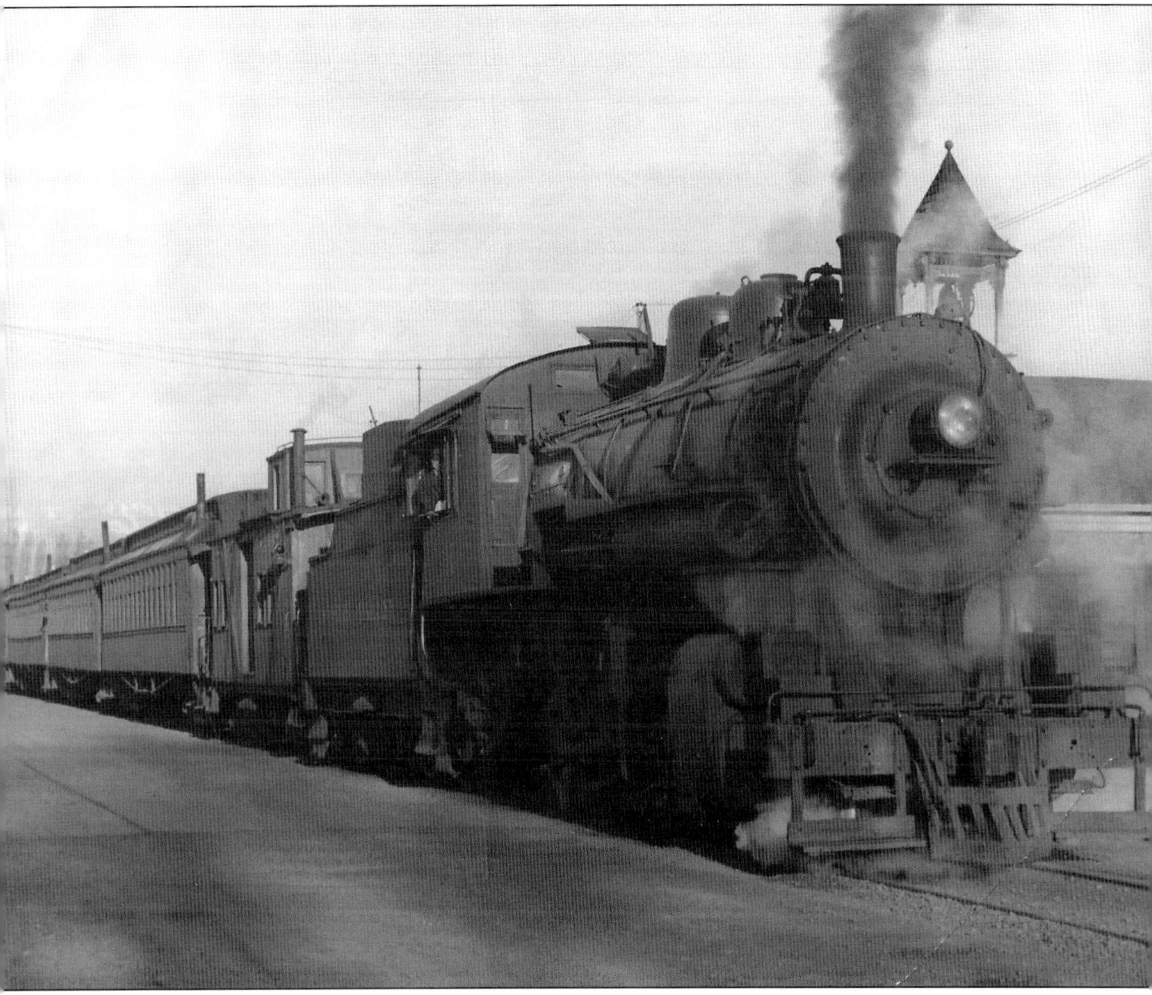

Engine No. 11 steams up Vine Street with a load of passenger coaches in tow. The steepled building in the background is one of Tooele's oldest. Residents built it in 1867 to serve as the city hall, the city jail, the courthouse, and to accommodate various public gatherings. Today, it houses a museum. (Courtesy of the Tooele Valley Railroad Museum.)

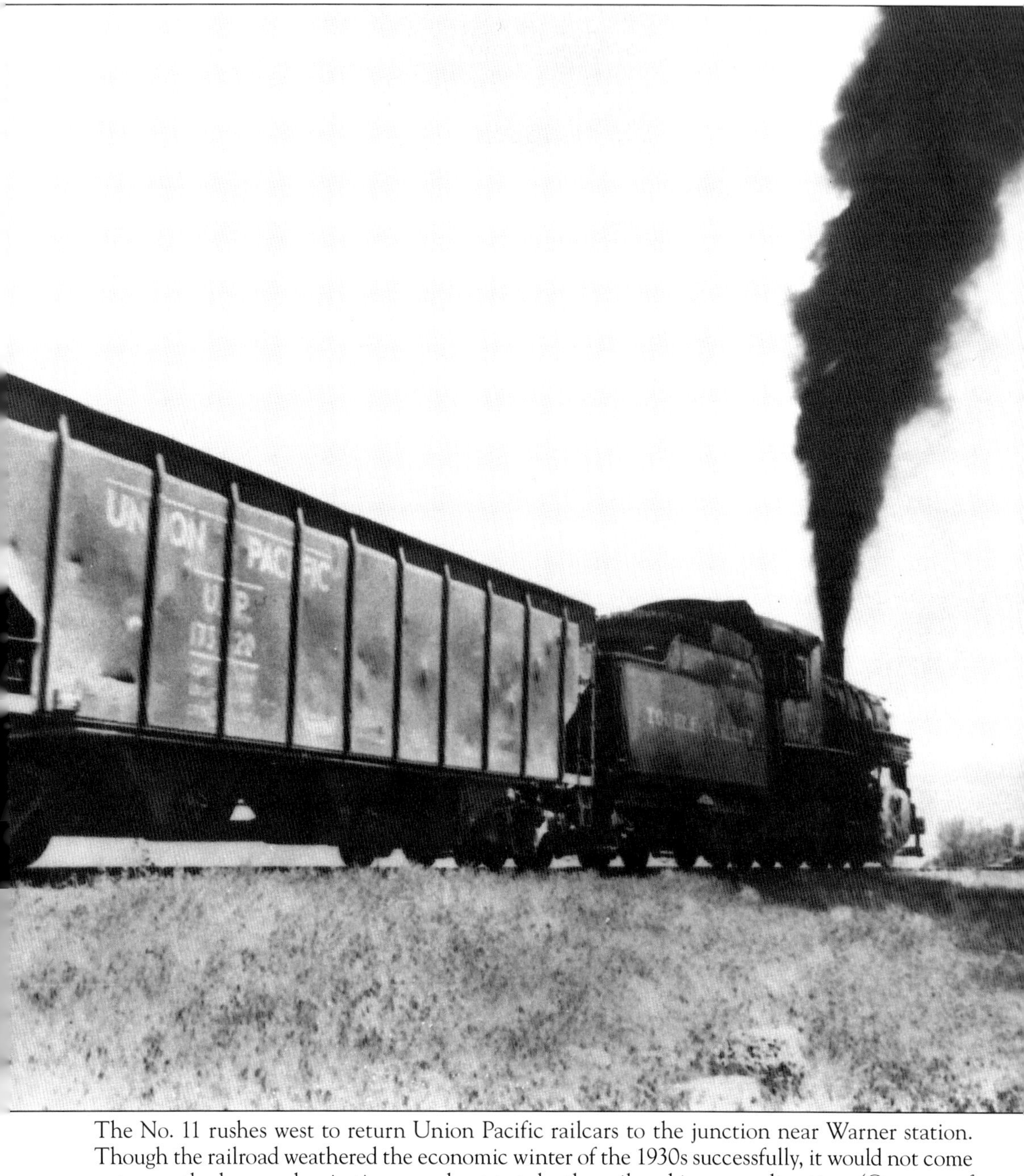

The No. 11 rushes west to return Union Pacific railcars to the junction near Warner station. Though the railroad weathered the economic winter of the 1930s successfully, it would not come out unscathed, as modernization was about to take the railroad in a new direction. (Courtesy of the Tooele Valley Railroad Museum.)

Four

War and Recovery 1942–1959

Despite Elton's investment in Tooele, local industry found itself struggling less than a year after his tunnel's grand opening. The Elton Tunnel, though expensive, provided little in return. Even the water it brought to the desert valley—approximately 4,000 gallons per minute, as promised—was contaminated and, according to locals of the time, the approximate color of mustard. In 1942, the annual Tunnel Day was canceled.

Five years later, after various attempts to make the project profitable, the short-lived Elton Tunnel was quietly closed. The end of World War II–era subsidies for lead and copper finally bankrupted the National Tunnel and Mines Company, and on October 4, 1948, the entire company, valued at some $6 million, was sold at auction for $500,000 to Anaconda Copper.

Despite its changed parent company, the Tooele Valley Railway proved resilient. The growing popularity of automobiles ended all passenger services, and 24-hour operation was discontinued, but the Tooele Valley Railway found work hauling not only ore but also various other bulk shipments, including oil, newsprint, and even cars.

During the mid-1950s, the railroad decided to retire steam power in favor of the increasingly efficient diesel engines. The first diesel, engine No. 100, came to Tooele in 1955. The oldest engines, No. 9 and No. 10, were both retired and scrapped in the early 1950s. In 1956, engine No. 12 was scrapped and converted into a much-needed snowplow.

Engine No. 11, which the Tooele Valley kept on hand as an alternate for the diesel, remained in service for nearly another decade. Its final run, on May 20, 1963, made it the last steam engine to operate in the state of Utah. When its boiler was finally condemned by the state inspector, the engine was disabled and retired to a monument in the Tooele city park. A second diesel, engine No. 104, was purchased to replace it.

A 1958 joint agreement between International's final competitor, a lead smelter in Midvale, brought an increase in rail traffic to Tooele and proved a boon to the railroad company. According to the terms of the agreement, the Midvale facility would mill and concentrate ores and International would smelt them. Responsibility for shipping the ore between these two facilities fell to the Union Pacific and the Tooele Valley Railway. Tooele's little railroad was again on a track for success.

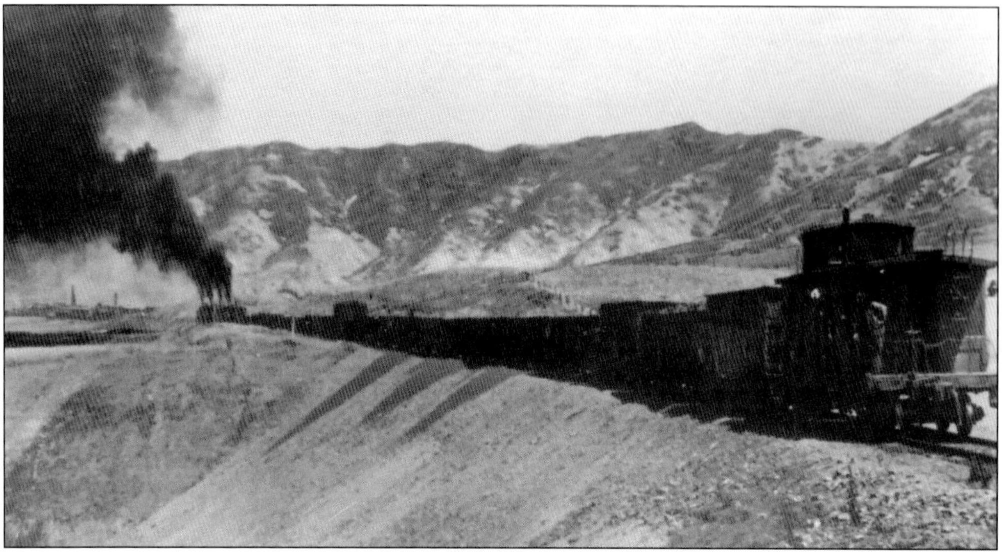

A four-engine train crosses the Middle Canyon trestle with finished goods from International on its way to Warner for distribution. The railroad filled in the trestle with waste rock from the Elton Tunnel in 1943, which increased the allowable speed over the gorge from 8 miles per hour to 15 miles per hour. (Courtesy of the Tooele Valley Railroad Museum.)

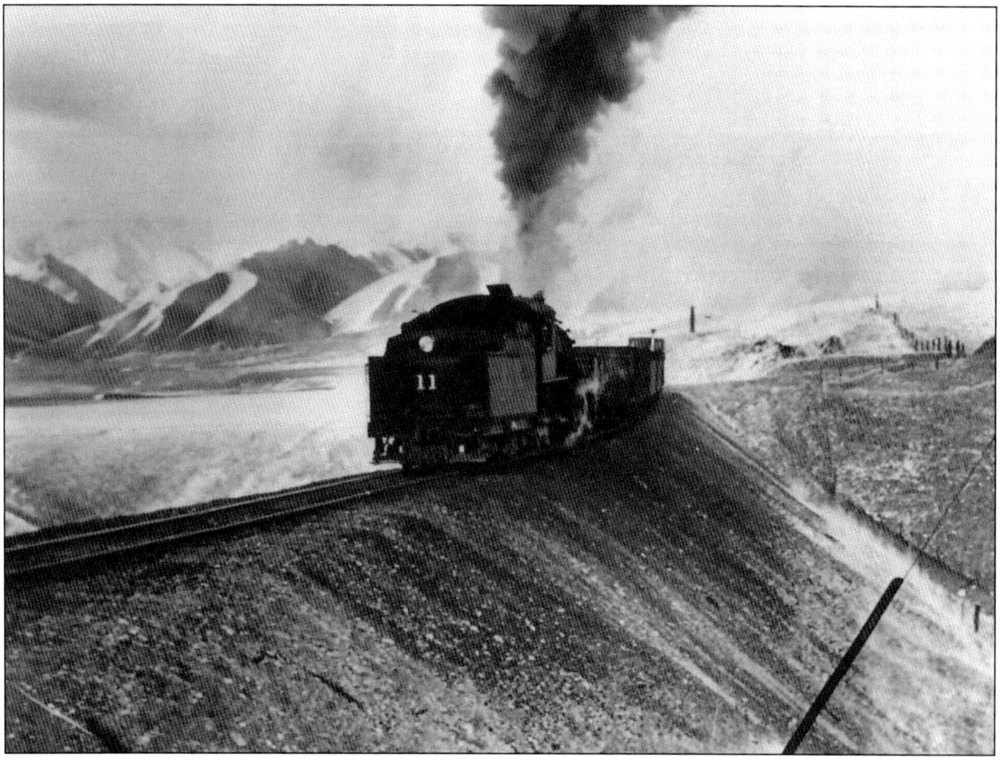

Engine No. 11 pushes a load of ore over the newly filled Middle Canyon trestle. Railroad officials knew the trestle was unstable in the mid-1920s, long before they had it filled. The Elton Tunnel ultimately failed to deliver, but the railroad welcomed this solution to a long-standing problem. (Courtesy of the Tooele Valley Railroad Museum.)

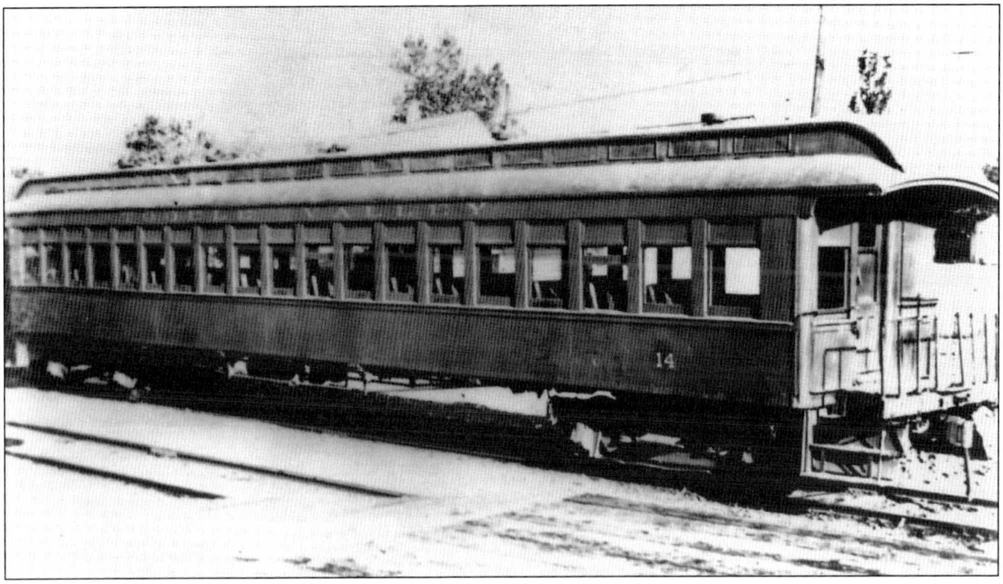

These new passenger coaches were photographed in the 1940s. It is not entirely clear when the Tooele Valley Railway updated its coaches, but passenger cars in earlier photographs show that a different model was in use prior to the 1940s. Despite the upgrade, railroad officials announced plans to discontinue general passenger services in September 1941. Originally, an anticipated increase in freight traffic, driven by the predicted success of the Elton Tunnel, was the railroad's stated reason. Later, company officials attributed the change to the automobile's newfound popularity. Passenger service for International employees continued, and the railroad picked up bulk shipping to make up the difference. (Both courtesy of the Tooele Valley Railroad Museum.)

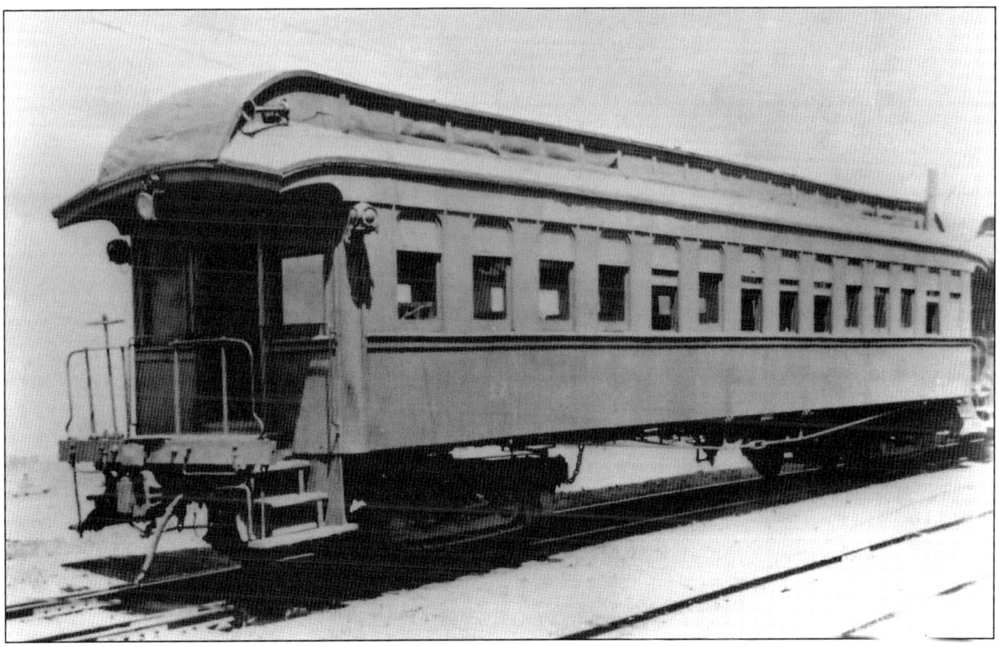

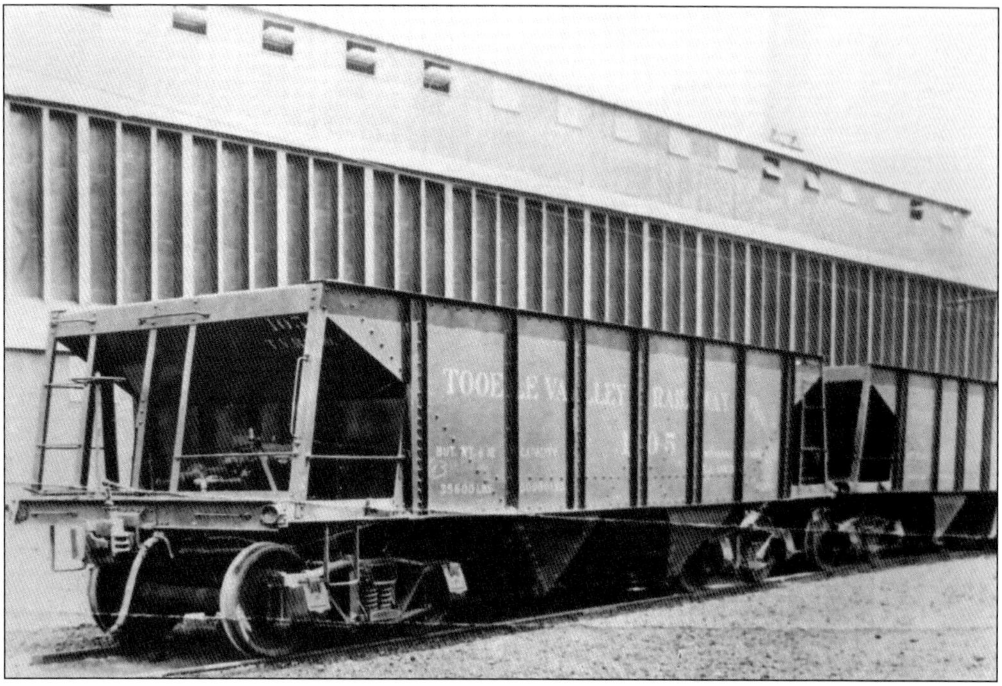

Hopper cars for transporting ore are seen here outside the International smelter in the 1940s. In the mid-1920s, the Interstate Commerce Commission counted about 60 freight cars, including boxcars and hopper cars, in the railroad's possession. Freight cars from other railroads also frequented the Tooele Valley line. (Courtesy of the Tooele Valley Railroad Museum.)

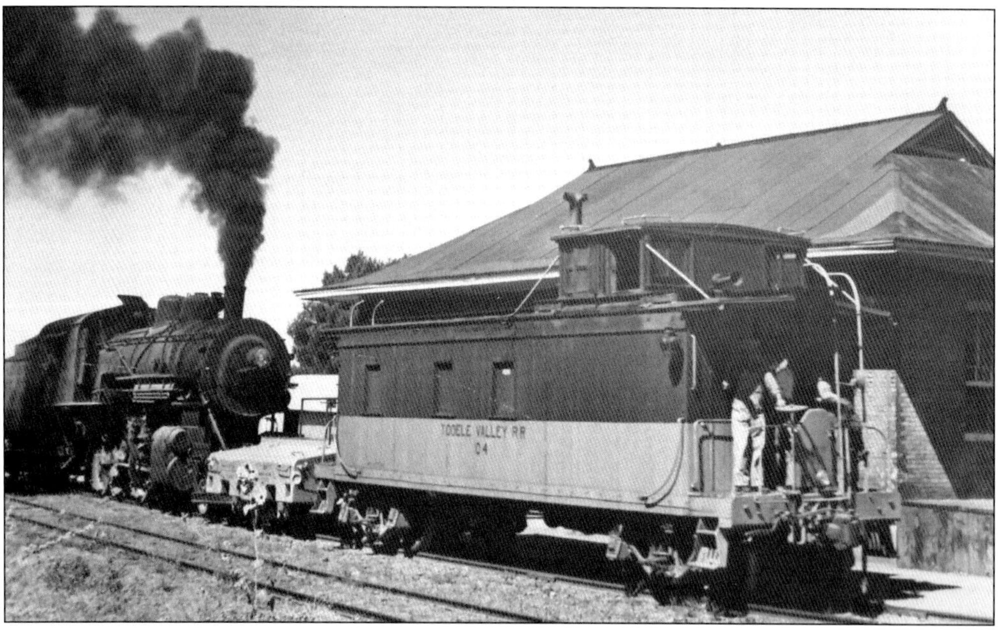

Caboose No. 4 pauses at the Tooele station on Broadway and Vine Street. This was the last caboose operating on the Tooele Valley line. The railroad purchased it secondhand in 1957 and it remained on the company's roster until 1982. Caboose No. 3 remained in service until earlier in 1982. (Courtesy of the Tooele Valley Railroad Museum.)

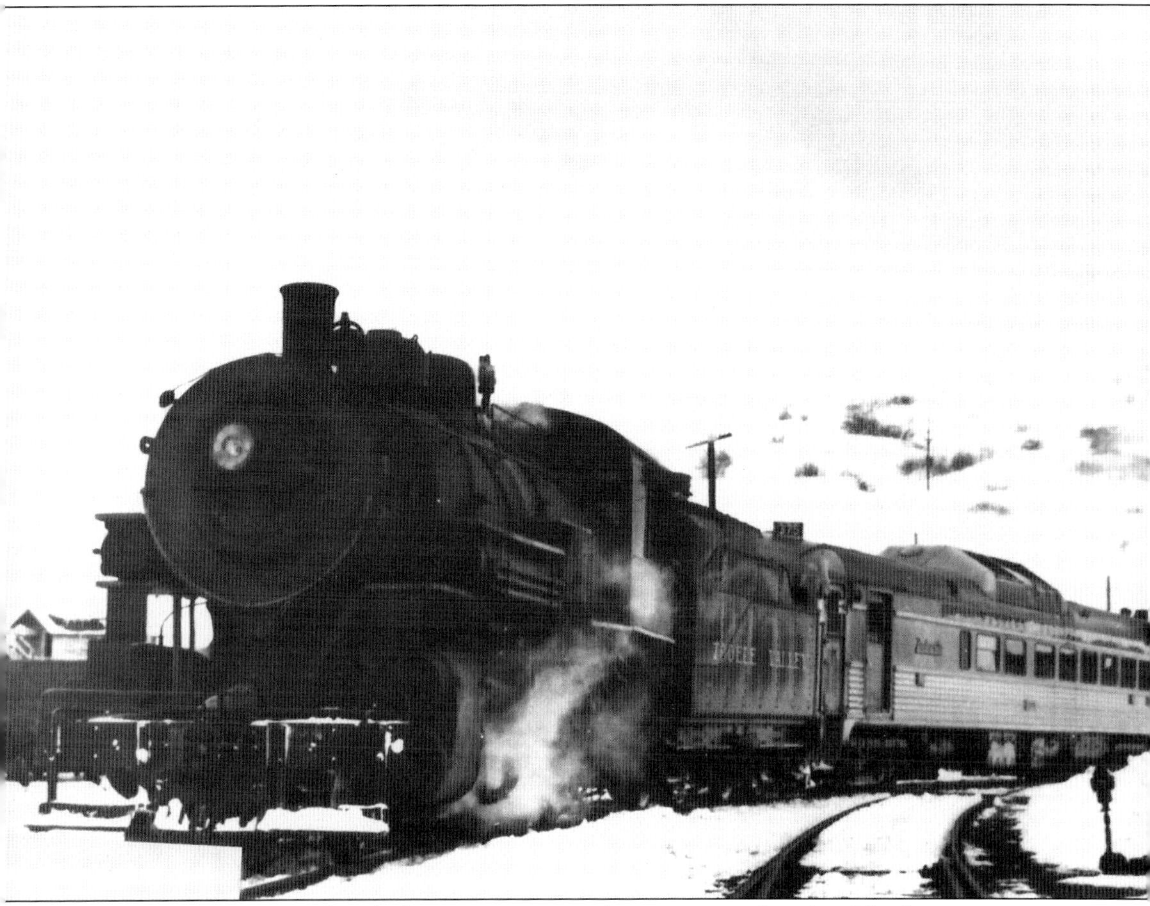

Engine No. 11 pulls an unidentified passenger car near the International smelter. The discontinuation of passenger services was perhaps a signal of bigger changes happening at the smelter. Copper smelting was no longer profitable, and International leaned more heavily on lead smelting and zinc products from its newly built slag treatment plant. (Courtesy of the Tooele Valley Railroad Museum.)

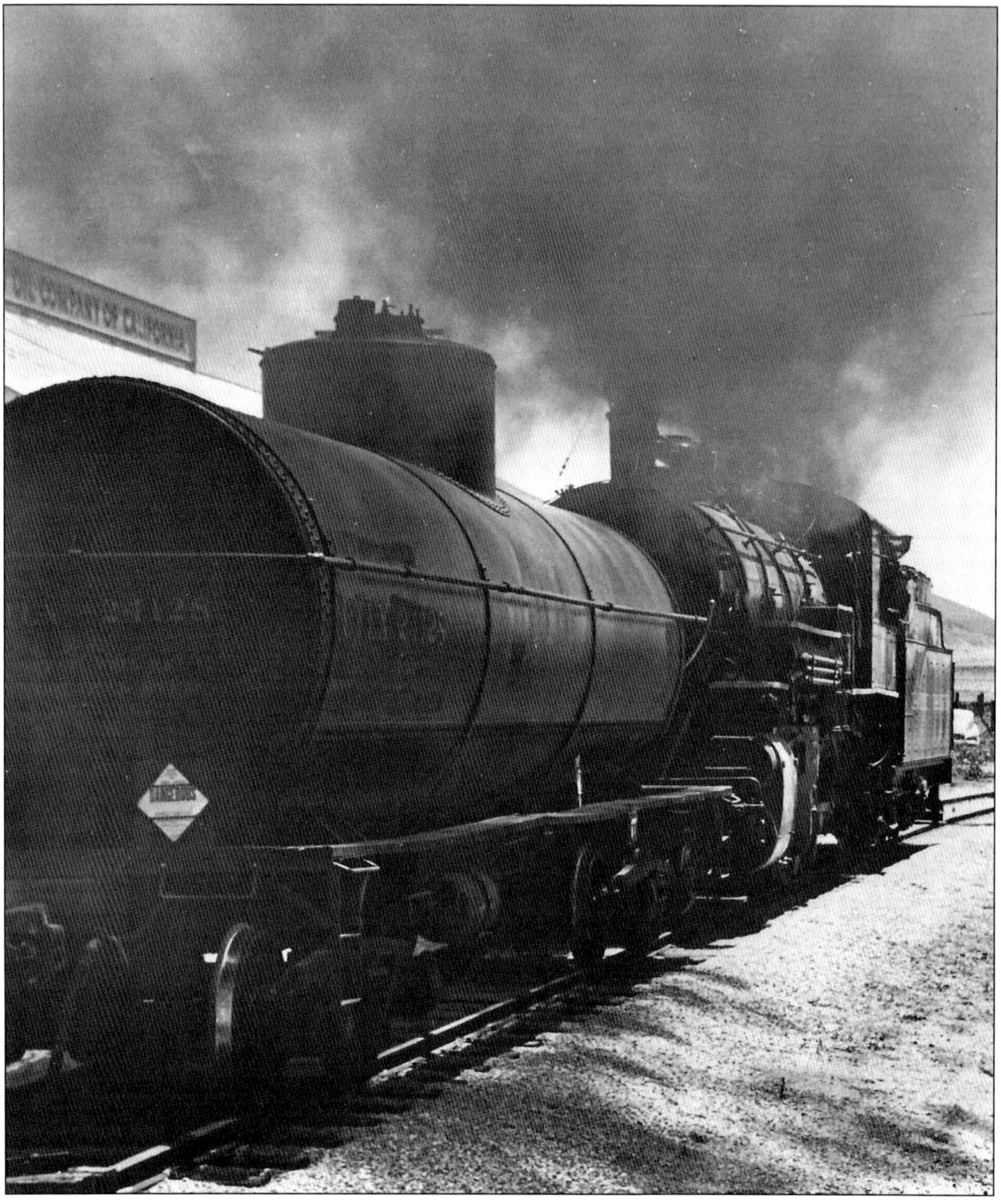

Without ticket sales to help the railroad pull a profit, the Tooele Valley turned to bulk shipping as an alternate source of revenue. Common loads included newsprint and oil for Tooele businesses. The smelter itself did not use the oil; it switched to natural gas in 1928 because the company found it was both cheaper and easier to handle than other fuels. (Courtesy of the Tooele Valley Railroad Museum.)

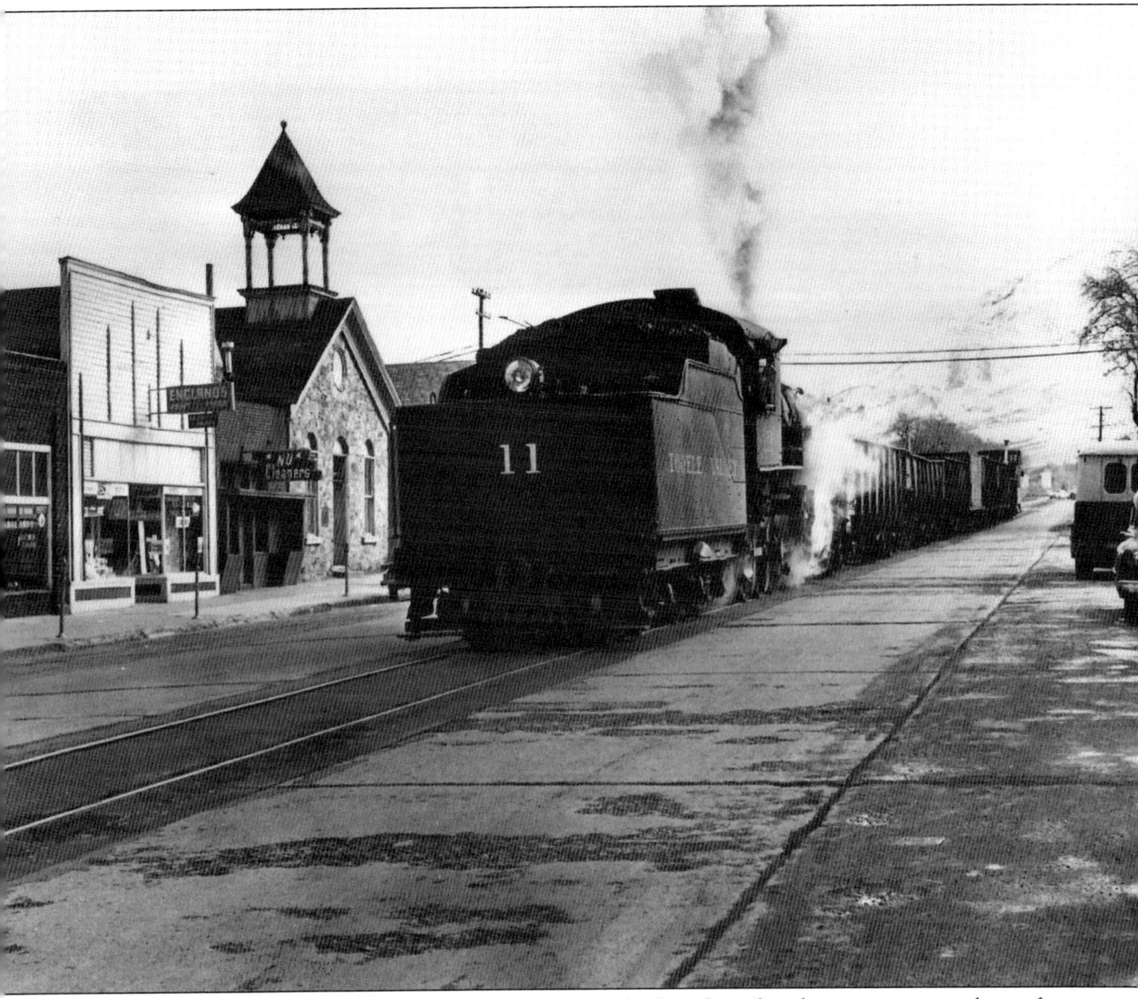

The Tooele Valley Railway is seen here on Vine Street, which it shared with increasing numbers of automobiles in the 1940s and 1950s. Originally, International planned to launch a subsidiary called the International Bus Company to replace discontinued passenger service on the railroad, but it is unclear exactly what became of those plans. (Courtesy of the Tooele Valley Railroad Museum.)

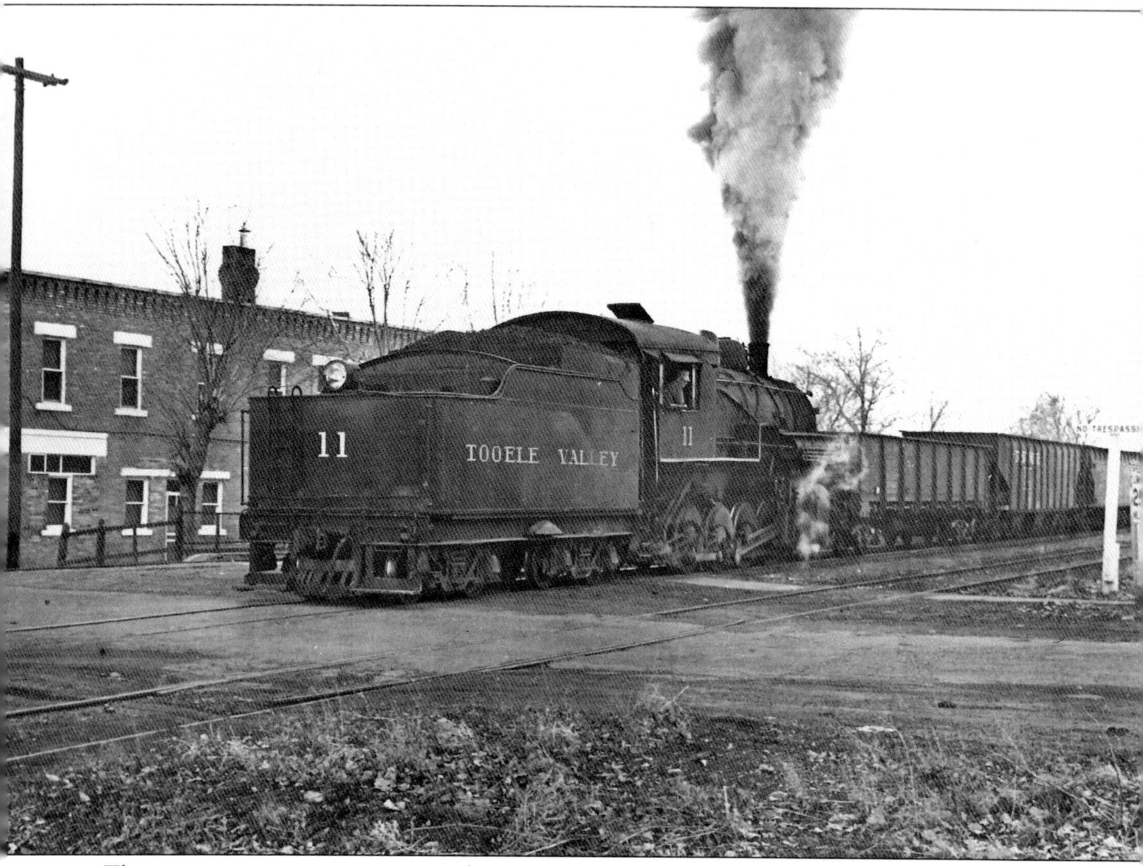

The train continues on its eastward journey up Vine Street, passing a bustling neighborhood of immigrants who worked at the smelter. For years, this area, called Newtown by locals, acted as a second downtown for Tooele. Much of this section of town was later demolished or abandoned. (Courtesy of the Tooele Valley Railroad Museum.)

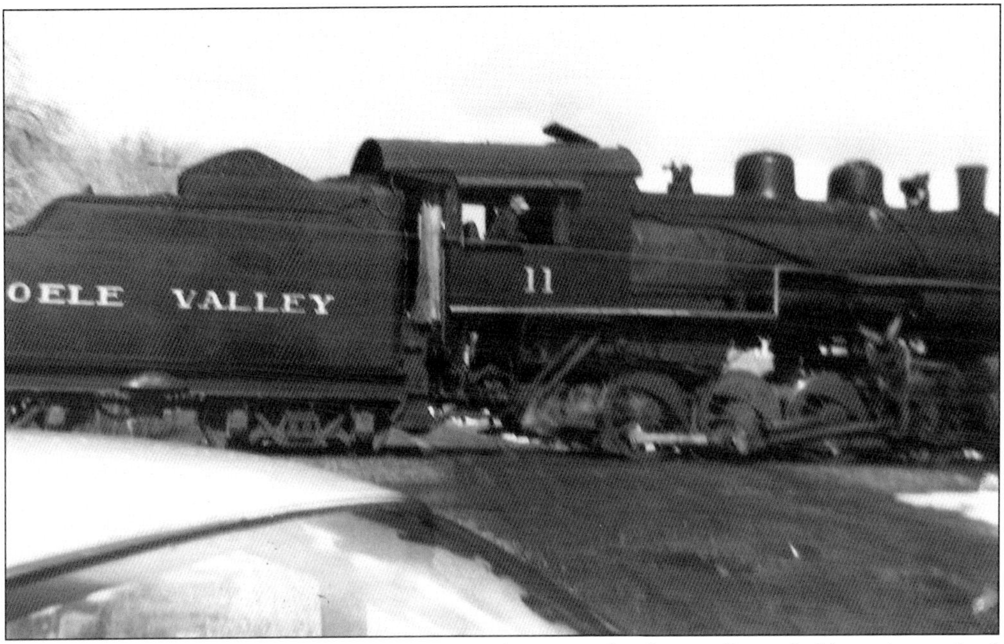

Cars wait for engine No. 11 to cross a street on the west side of town. Remarkably, only one fatal accident involving a train and an automobile was recorded on the Tooele Valley line. The accident occurred on the east edge of town when a woman drove her car into the path of an oncoming train. The impact killed one of her children. (Courtesy of the Tooele Valley Railroad Museum.)

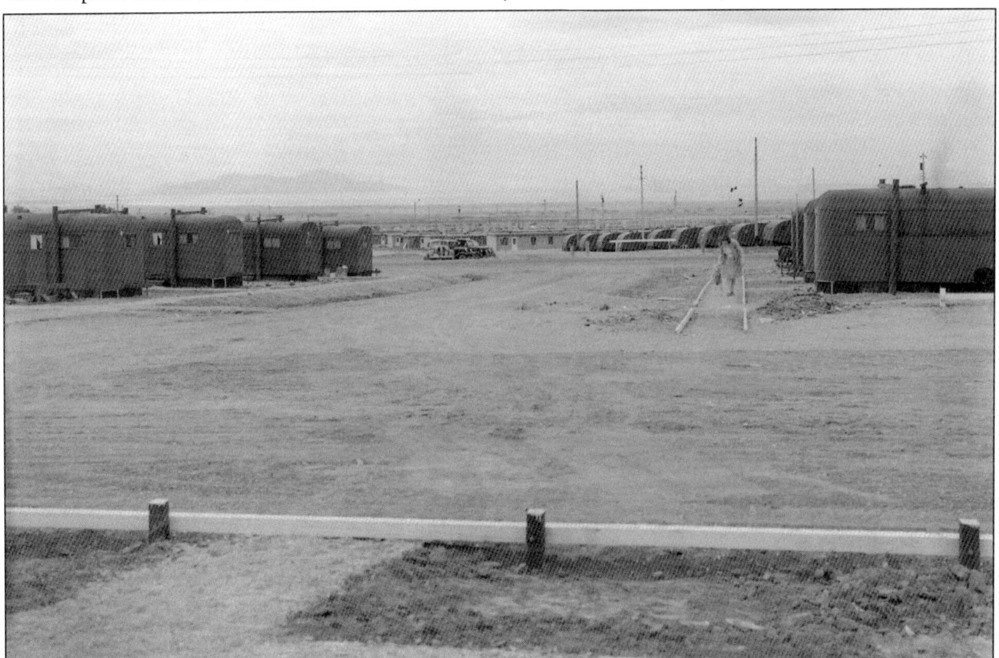

This snapshot from 1943 shows a trailer park that International Smelting set up to house some of its employees. Housing projects such as this, usually sponsored by International, helped solve Tooele's housing problem and allowed the company to fill its employee roster each year. (Courtesy of the Utah State Historical Society.)

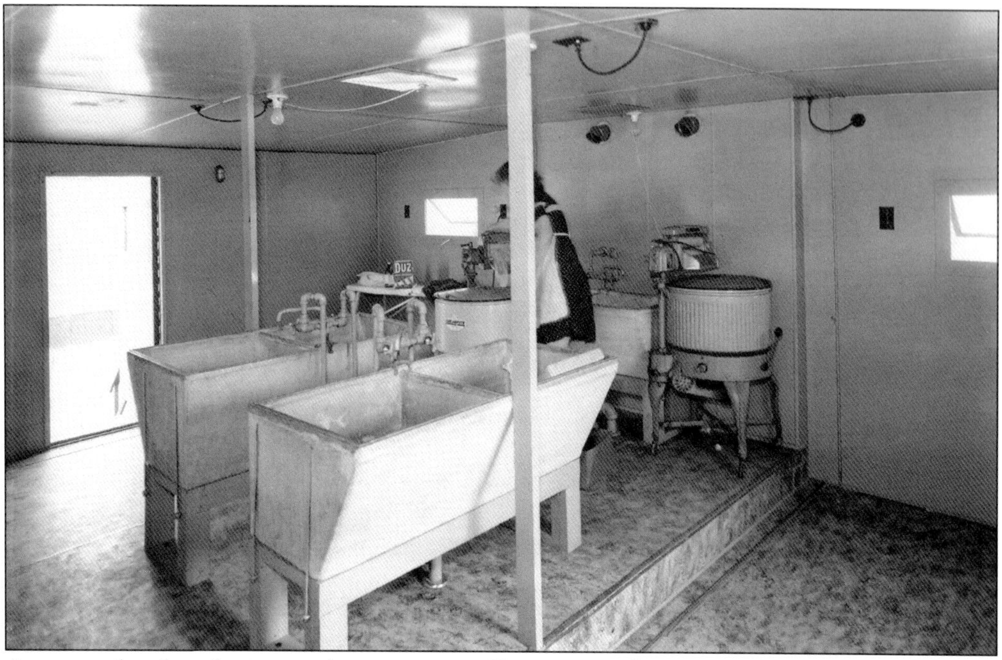

A woman does laundry in a washroom at one of International's company housing projects. Many of the families that worked at the smelter were immigrants from Southern European countries, especially Italy and Greece, and they often arrived with few belongings to their names. (Courtesy of the Utah State Historical Society.)

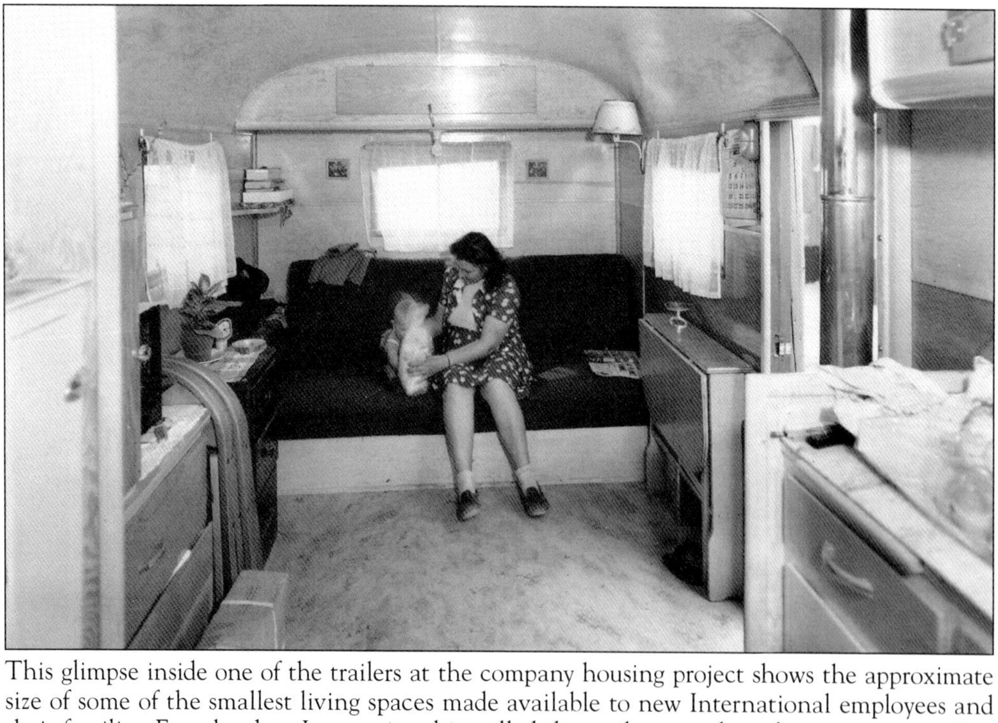
This glimpse inside one of the trailers at the company housing project shows the approximate size of some of the smallest living spaces made available to new International employees and their families. Exactly when International installed the trailers, or when they were removed, is unknown. (Courtesy of the Utah State Historical Society.)

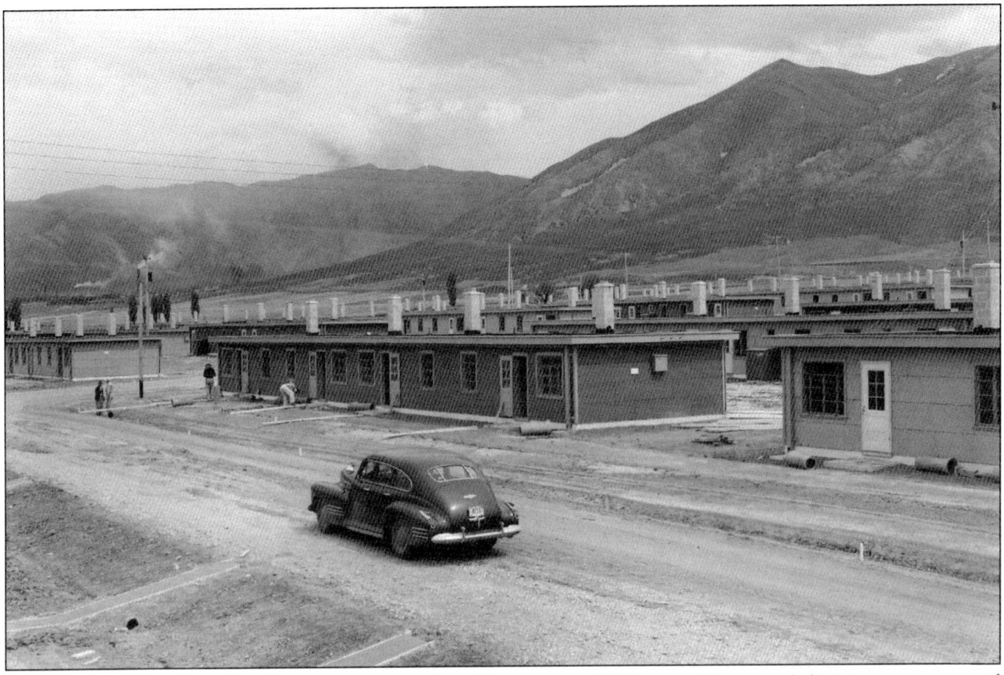

Rows upon rows of simple, cheap apartments lined the streets of this early Tooele subdivision, constructed for employees of the International company. These homes were a step up from the trailers, which coexisted with the apartments at the time. (Courtesy of the Utah State Historical Society.)

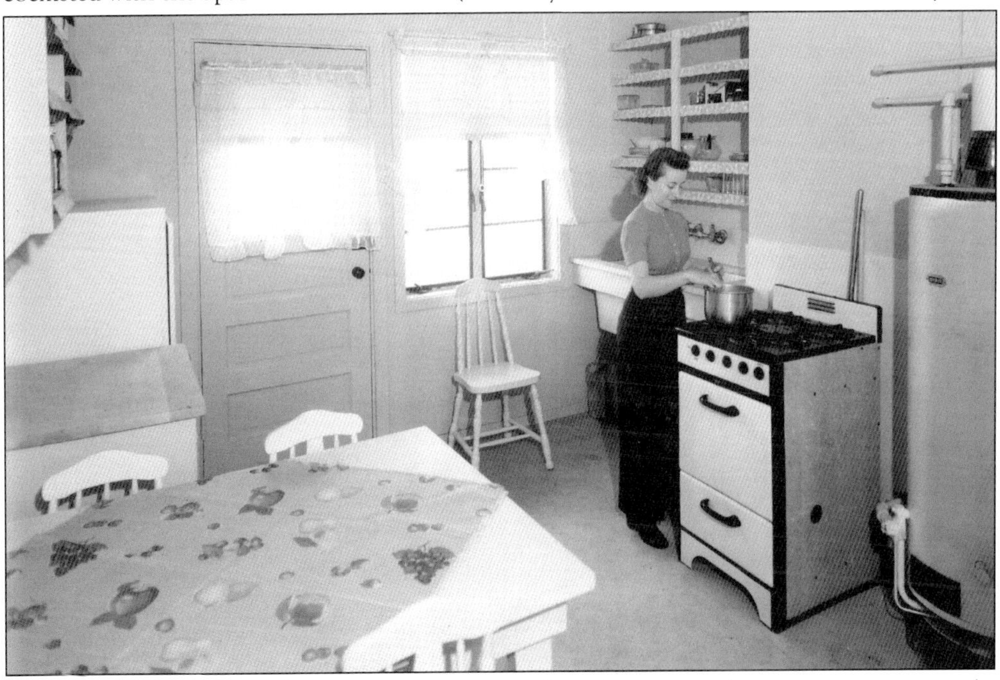

A woman cooks on a small stove in the kitchen of an International company apartment. As with the trailers, it is unclear when or why the apartments were removed. When they were still standing, they provided a warm place to sleep for hundreds of immigrant workers and their families. (Courtesy of the Utah State Historical Society.)

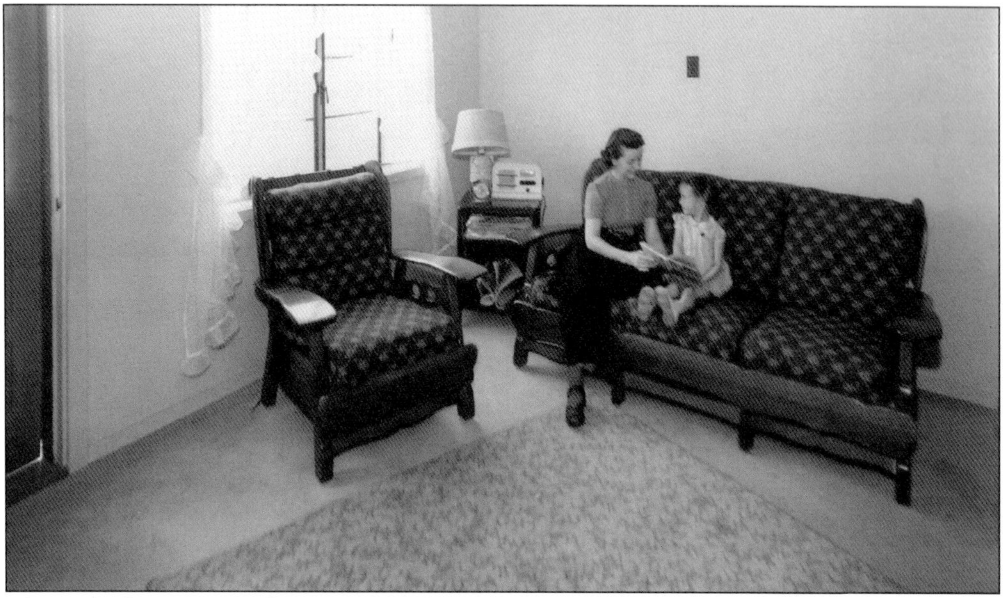

This is the living room of an apartment home built by the International company in Tooele for its employees. The living room was simply the other end of the kitchen. Divisions between the two rooms were arbitrary, and this family marked the difference with a rug. (Courtesy of the Utah State Historical Society.)

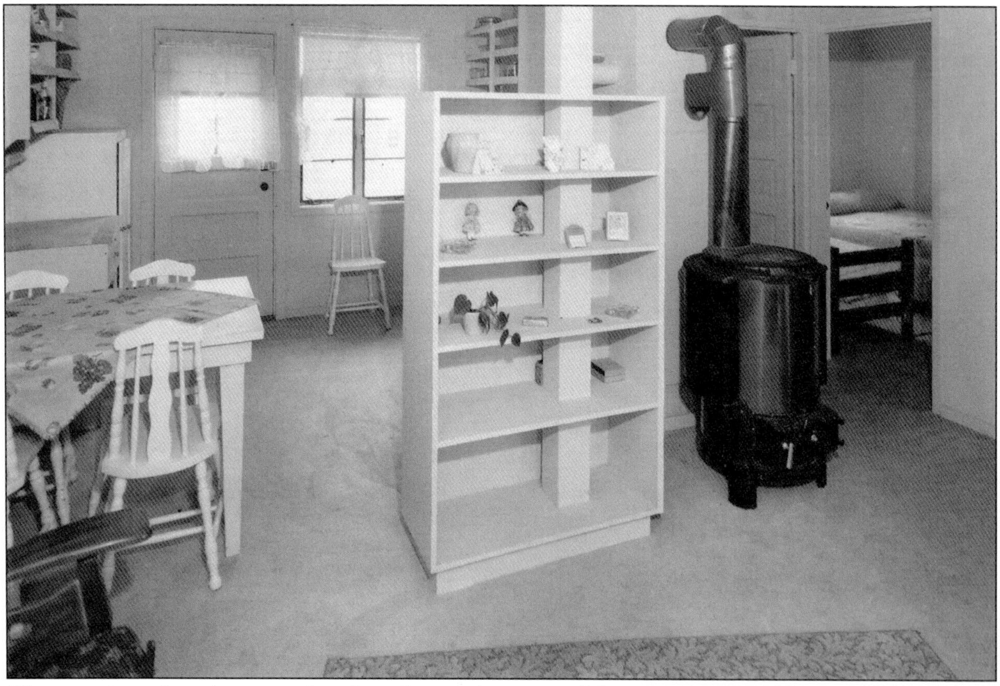

The number of workers employed at the smelter varied from one year to the next, depending on whether the company was turning a profit. Typically, the number of names on the payroll was somewhere between 500 and 600, a relatively small number for an operation the size of the International smelter. How many of those workers lived in company housing is not known. (Courtesy of the Utah State Historical Society.)

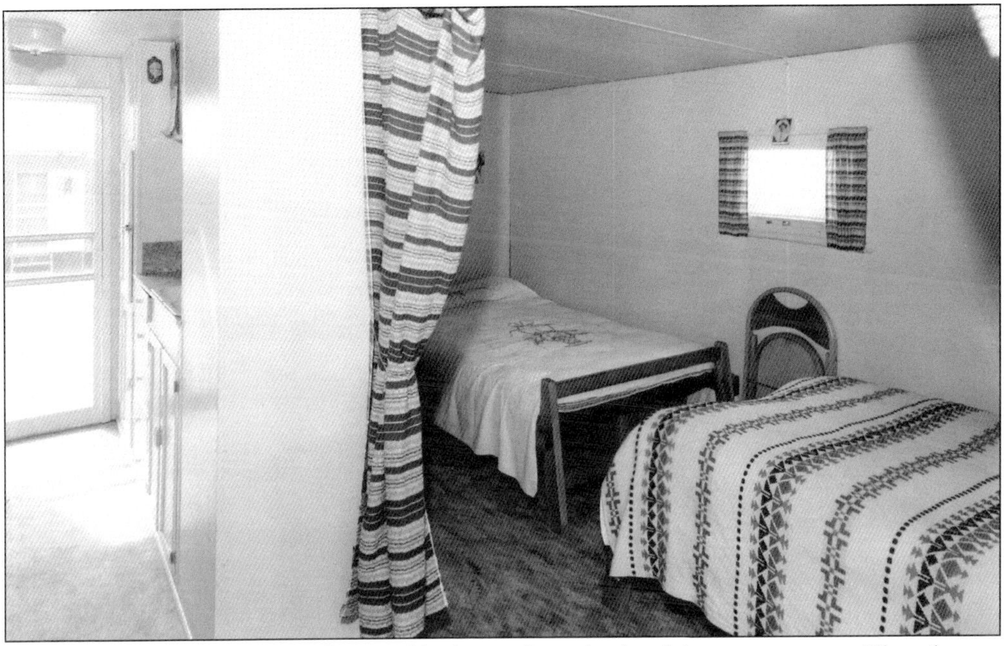

Above, a curtain divides a small second bedroom from the family's common areas. These homes had two bedrooms, but the master bedroom (below) was the only room that was entirely closed off from the rest of the apartment. Though many of the families that came to Tooele emigrated from Southern Europe, a diversity of other countries, ranging from Austria to Japan, were represented in smaller numbers. Immigrants rarely interacted with families descended from the valley's original settlers, but the entire town came together to celebrate during the Fourth of July parade, where marchers were invited to carry the colors of their native countries. (Both courtesy of the Utah State Historical Society.)

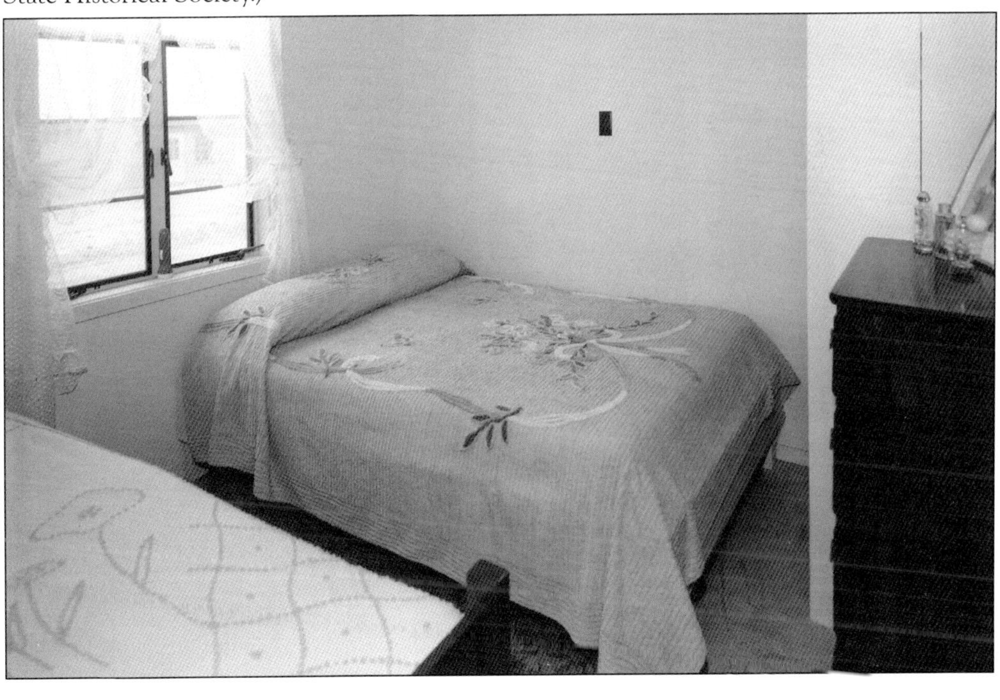

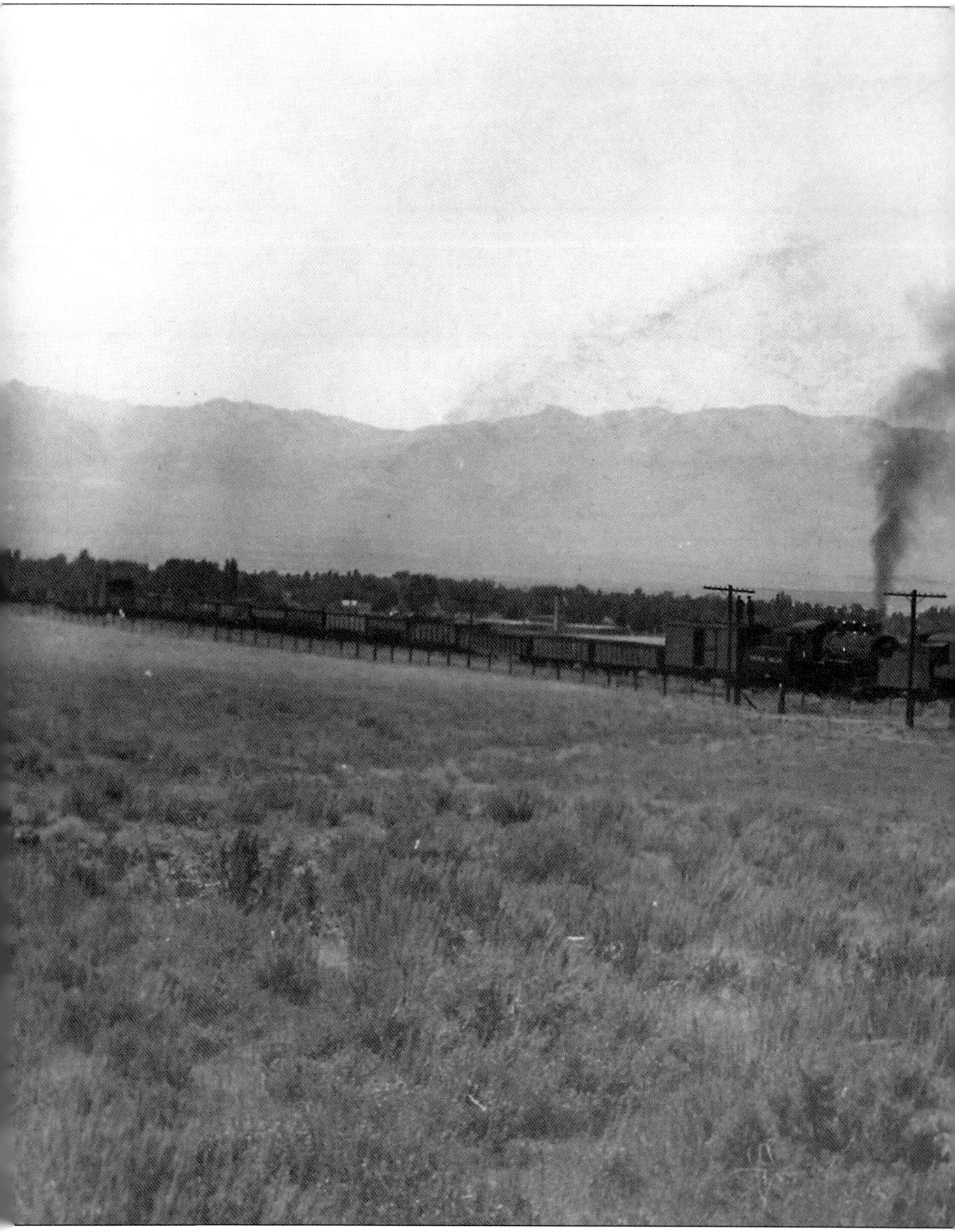

This spectacle—a train with the combined power of all four Tooele Valley engines—caught the eye of a photographer as it passed through town. The steam engines were on their way out in

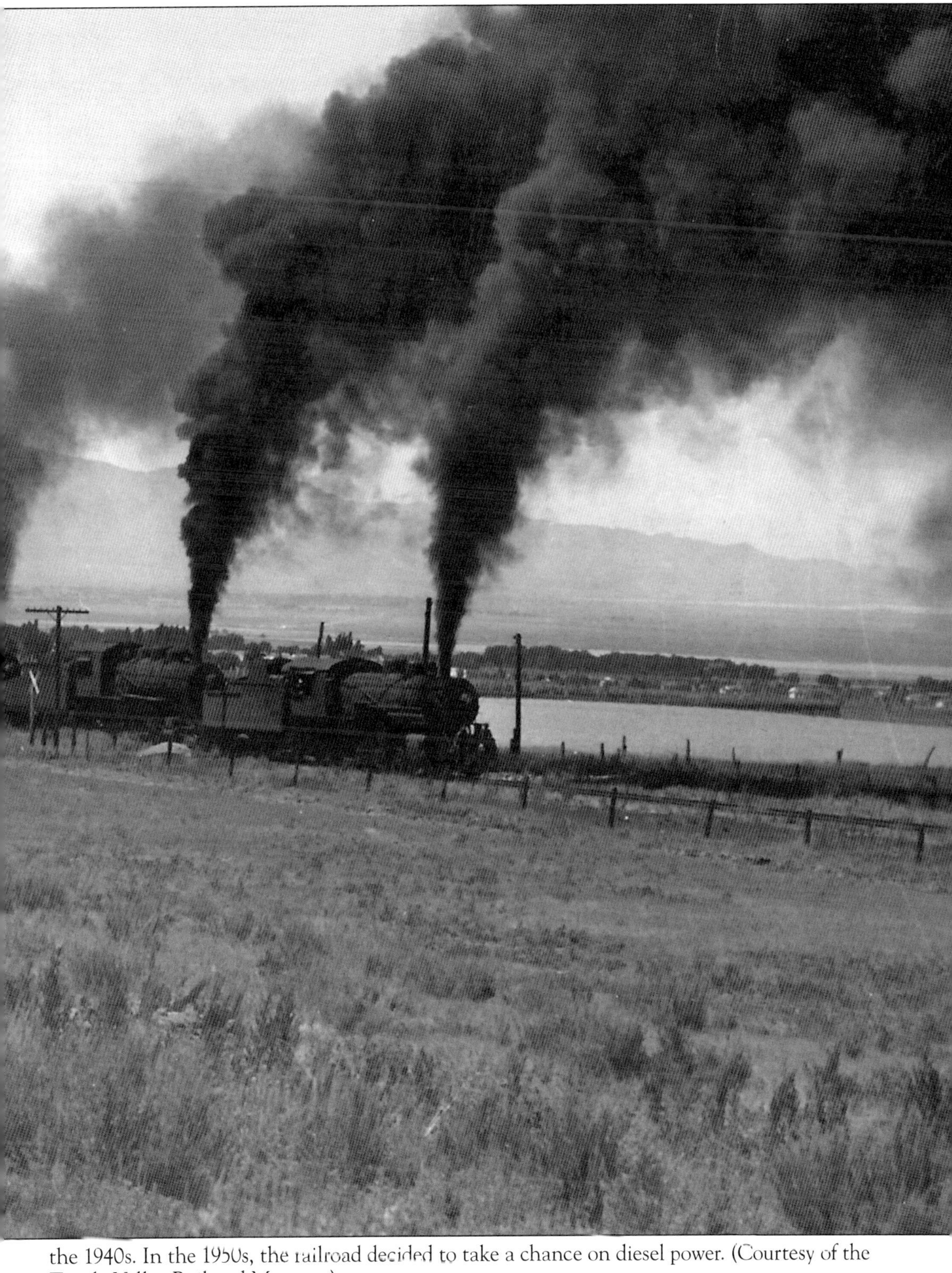

the 1940s. In the 1950s, the railroad decided to take a chance on diesel power. (Courtesy of the Tooele Valley Railroad Museum.)

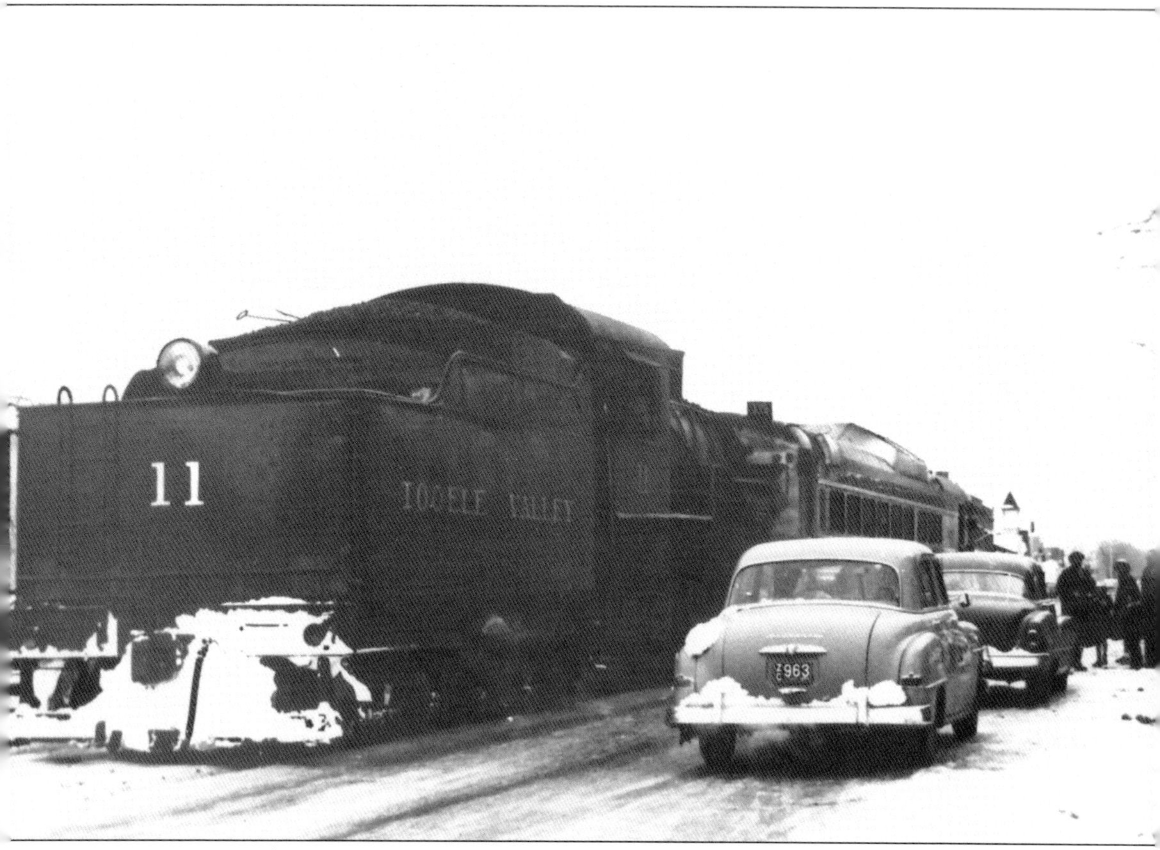

Engine No. 11 shares Vine Street with automobile and pedestrian traffic as it approaches Main Street. By the late 1940s, dynamics in the town were clearly changing. The International smelter was no longer a homegrown, independent company, having been bought out by Anaconda Copper in October 1948. (Courtesy of the Tooele Valley Railroad Museum.)

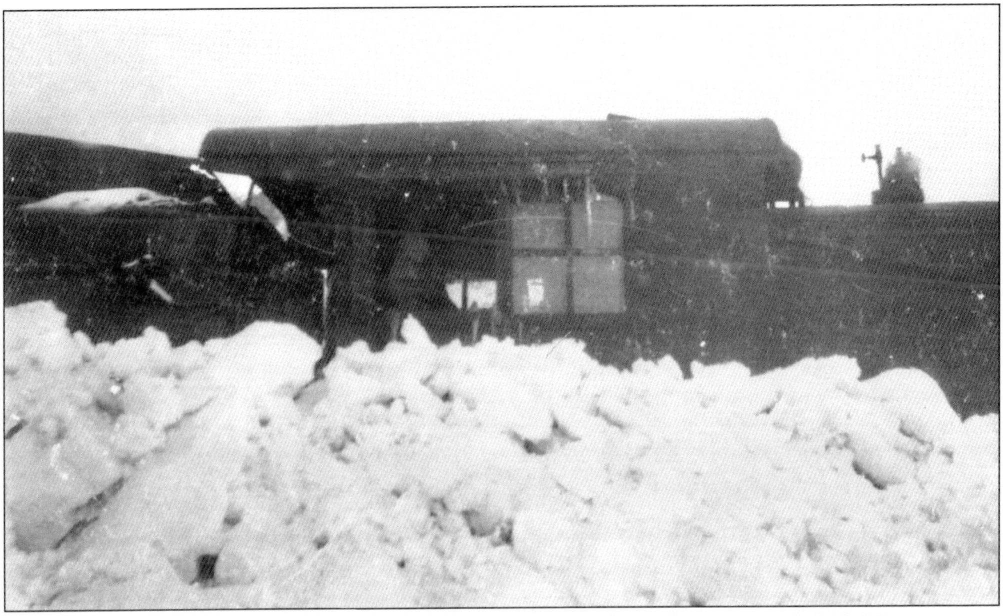

A second round of record-breaking winter storms hit Tooele in the winter of 1948. No trains got stuck that year, but snow once again piled into drifts half as tall as a locomotive. This grinning railroad worker does not seem to mind—but then, he was not assigned to snow removal. (Courtesy of the Tooele Valley Railroad Museum.)

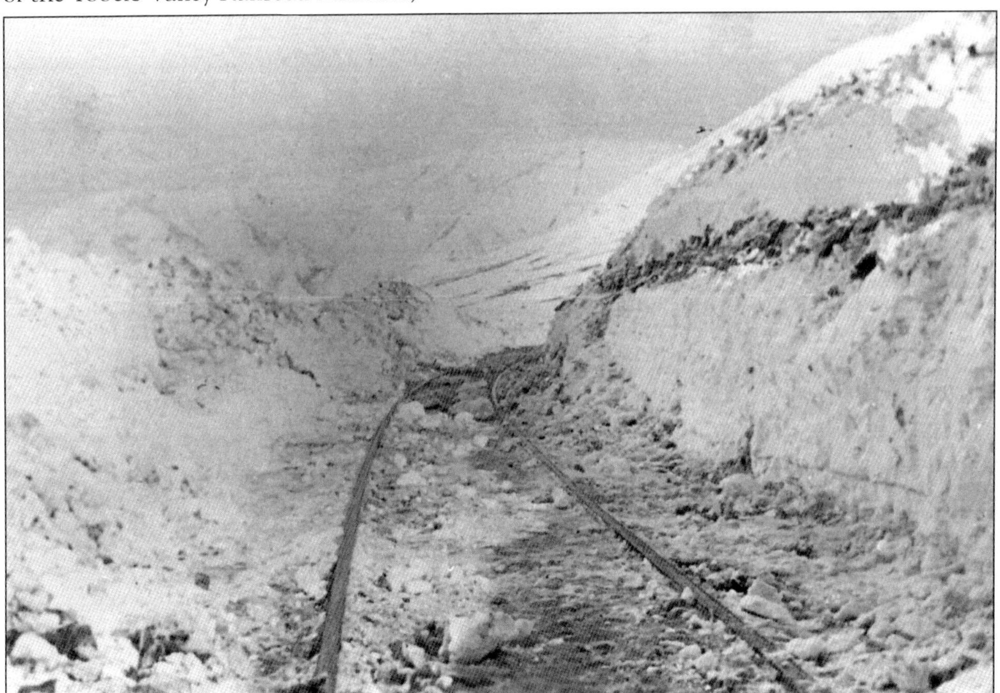

Snow collects in sedimentary cliff-like formations around the Tooele Valley Railway tracks approaching Pine Canyon. The railroad fought to keep snow off the tracks here in the foothills outside town, where windblown snow from the canyon collected on top of the original snowfall. (Courtesy of the Tooele Valley Railroad Museum.)

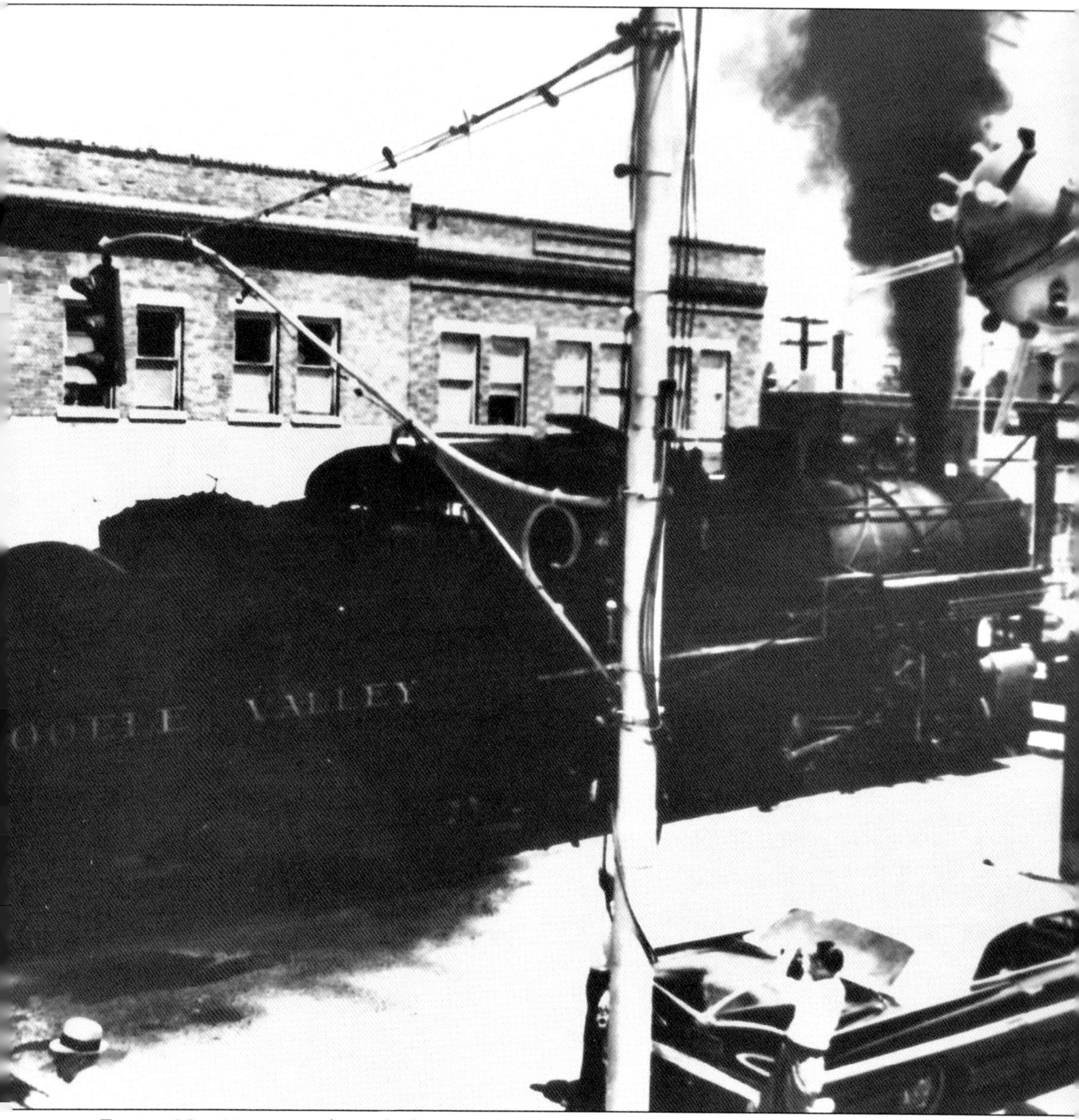

Engine No. 11 steams through downtown Tooele, a sight that was becoming increasingly less common. The Tooele Valley ceased 24-hour operation in 1950, and the company began to downsize its roster of engines. The company retired and scrapped engine No. 9 that same year. (Courtesy of the Tooele Valley Railroad Museum.)

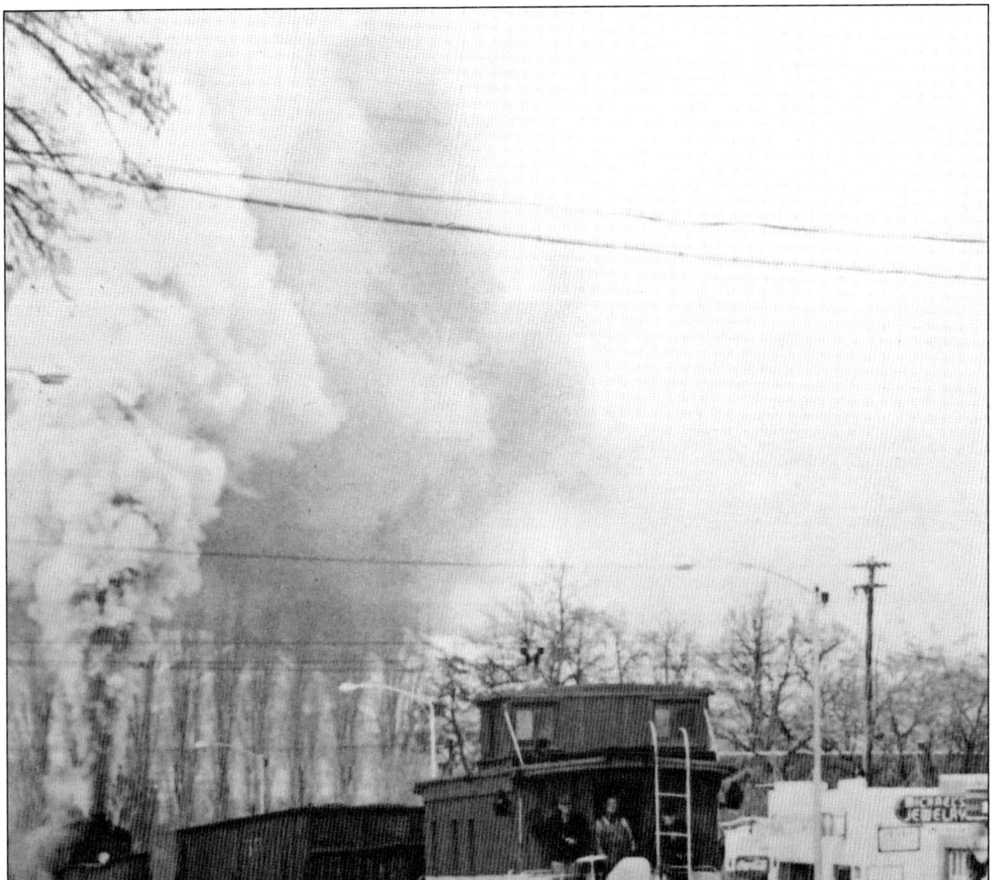

While bulk shipping and an agreement with another smelter in Salt Lake City kept the Tooele Valley in business in the 1950s, the railroad also discontinued shipping orders that were less than a carload at that time. In 1942, the Tooele Valley received, on average, about three carloads of miscellaneous freight per week. By 1950, that volume had decreased to less than one car per week. (Courtesy of the Tooele Valley Railroad Museum.)

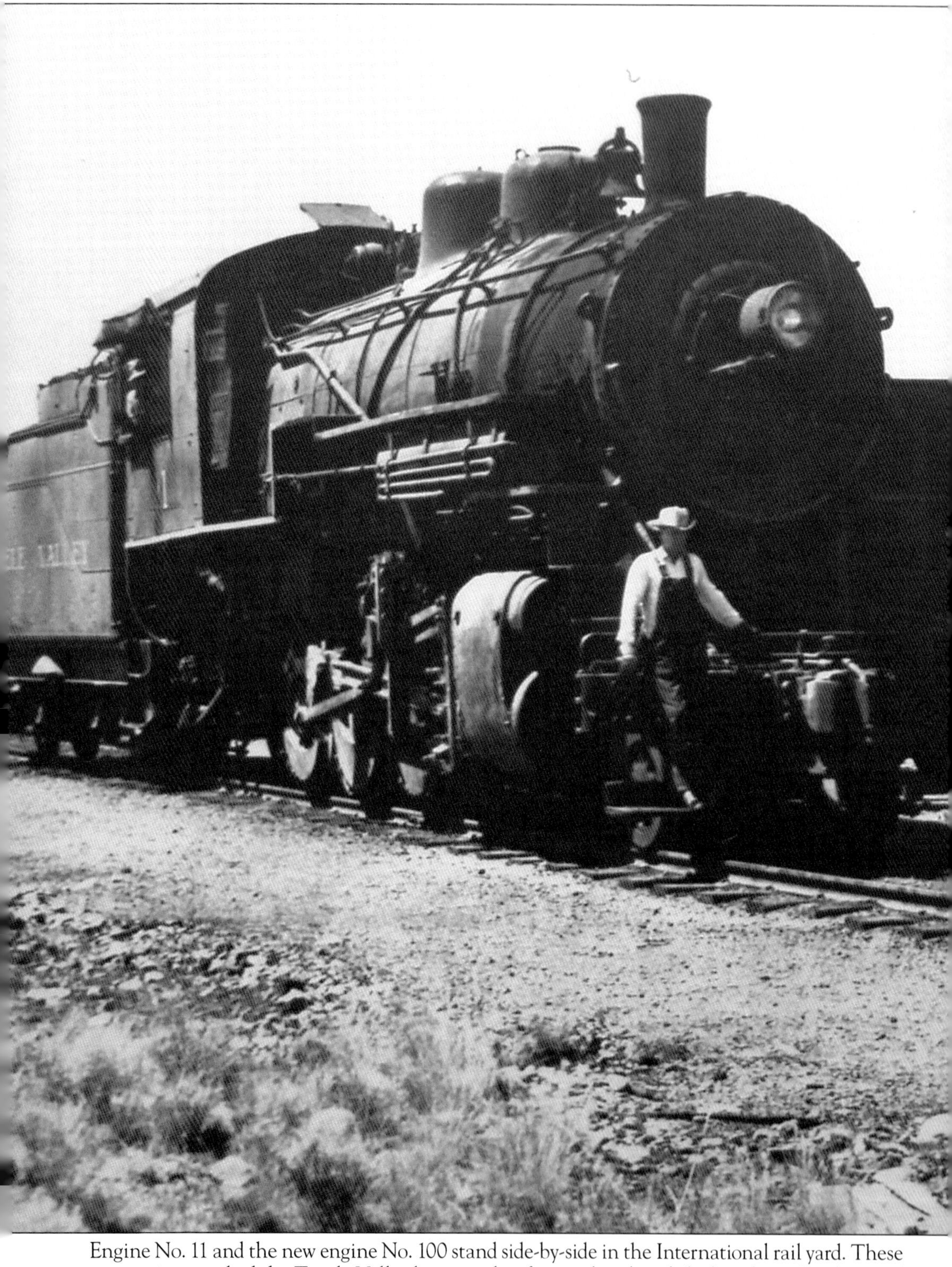

Engine No. 11 and the new engine No. 100 stand side-by-side in the International rail yard. These two engines worked the Tooele Valley line together for nearly a decade before the railroad retired

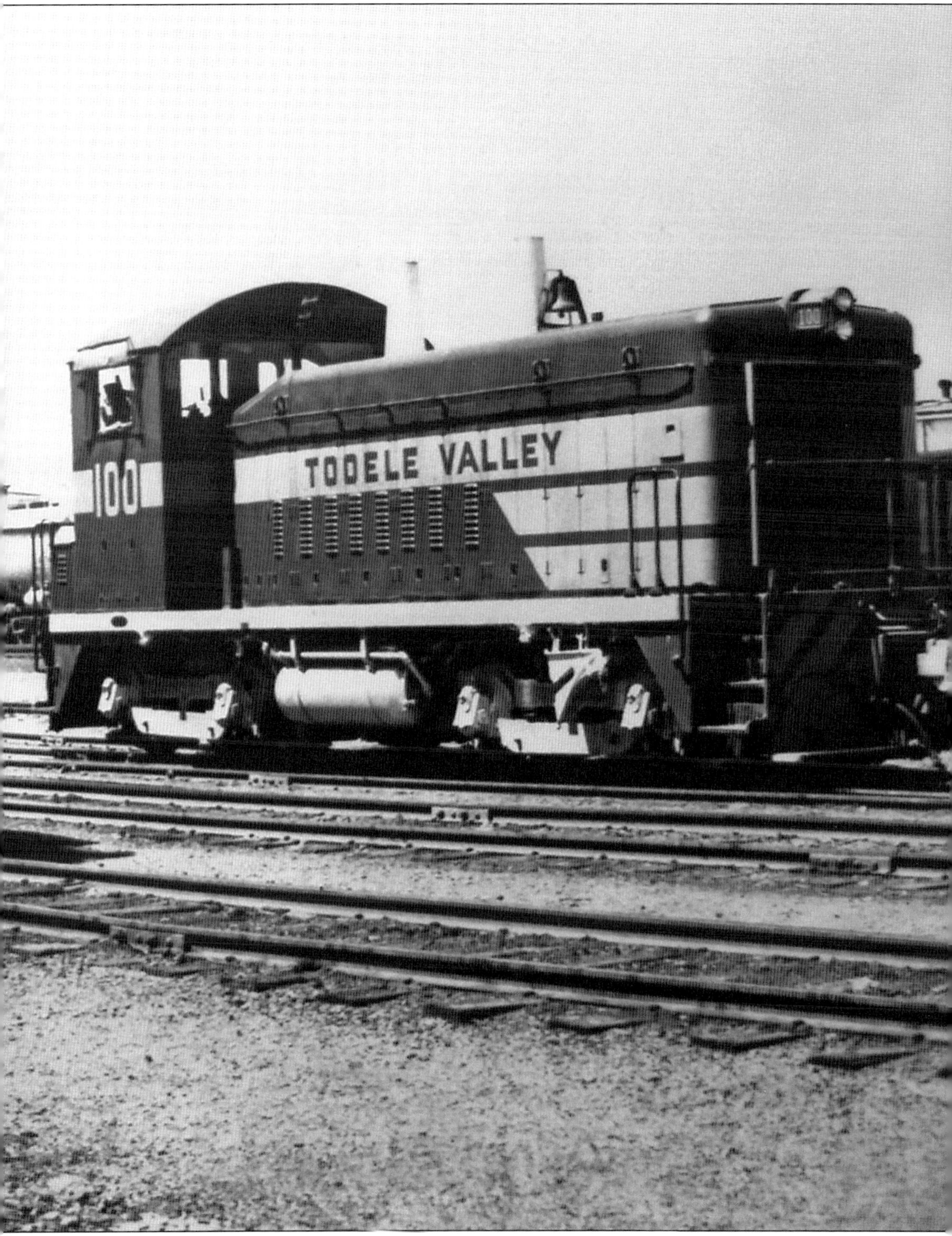

engine No. 11 in the early 1960s. During that time, No. 100 was the primary engine, with No. 11 on standby. (Courtesy of the Tooele Valley Railroad Museum.)

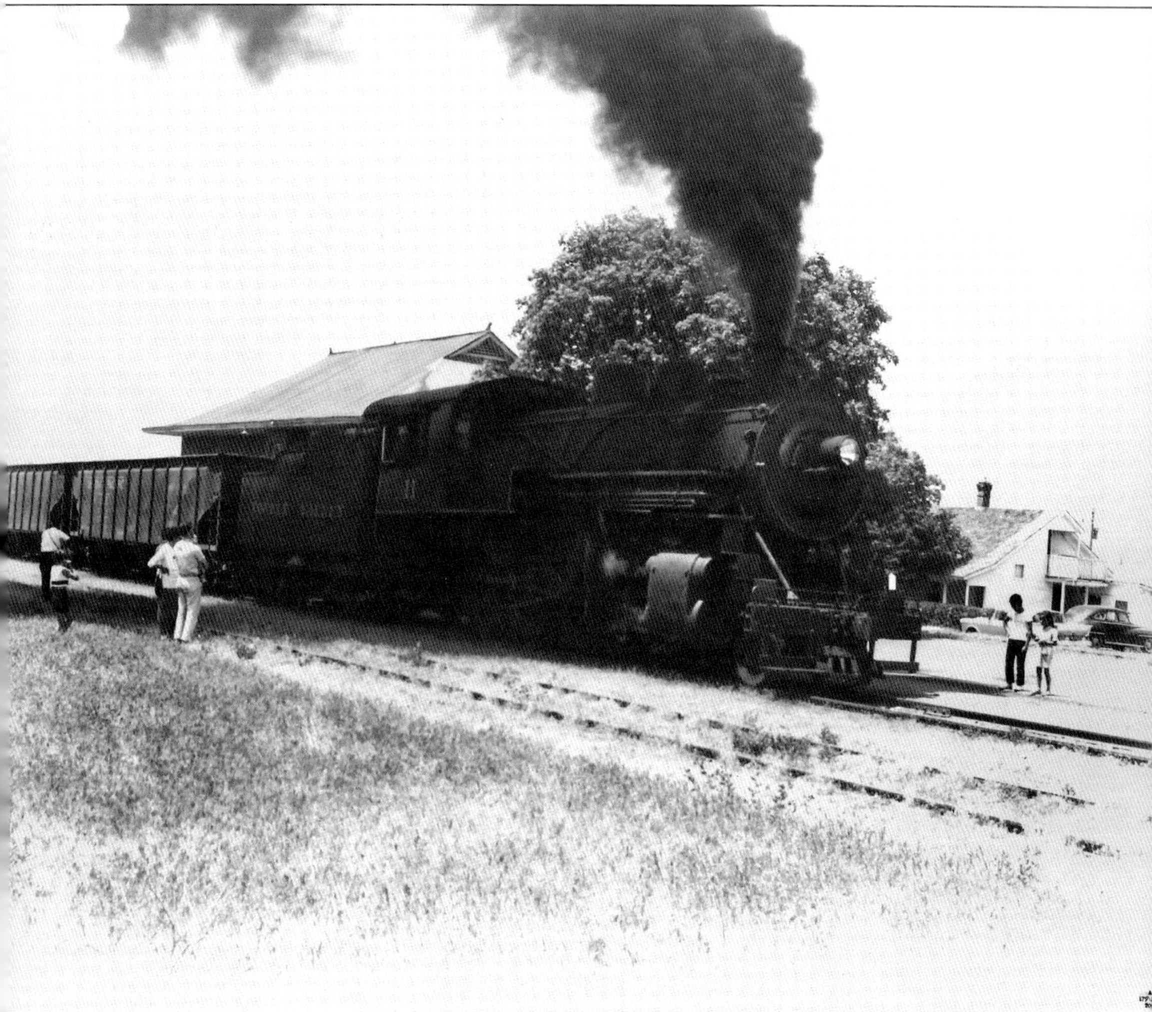

Tooele Valley engine No. 11 pulls a load of hopper cars past the Tooele station on its way to the smelter. Once the railroad decided that the time had come to purchase a new diesel engine, company administrators took a second look at the steam engines on their roster and decided to keep the No. 11, which was in better shape than the others. (Courtesy of the Tooele Valley Railroad Museum.)

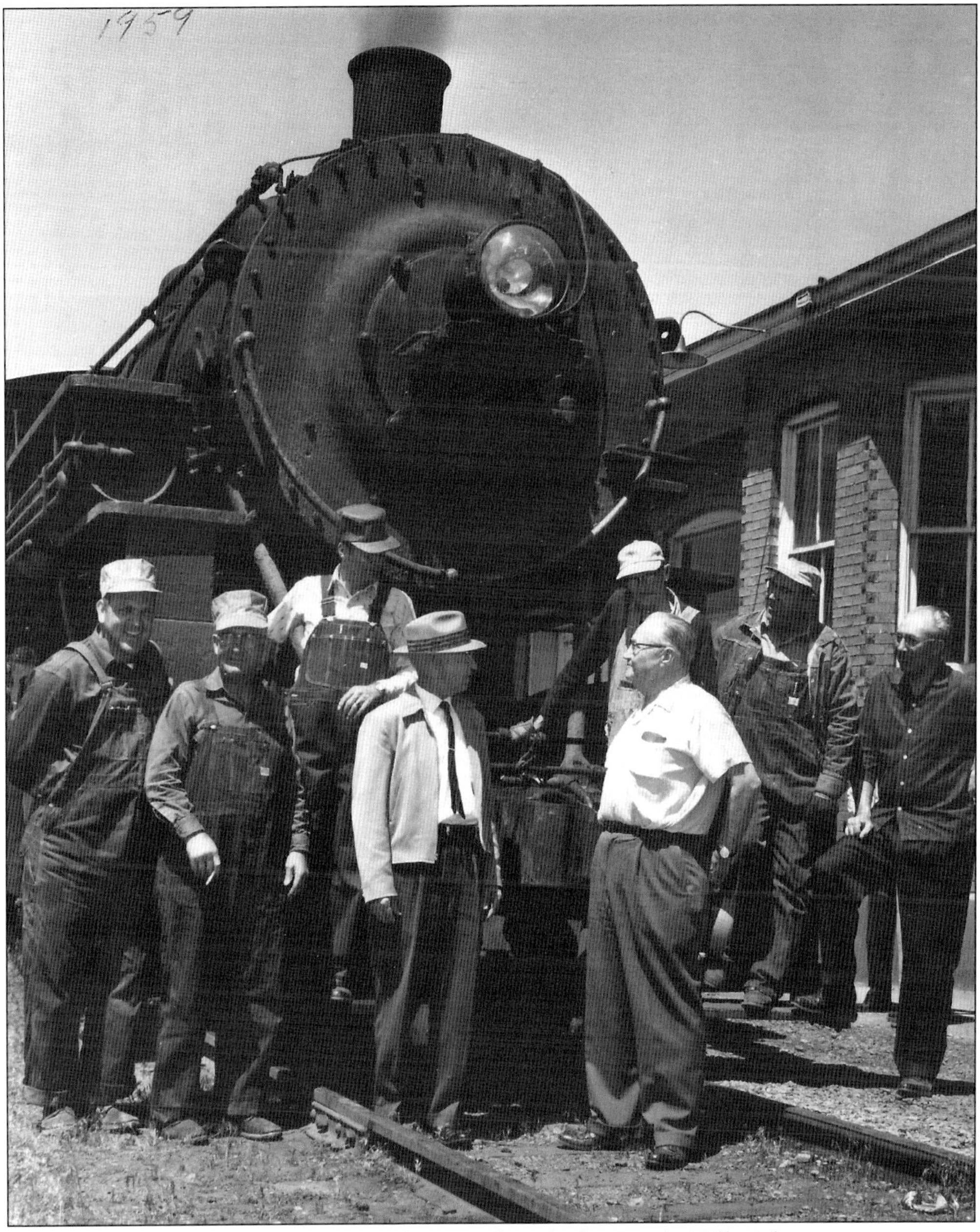

Railroad employees gather for a final photograph with the Tooele Valley's last operating steam engine, the No. 11. The photograph is dated 1959, but strikingly similar photographs place it at the engine's retirement ceremony, on May 20, 1963. The engine remained in operation until 1963, when state inspectors condemned the boiler. (Courtesy of the Tooele Valley Railroad Museum.)

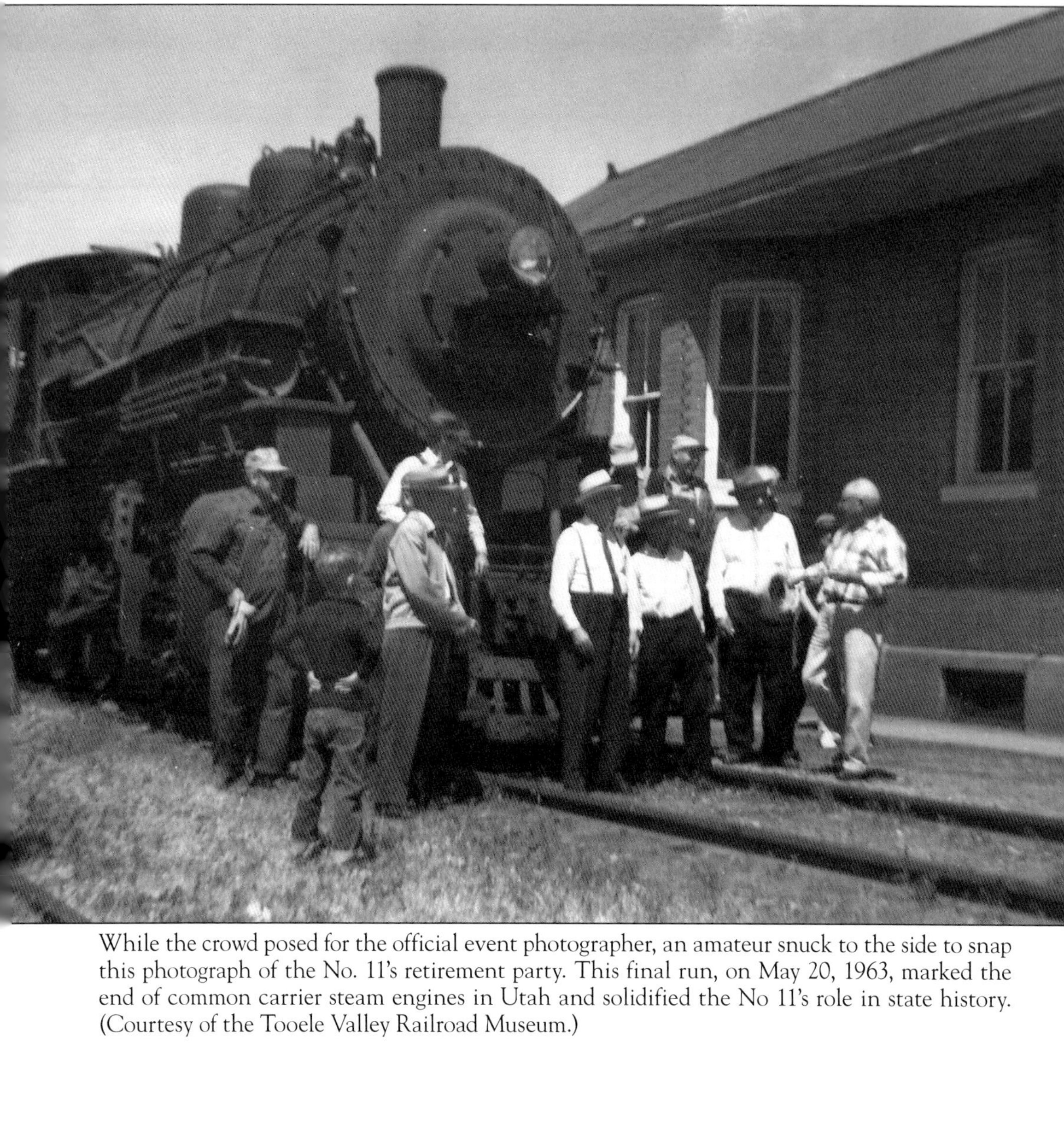

While the crowd posed for the official event photographer, an amateur snuck to the side to snap this photograph of the No. 11's retirement party. This final run, on May 20, 1963, marked the end of common carrier steam engines in Utah and solidified the No 11's role in state history. (Courtesy of the Tooele Valley Railroad Museum.)

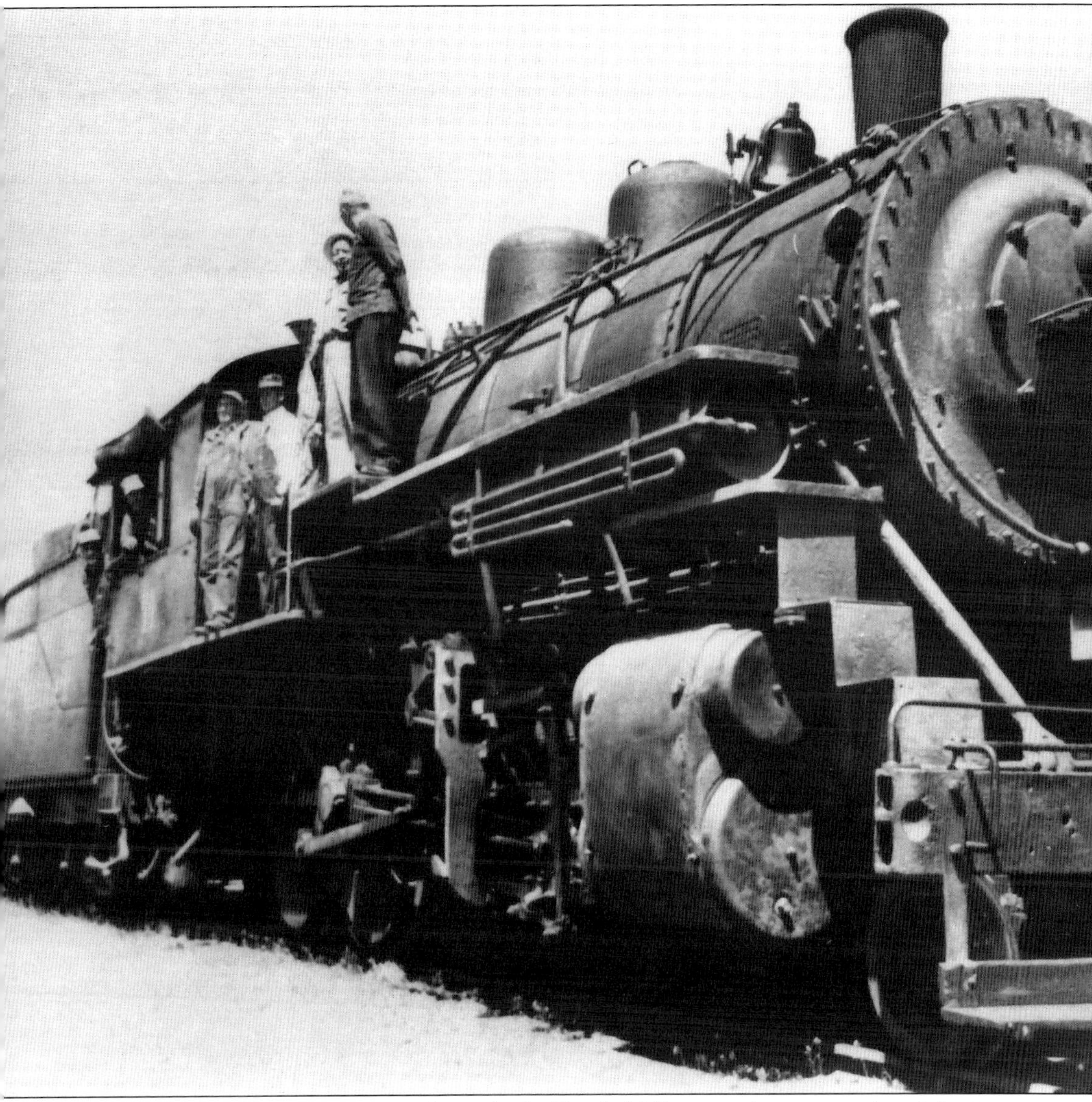

Retiring the No. 11 in 1963 temporarily made the Tooele Valley a single-engine railroad, forcing it to rent engines from nearby railroads if something happened to the No. 100, a model SW1200 diesel that the Tooele Valley acquired directly from General Motors in June 1955. (Courtesy of the Tooele Valley Railroad Museum.)

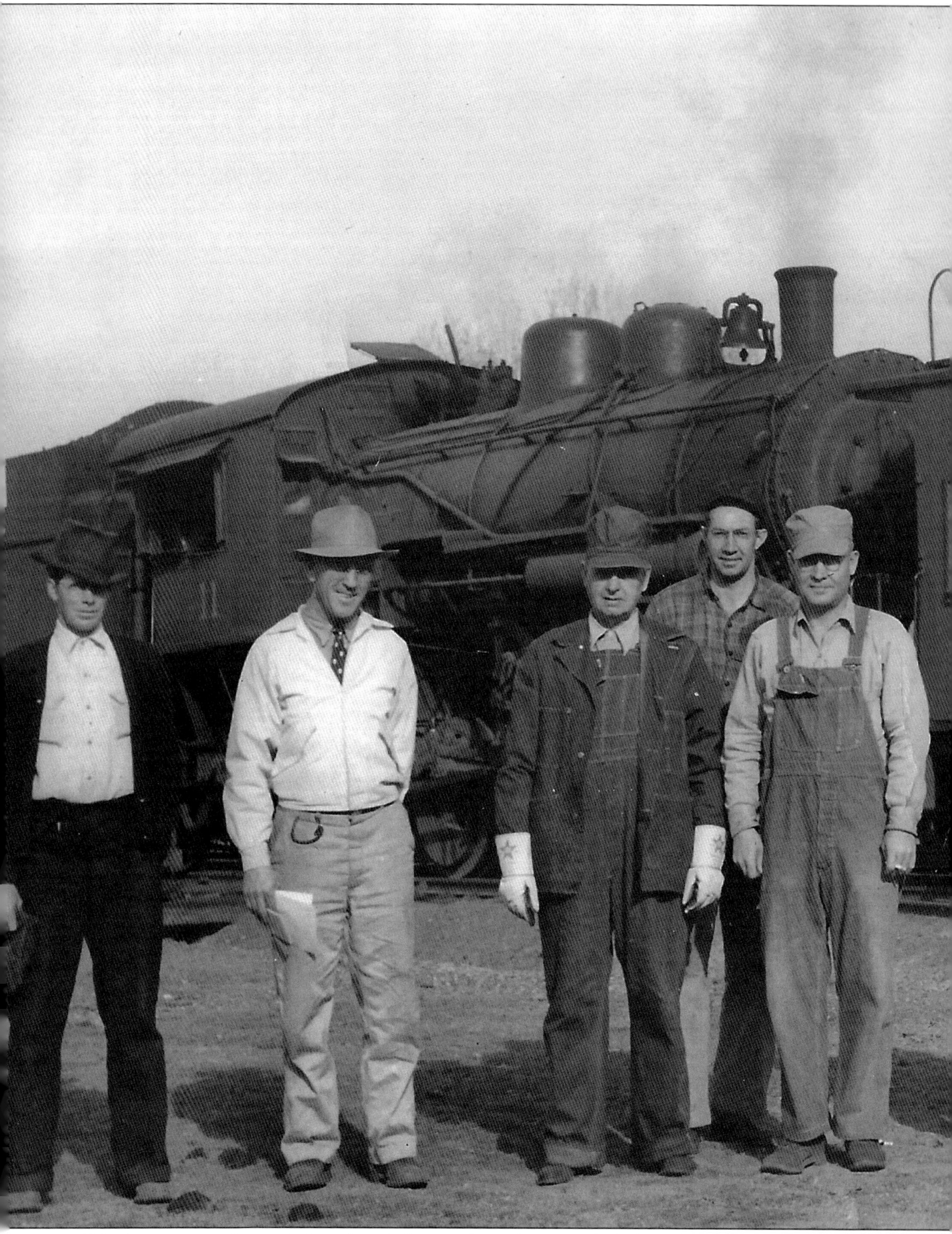

Workers pose in front of the No. 11 for one last photograph before the steam engine officially entered retirement. Don Lee, who became the railroad's last superintendent, is present. The

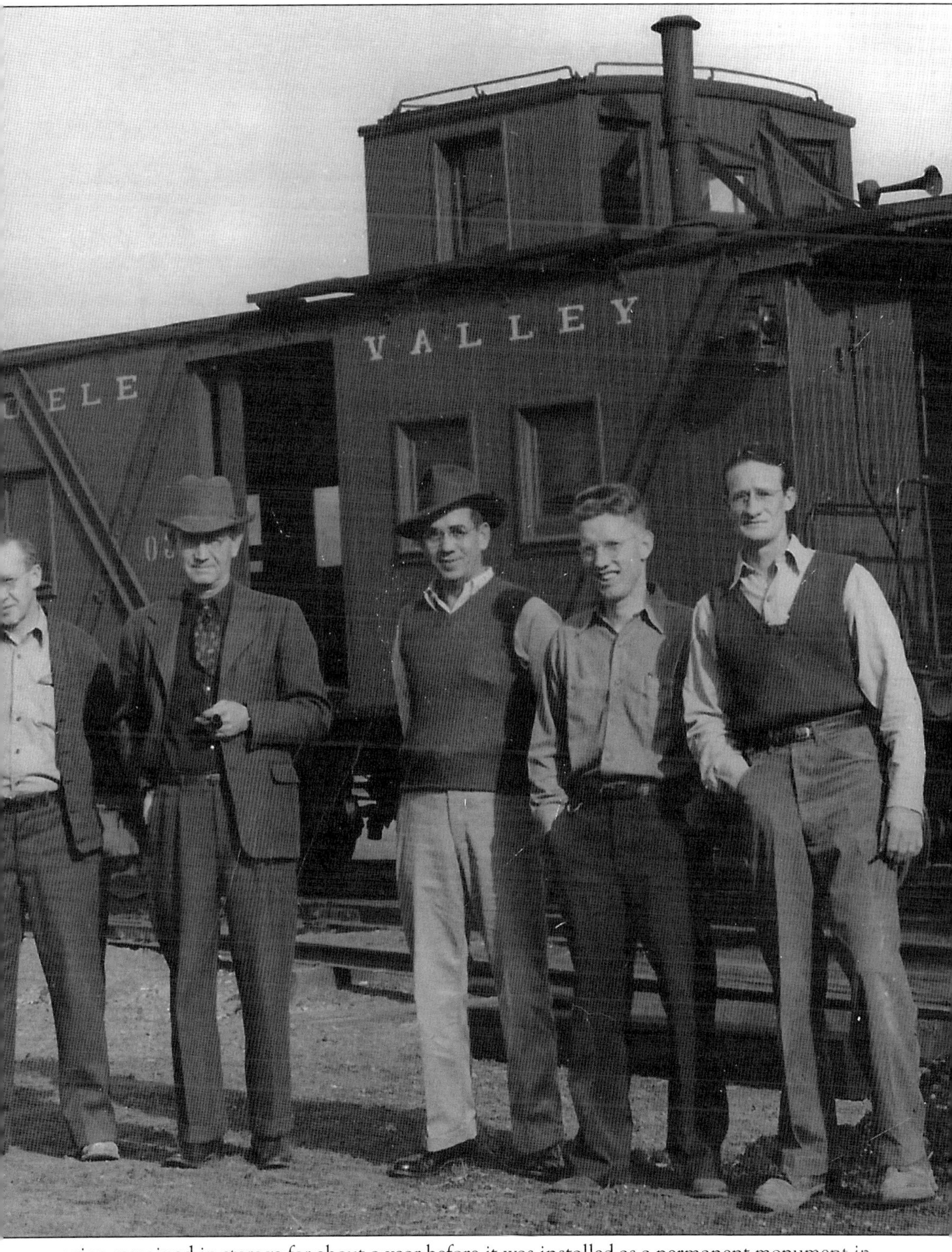

engine remained in storage for about a year before it was installed as a permanent monument in the Tooele city park in September 1964. (Courtesy of the Tooele Valley Railroad Museum.)

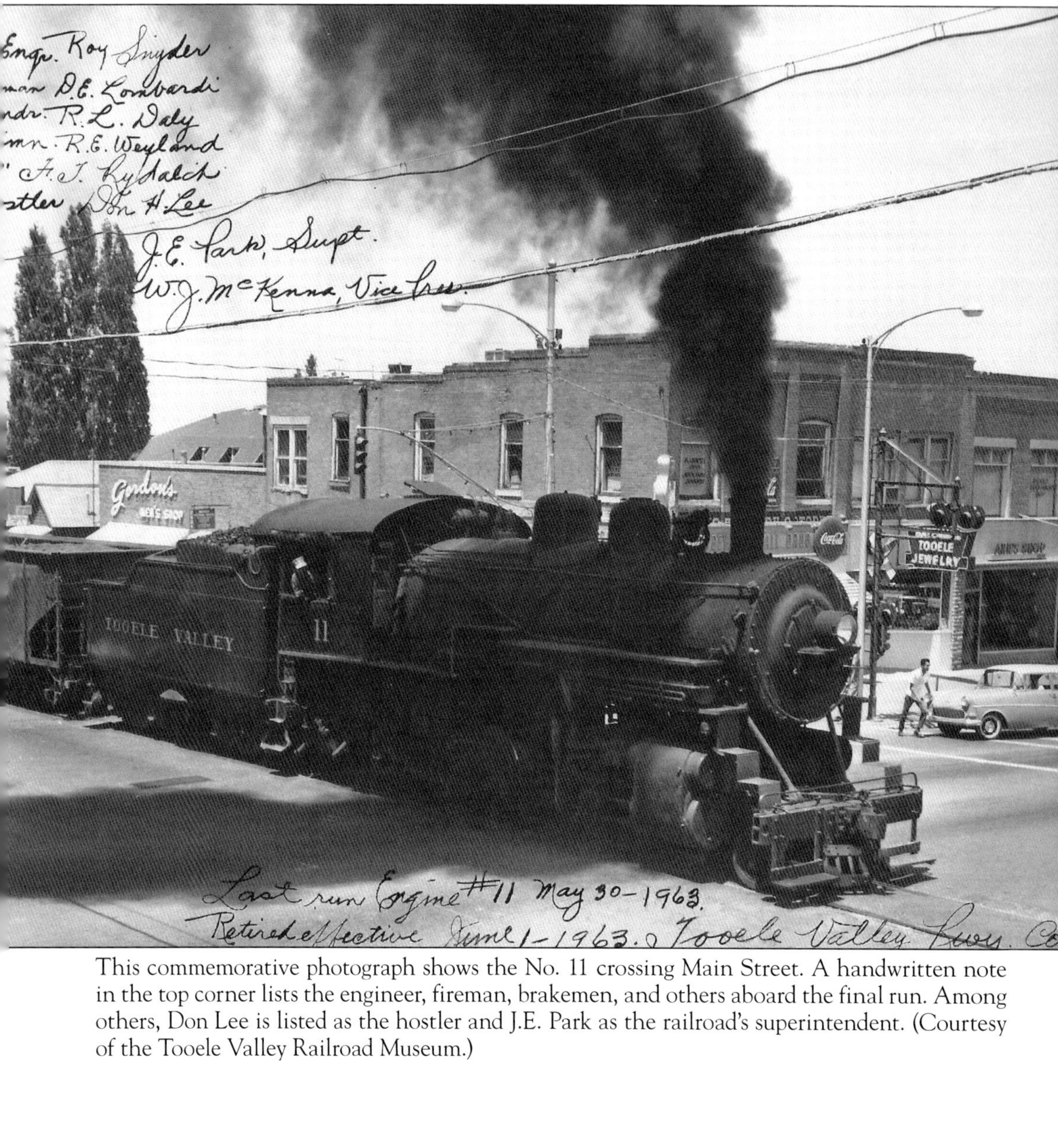

This commemorative photograph shows the No. 11 crossing Main Street. A handwritten note in the top corner lists the engineer, fireman, brakemen, and others aboard the final run. Among others, Don Lee is listed as the hostler and J.E. Park as the railroad's superintendent. (Courtesy of the Tooele Valley Railroad Museum.)

Five

CLOSURE AND POSTERITY 1960–1982

Though created expressly to serve the International smelter, the Tooele Valley Railway ultimately outlived it. Without government subsidies, the value of raw metal continued to decrease in the 1960s and into the 1970s. International had already become Utah's sole lead smelter in 1967, but even its near monopoly on the local market could not save it.

The nationalization of the copper industry in Chile, where Anaconda Copper had invested millions, dealt the company a fatal blow. The International smelter, which Anaconda closed in 1972 as it scrambled to reorganize, was simply collateral damage.

Tooele locals first heard the news on November 5, 1971, when Anaconda announced that International would close at the end of the year. Work continued three weeks longer than expected, but Anaconda eventually made good on its promise. The closure immediately impacted the 350 or so remaining International employees, who all lost their jobs simultaneously. But the effect rippled outward to the rest of Utah's mining industry. With no smelter to service their needs, another 30 mines ceased operations.

Of course, with the closure came rumors of the railroad's imminent demise. Newspapers actually reported the railroad's final run on January 28, eliciting great dismay from Tooele Valley Railway executives who intended to maintain service, running trains two or three times a week.

A single glimmer of hope remained for the little railroad: Anaconda's newly-built Carr Fork mine and mill. Exploratory drilling for the project had begun as early as 1967, but the mine did not officially open until 1974. Even after administrators got the project off the ground, low productivity and falling copper prices continued to plague the new mine.

For the next few years, the Tooele Valley Railway stayed afloat hauling scrap from the decommissioned International smelter and running occasional errands for Carr Fork and other local businesses. Trouble struck again in late 1975, this time hitting the railroad directly when the Warner station was destroyed by a fire on December 8.

The railroad recovered and continued sparse operations for another five years. The last known freight run took place on July 7, 1980, when the Tooele Valley Railway delivered a shipment of newsprint for the *Tooele Transcript-Bulletin*. Two years then passed without a single customer. Finally, in 1982, the railroad was formally abandoned by its new parent company, Atlantic Richfield, but not before dedicated locals struck a deal to preserve the railroad's history for future generations.

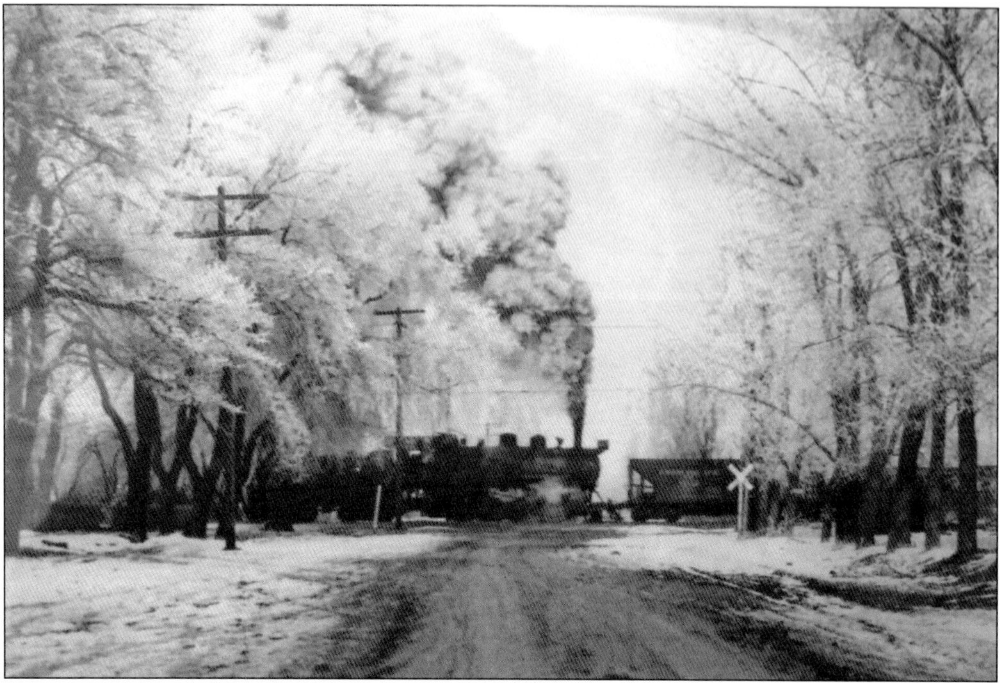

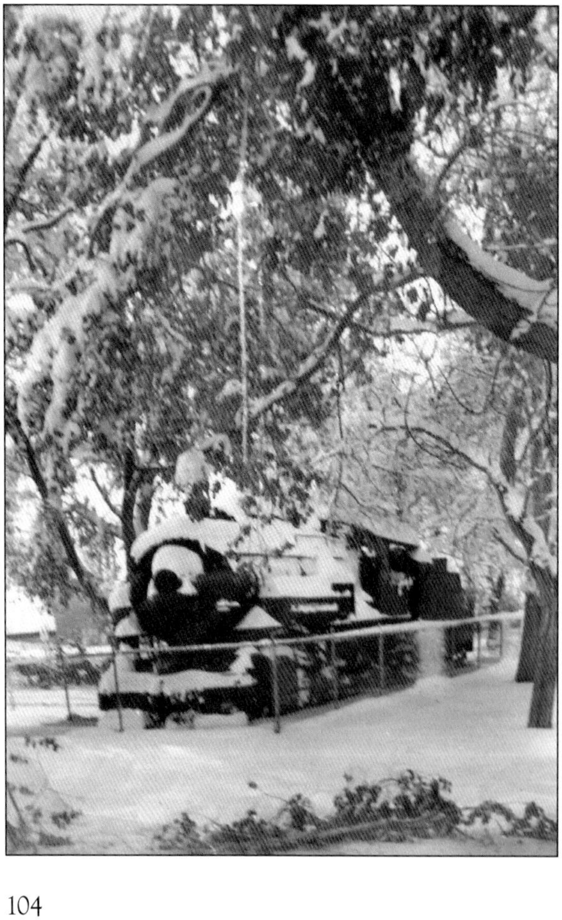

This photograph shows a Tooele Valley steam engine passing through town during a more typical winter, with slushy roads and frosted trees. Though the railroad no longer operated steam engines, the image of a steam train downtown remained ingrained in local memory. (Courtesy of the Tooele Valley Railroad Museum.)

Engine No. 11 is seen here in its new home, protected by a fence in the Tooele city park. Originally, the railroad brought the engine out of storage for a mining exhibition, but it was soon decided that it would make a fitting city monument. Two decades later, volunteers moved the steam engine one mile east, where it became a part of the Tooele Valley Railroad Museum. (Courtesy of the Tooele Valley Railroad Museum.)

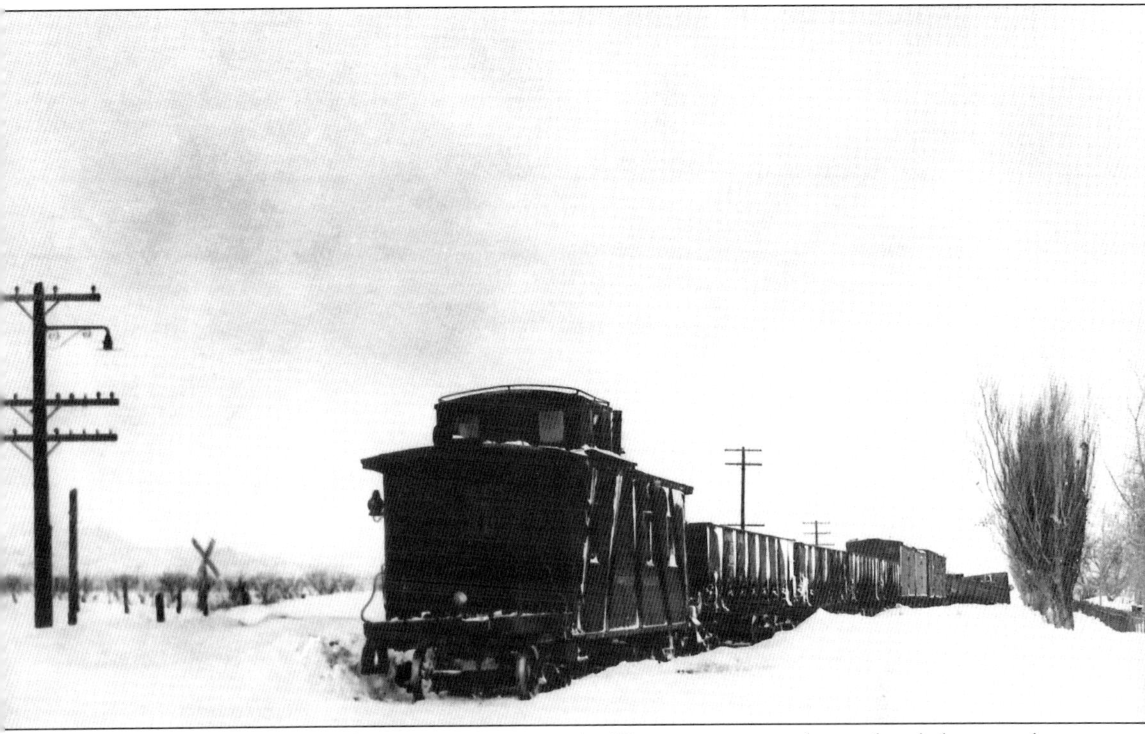

A snowy caboose and empty hopper cars return to the Warner station in this undated photograph. Even before Anaconda lost its Chilean properties in 1971, the fate of the International smelter and its railroad was questionable. International became the last custom smelter operating in the state in 1963, and it struggled to turn a profit as the value of metals continued to slide. (Courtesy of the Tooele Valley Railroad Museum.)

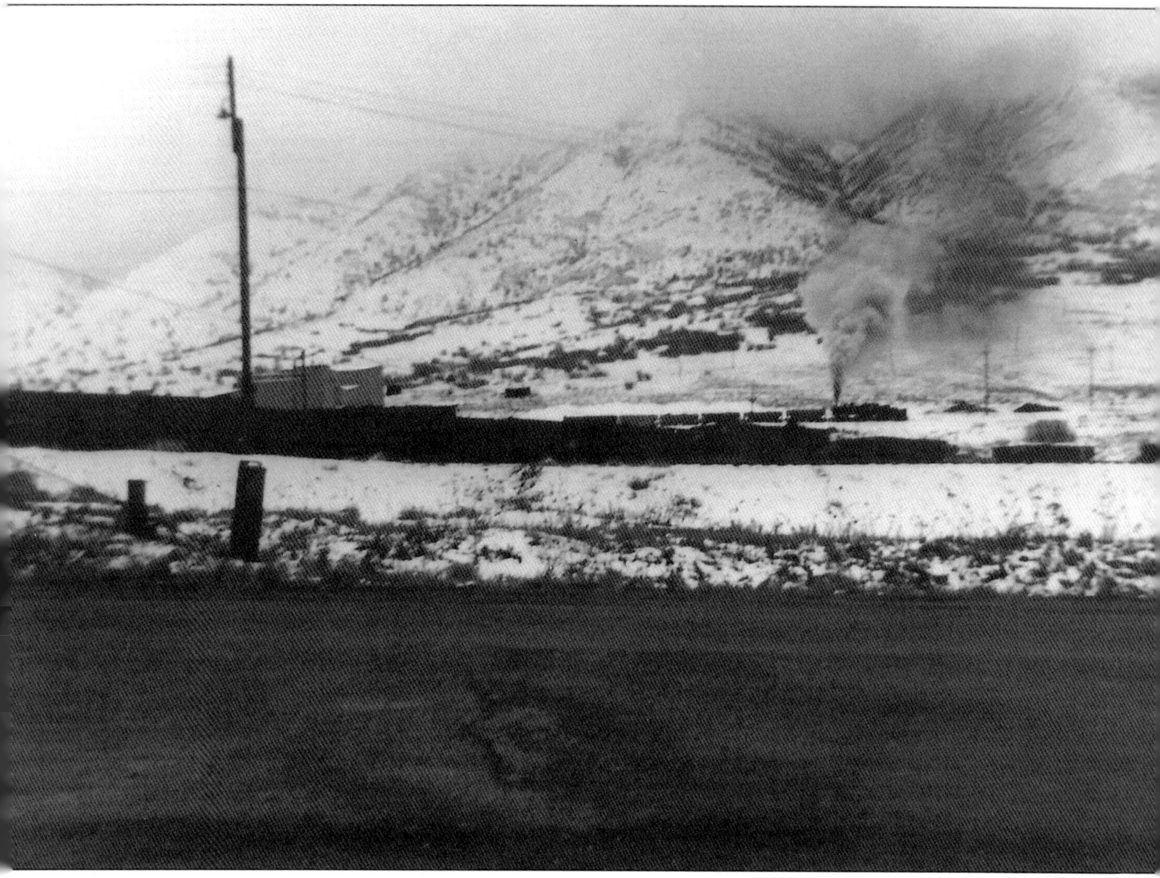

By the time the smelter closed in 1972, the railroad's demise was so widely anticipated that the local paper announced its final day of operation—about a decade too soon. Don Lee, the railroad's newly installed superintendent, planned to continue running trains twice a week, mostly shipping scrap metal from the smelter site on behalf of its new parent company, Atlantic Richfield. (Courtesy of the Tooele Valley Railroad Museum.)

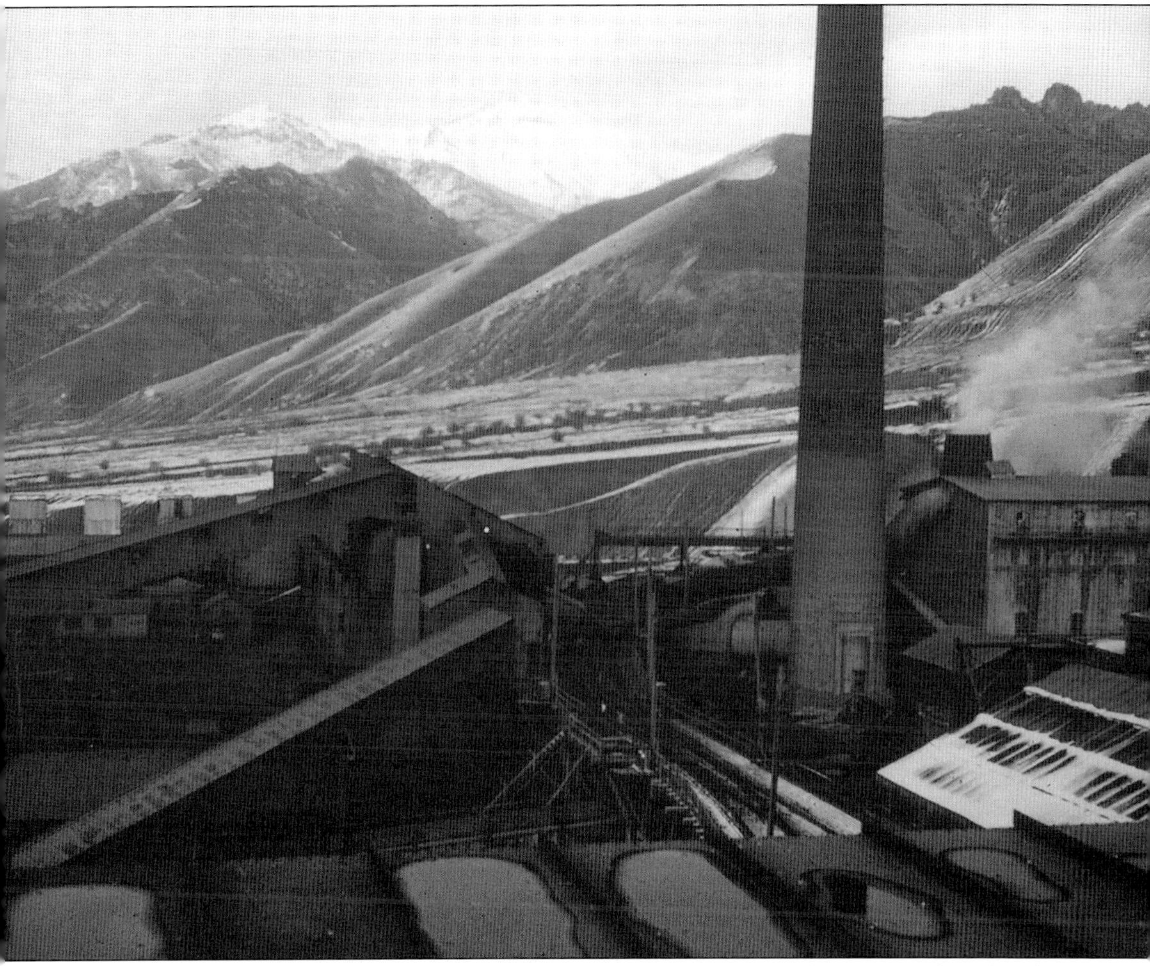

This photograph of the International smelter's copper-processing facilities was taken shortly after Anaconda announced the plant's closure in 1971. For most residents, the closure came rather abruptly, as official notice came little more than a month before the planned final day of operations. (Courtesy of the Tooele Pioneer Museum.)

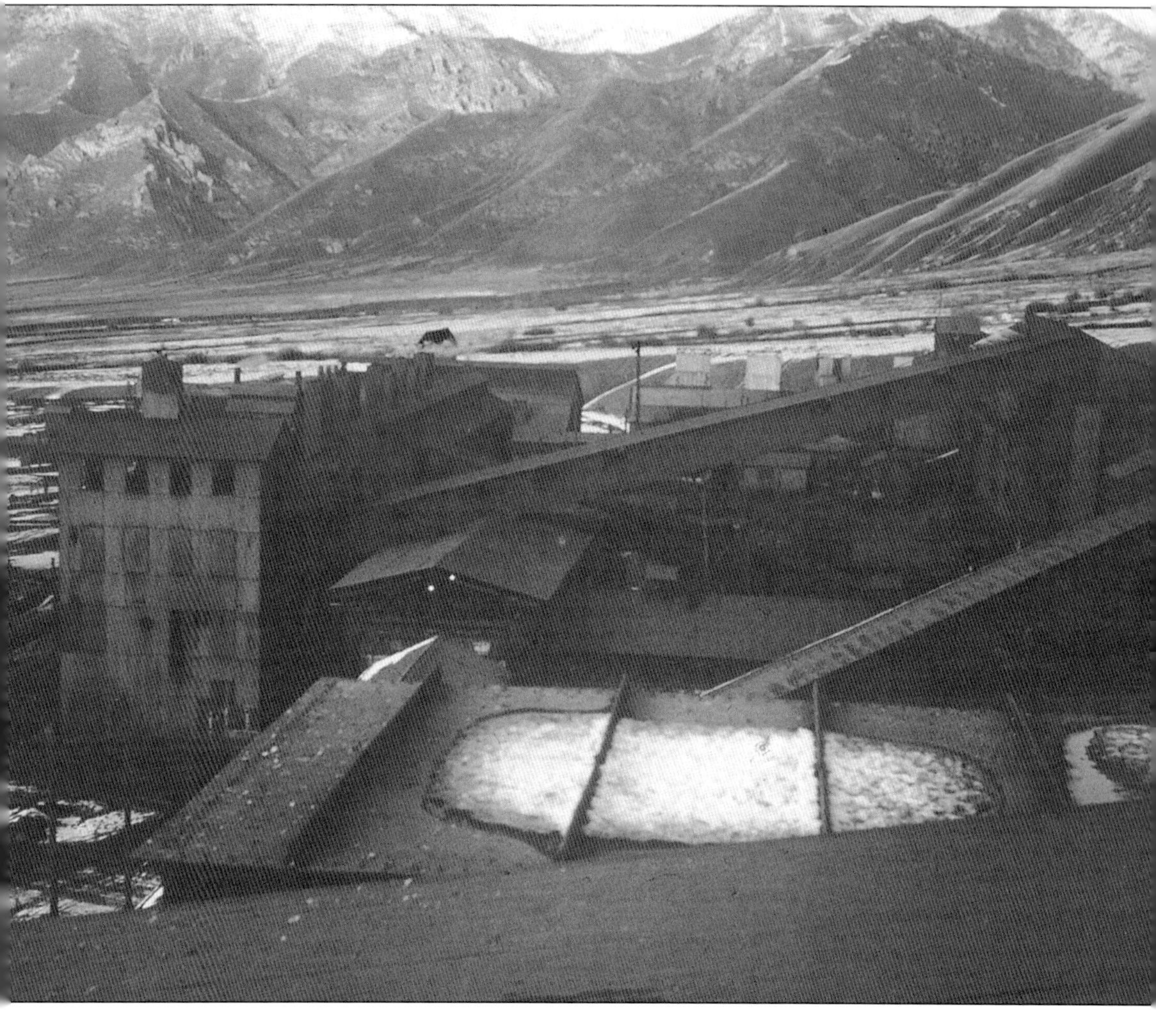

For those on the inside, the closure was perhaps less surprising. International had struggled to turn a profit for years in the face of the decreasing value of metal and increasing maintenance costs. Much of the smelter's equipment was never replaced, and repairing implements built in 1909 cost the company an estimated $20,000 per month. (Courtesy of the Tooele Pioneer Museum.)

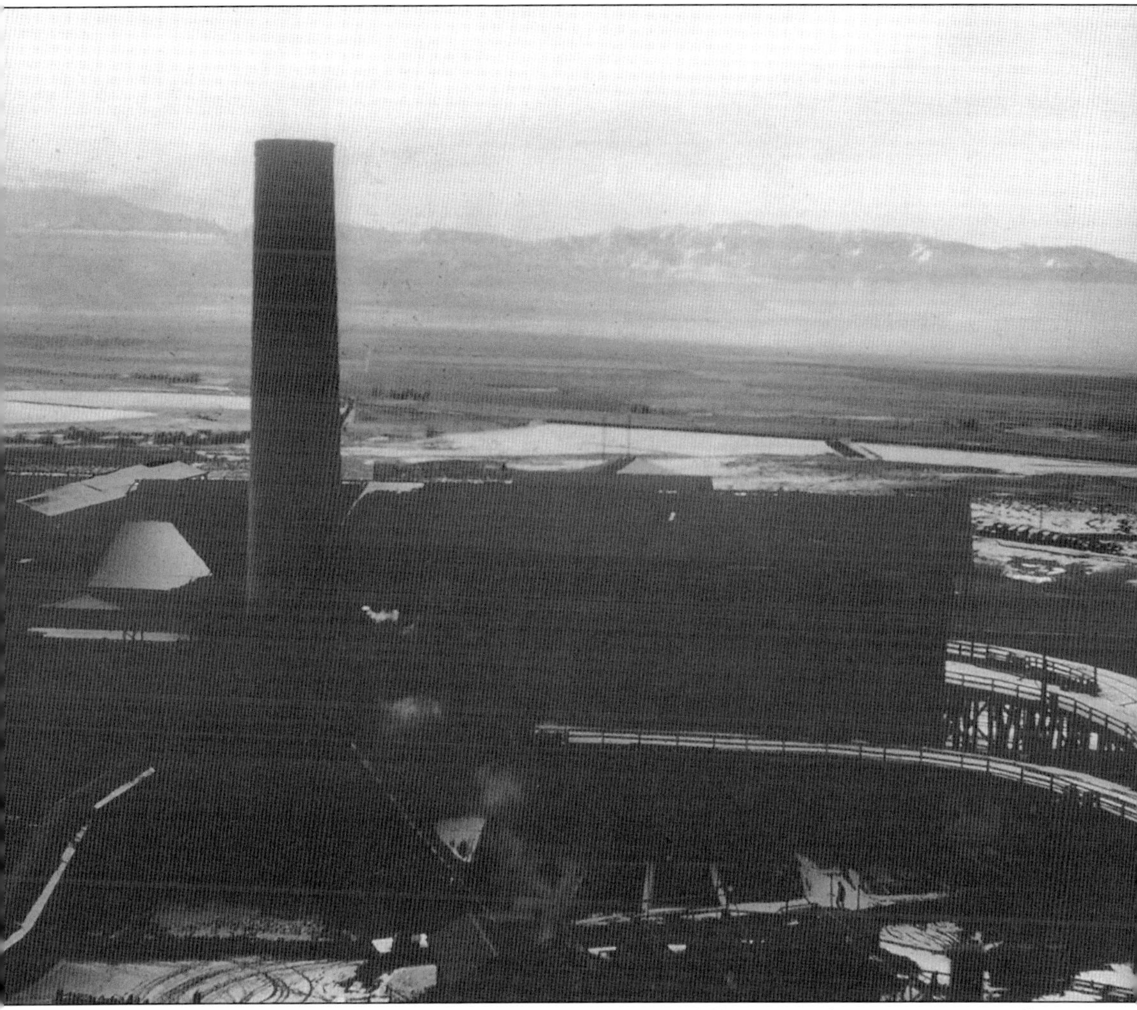

At the time of the closure, International still had about 350 full-time employees on its payroll, significantly less than the company had employed in the past. At peak operation, in the 1920s, the company employed about 2,000 men and supported more than 60 percent of the city's population. (Courtesy of the Tooele Pioneer Museum.)

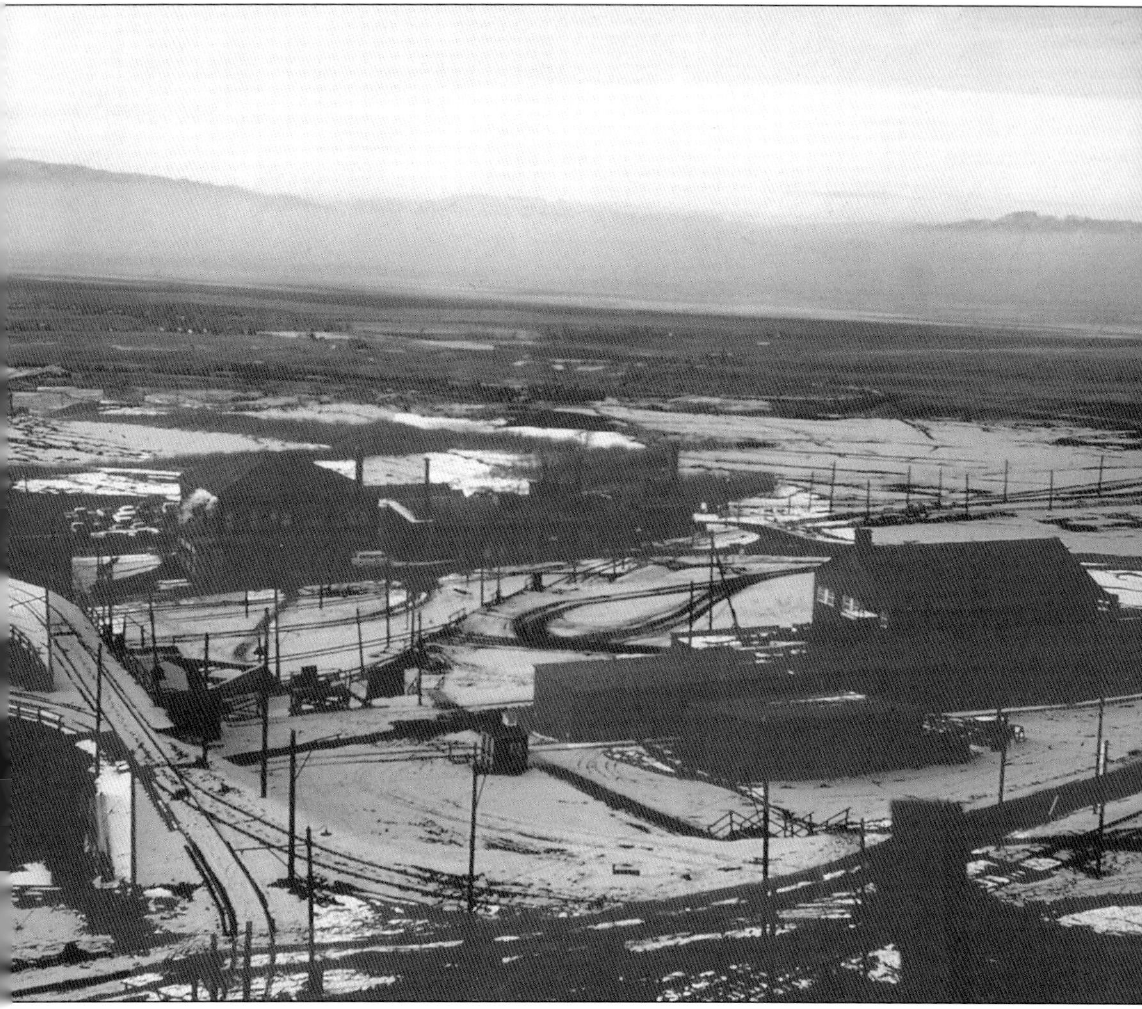

This overview of the rail yard at International was taken shortly after the smelter's closure in 1972. Though the Tooele Valley Railway continued operating for nearly a decade after the smelter's demise, many wondered how long it could last. For some, the trains evoked a deep sense of nostalgia, while others thought the trains a nuisance that could not go away soon enough. (Courtesy of the Tooele Pioneer Museum.)

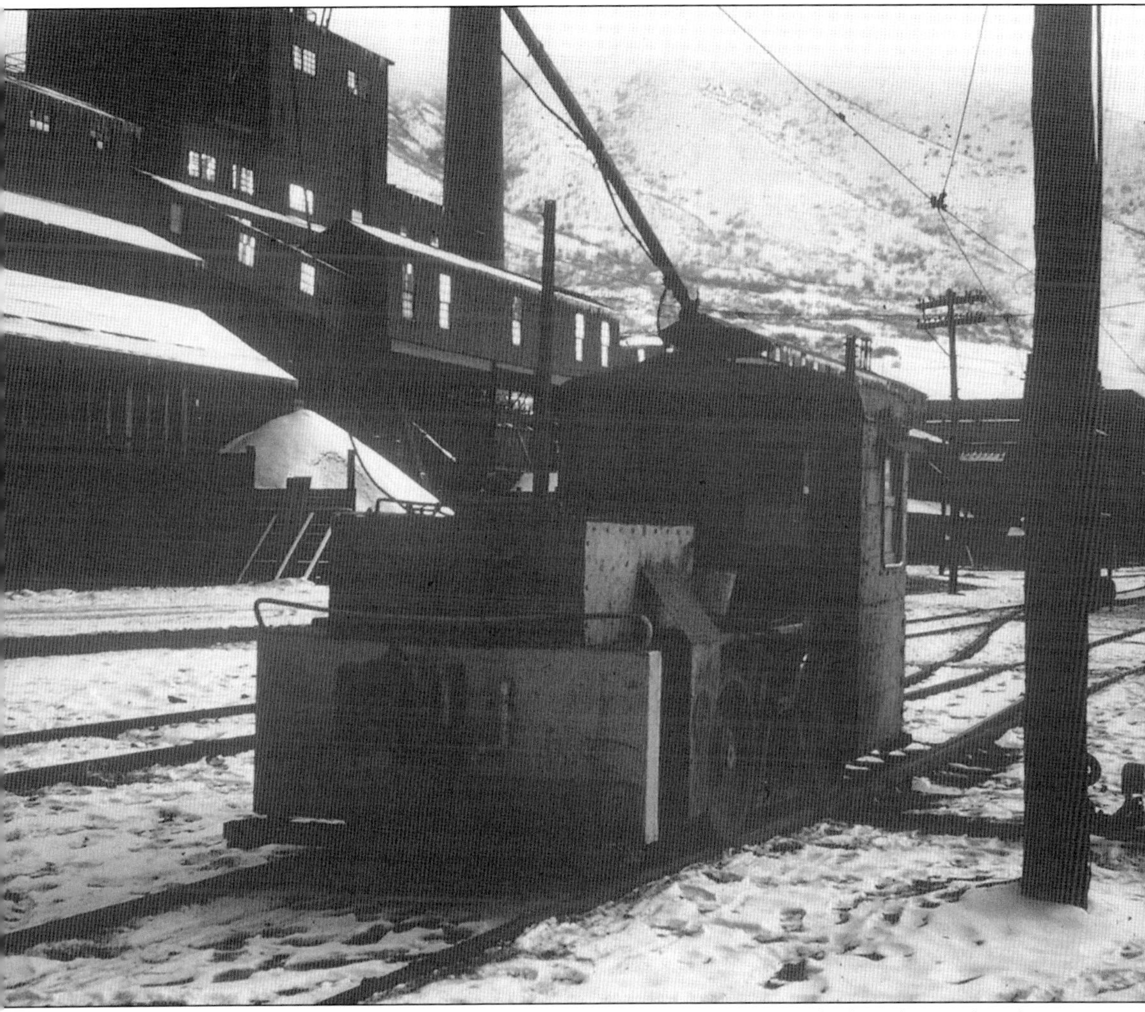

This electric switch car was abandoned by rail yard workers where it stood when the smelter shut down in 1972. Smelter workers who lost their jobs to the closure left various tools and bits of equipment strewn across the property for demolition crews to clean up after the fact. (Courtesy of the Tooele Pioneer Museum.)

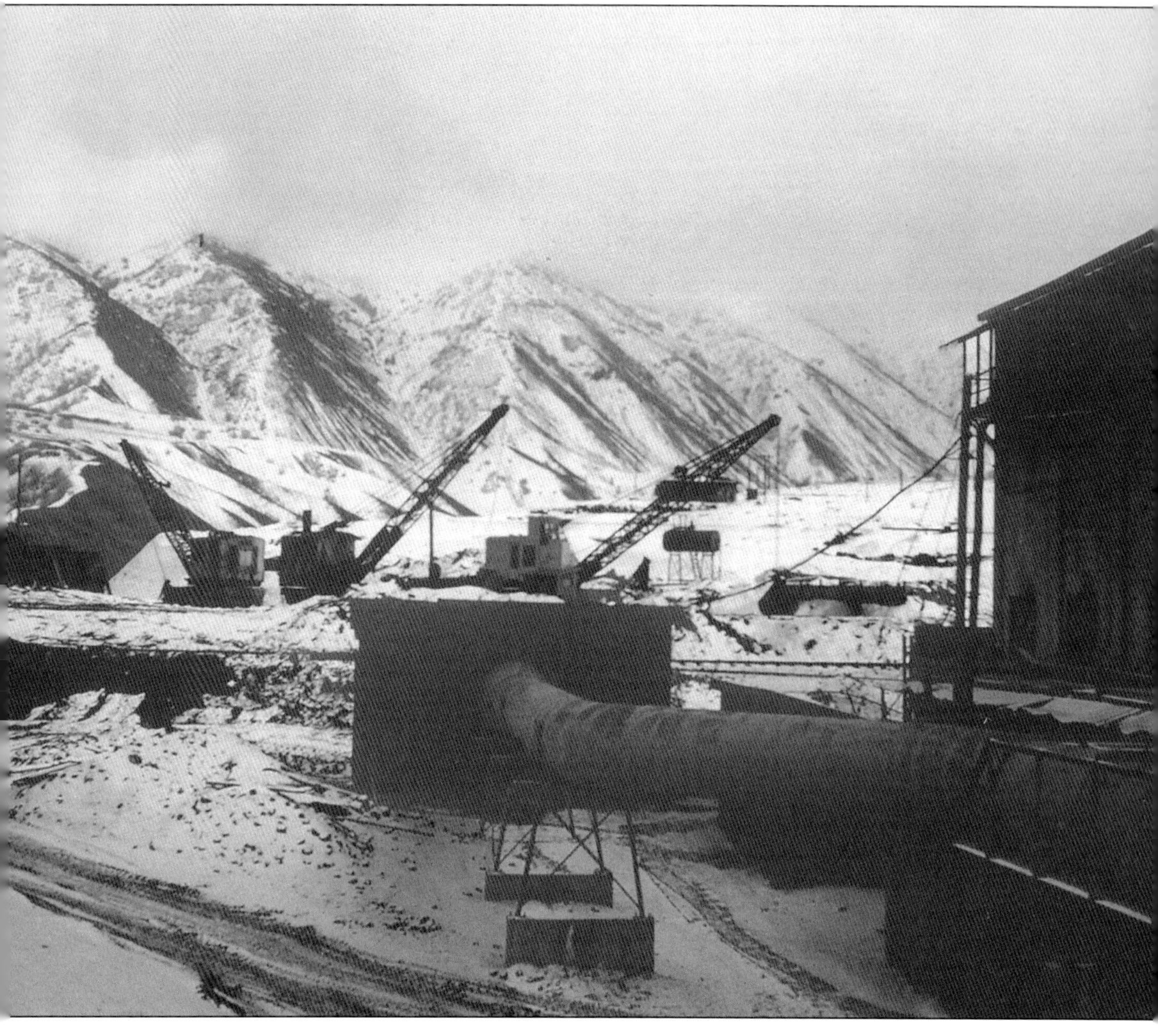

Cranes arrive to begin the demolition process. The oldest buildings were among the first that crews disassembled. While removing some of the smelter's many furnaces, the company discovered that trace amounts of valuable metals, including gold, had slipped through cracks in the furnace floors and built up beneath them during the smelter's 60 years. (Courtesy of the Tooele Pioneer Museum.)

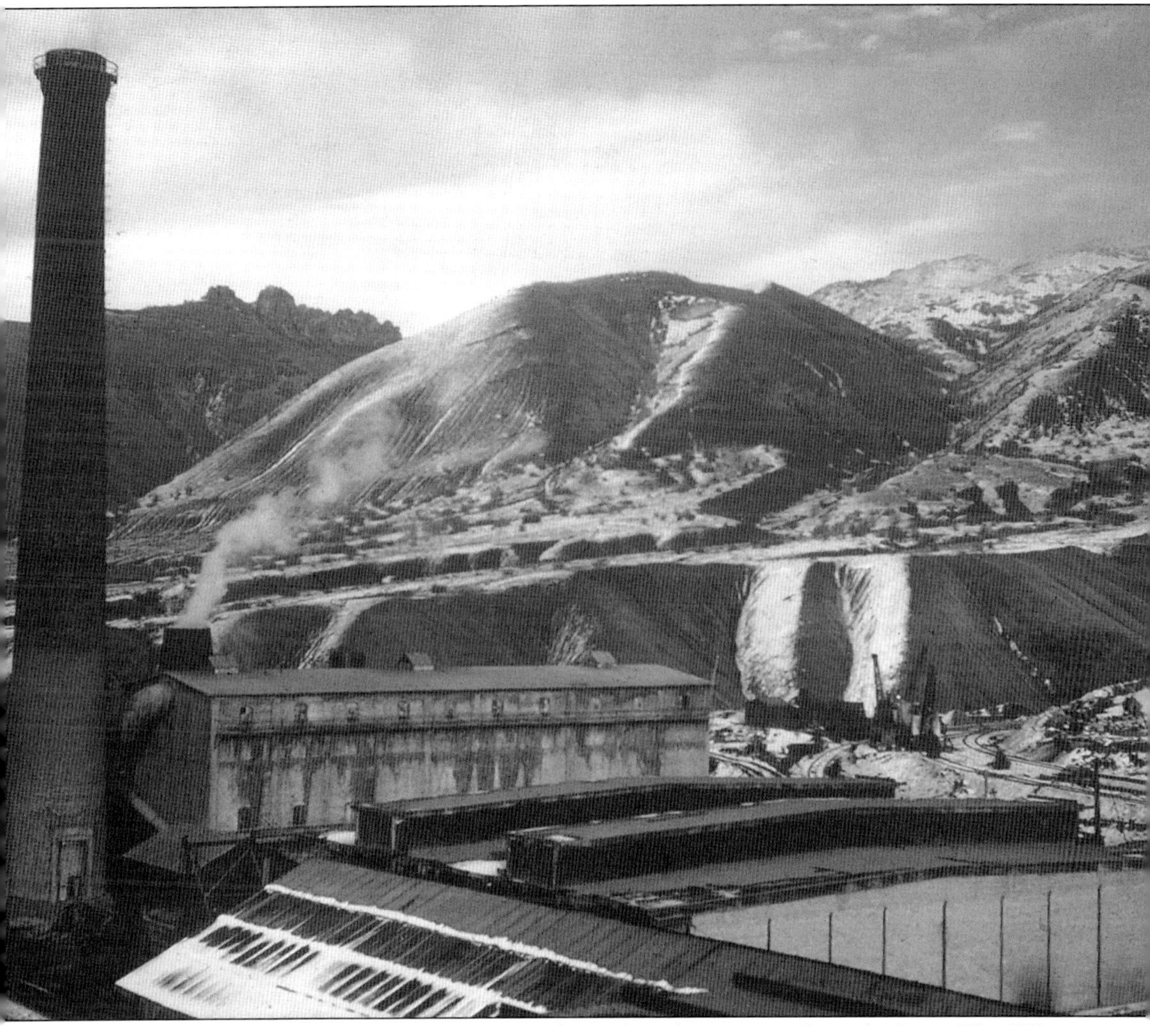

This is an overview of International's main smokestack and copper-smelting facilities. The 350-foot-tall smokestack was among the last structures removed from the site. After the bulk of the smelter came down, the railroad delivered construction supplies for the new Carr Fork mine in Pine Canyon. (Courtesy of the Tooele Pioneer Museum.)

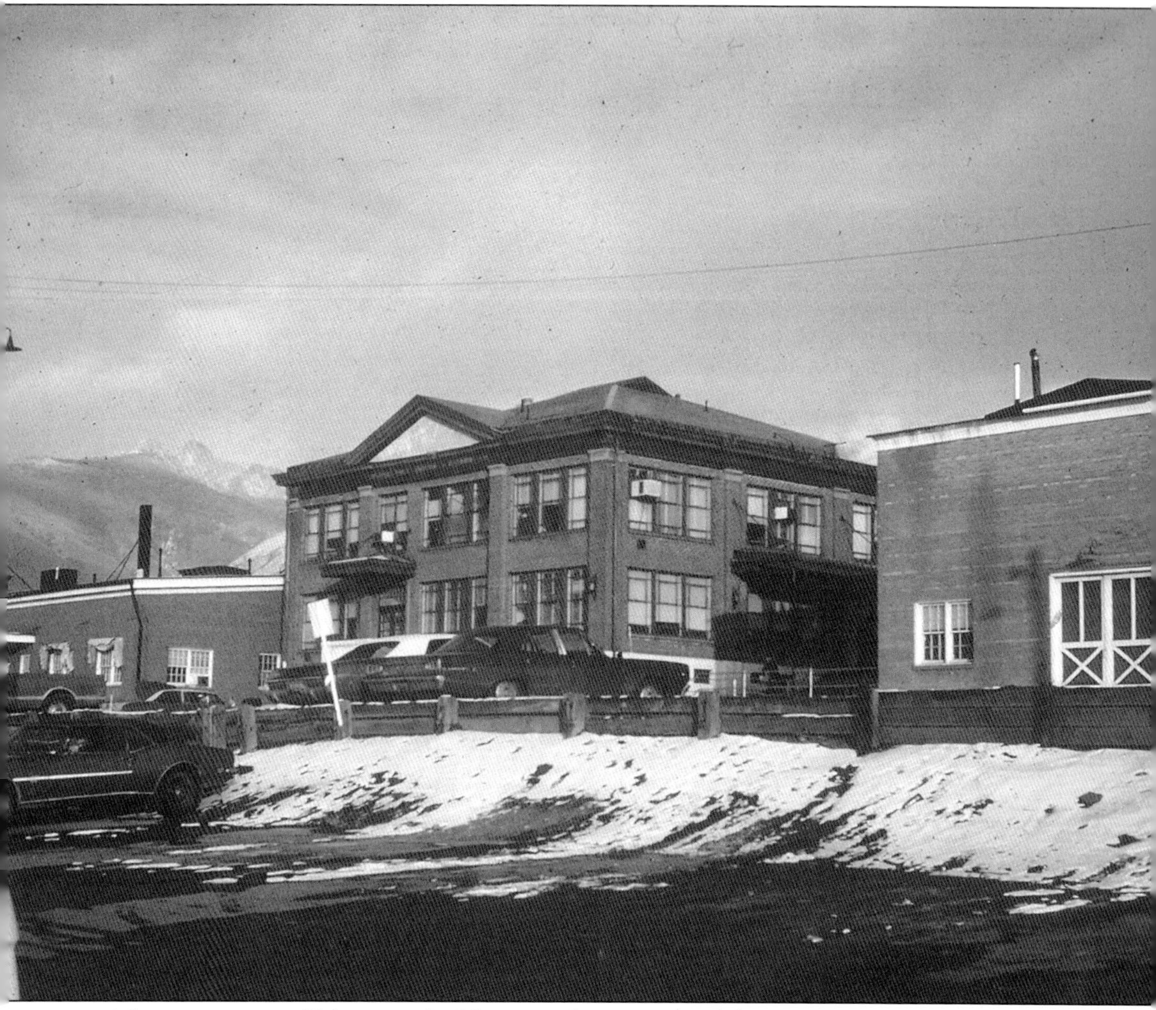

Administration and laboratory buildings on the west side of the International smelting complex are seen here. These buildings, also among the last to be removed, were some of the youngest structures on the site. The company had them rebuilt after a devastating fire destroyed the company laboratory on May 9, 1942. (Courtesy of the Tooele Pioneer Museum.)

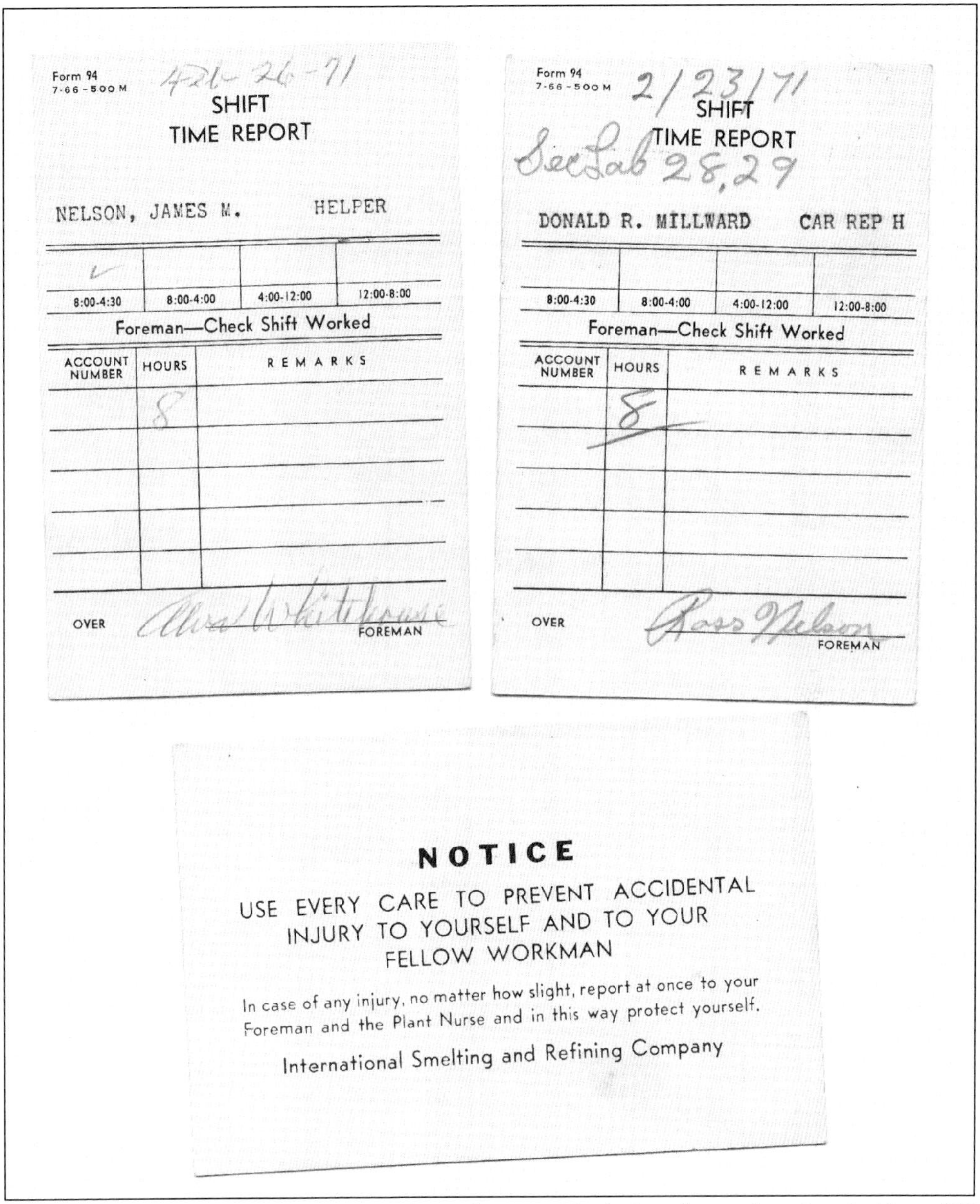

Form 94
7-66-500M
Feb-26-71
SHIFT
TIME REPORT

NELSON, JAMES M. HELPER

8:00-4:30	8:00-4:00	4:00-12:00	12:00-8:00
✓			

Foreman—Check Shift Worked

ACCOUNT NUMBER	HOURS	REMARKS
	8	

OVER FOREMAN

Form 94
7-66-500M
2/23/71
SHIFT
TIME REPORT
Sec Lab 28,29

DONALD R. MILLWARD CAR REP H

8:00-4:30	8:00-4:00	4:00-12:00	12:00-8:00

Foreman—Check Shift Worked

ACCOUNT NUMBER	HOURS	REMARKS
	8	

OVER Ross Nelson FOREMAN

NOTICE

USE EVERY CARE TO PREVENT ACCIDENTAL INJURY TO YOURSELF AND TO YOUR FELLOW WORKMAN

In case of any injury, no matter how slight, report at once to your Foreman and the Plant Nurse and in this way protect yourself.

International Smelting and Refining Company

These time cards are from shifts worked in February 1971, before the smelter closed. About 350 smelter employees lost their jobs a year later, and the loss of Utah's last custom smelter also forced 30 other mines in the area to close. With Tooele still struggling to recover, Anaconda laid off another 800 workers a decade later when the Carr Fork mine failed. (Courtesy of the Tooele Valley Railroad Museum.)

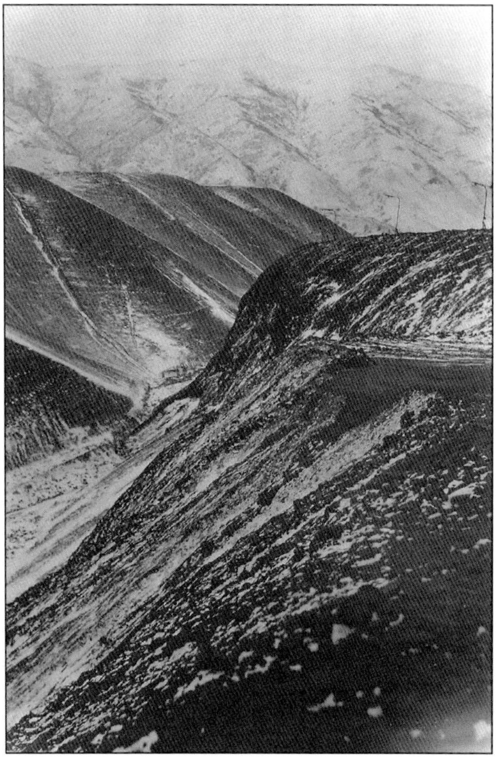

Mountains of slag reshaped the foothill cliffs at the mouth of Pine Canyon. The International smelter treated an estimated 750,000 tons of ore annually and produced 72,000 tons of lead, 10,000 tons of copper, and other byproducts, including nine million ounces of silver, according to *Mining, Smelting and Railroading in Tooele County*. Of course, it also produced the resulting slag associated with all those smelting processes. At first, the company dumped slag near the smelter site, but as the slag piles grew, it continued steadily up the canyon until the dumping completely altered the face of the mountain. (Both courtesy of the Tooele Valley Railroad Museum.)

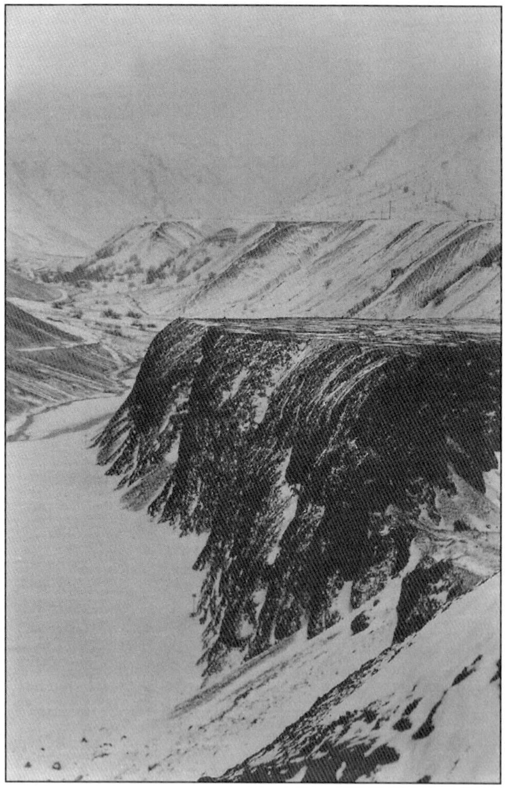

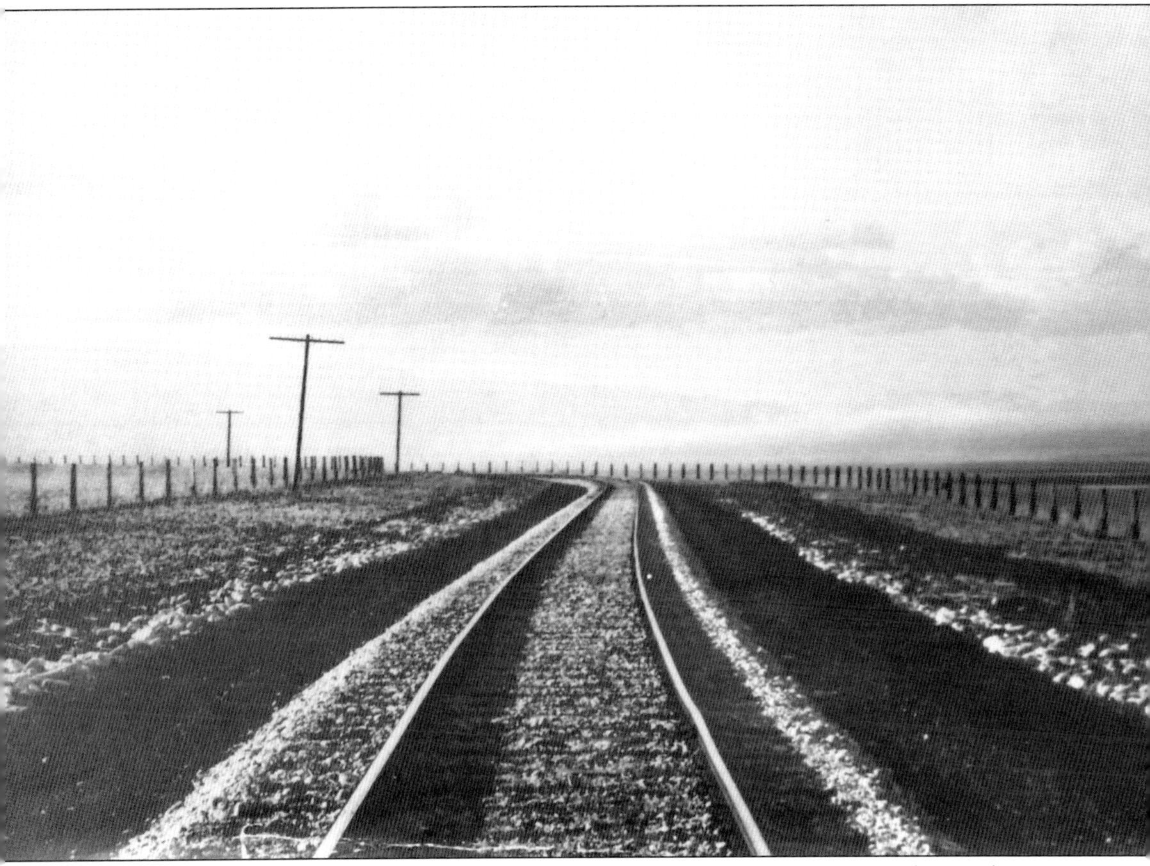

The end of the road for the Tooele Valley Railway came in the early 1980s when Atlantic Richfield announced its intention to abandon it. After formally abandoning its Tooele Valley Railway subsidiary, Atlantic Richfield paid K&N Salvage, a Portland-based company, to remove the tracks and repair Vine Street. Tooele City assisted to speed the process along. (Courtesy of the Tooele Valley Railroad Museum.)

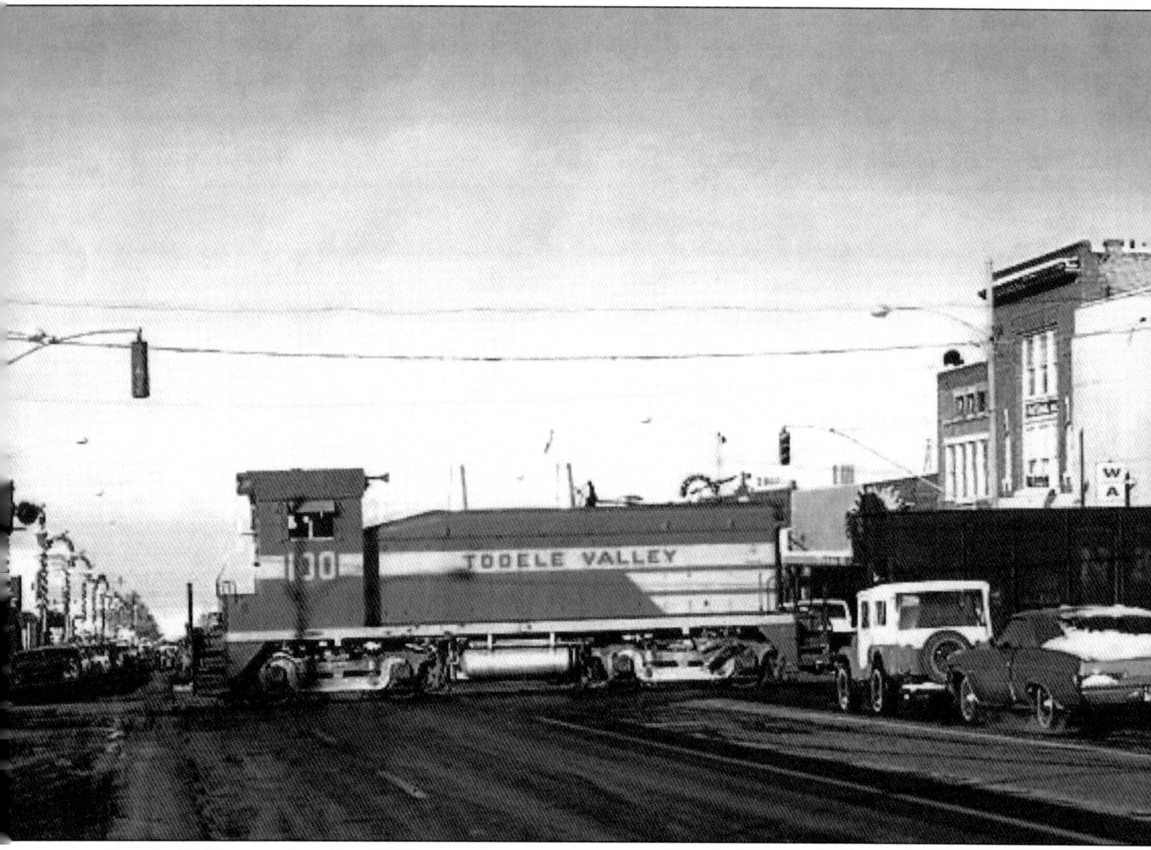

Tooele Valley engine No. 100 is seen here stopping traffic while crossing Main Street. Anaconda transferred this engine to another of its properties, Anaconda Aluminum Reduction Works, before it sold its properties in Tooele to Atlantic Richfield. This left the Tooele Valley Railway with the smaller of the two diesel engines, No. 104, during its final years. (Courtesy of the Tooele Valley Railroad Museum.)

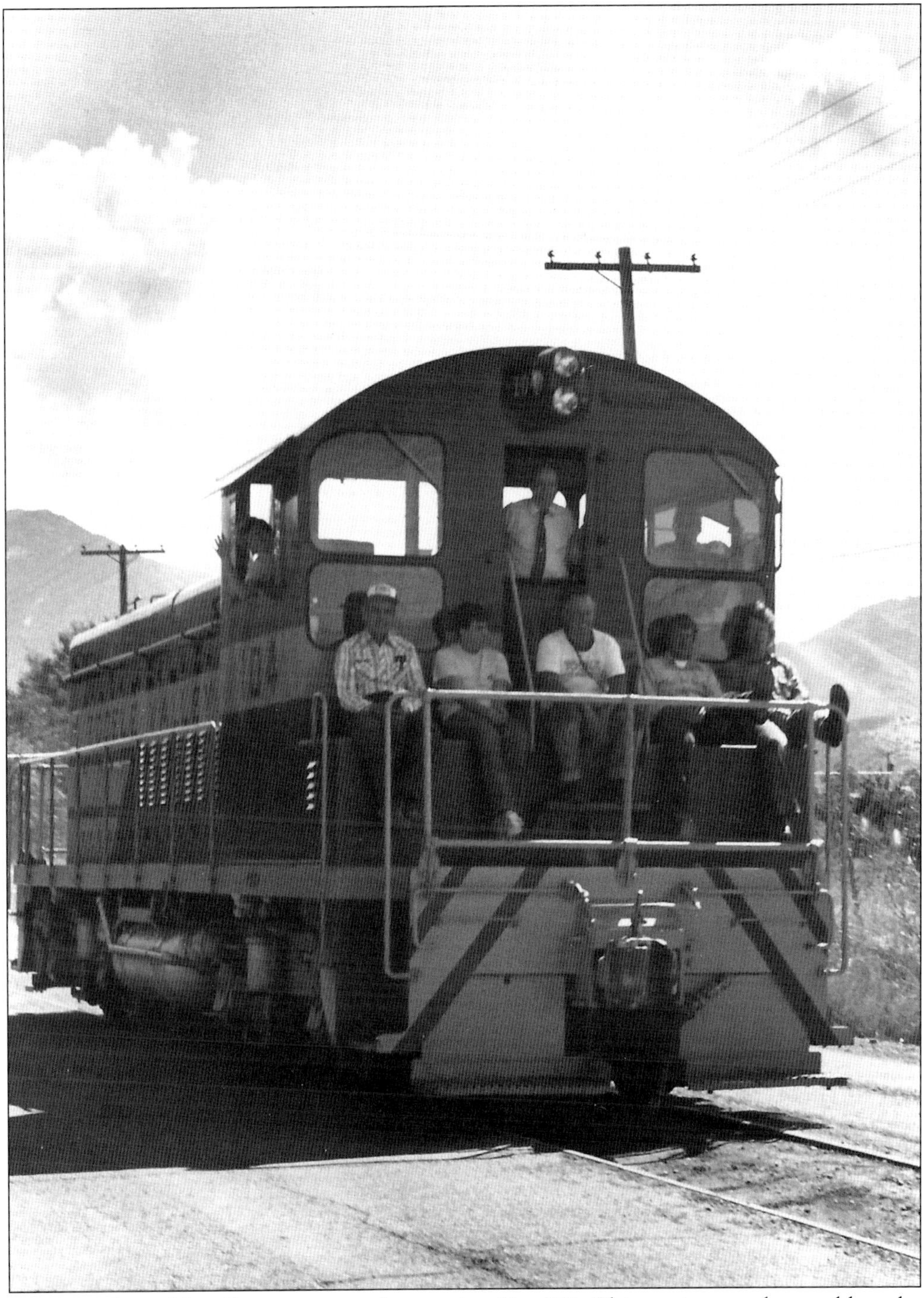

Visitors ride up Vine Street on a car-less engine No. 104. This engine was later sold to the Minnesota Corn Products Company and shipped out of Tooele on March 19, 1983. For several years prior to its sale, the engine had little work to do—the railroad served its last customer six months before Atlantic Richfield announced plans to abandon the line. (Courtesy of the Tooele Valley Railroad Museum.)

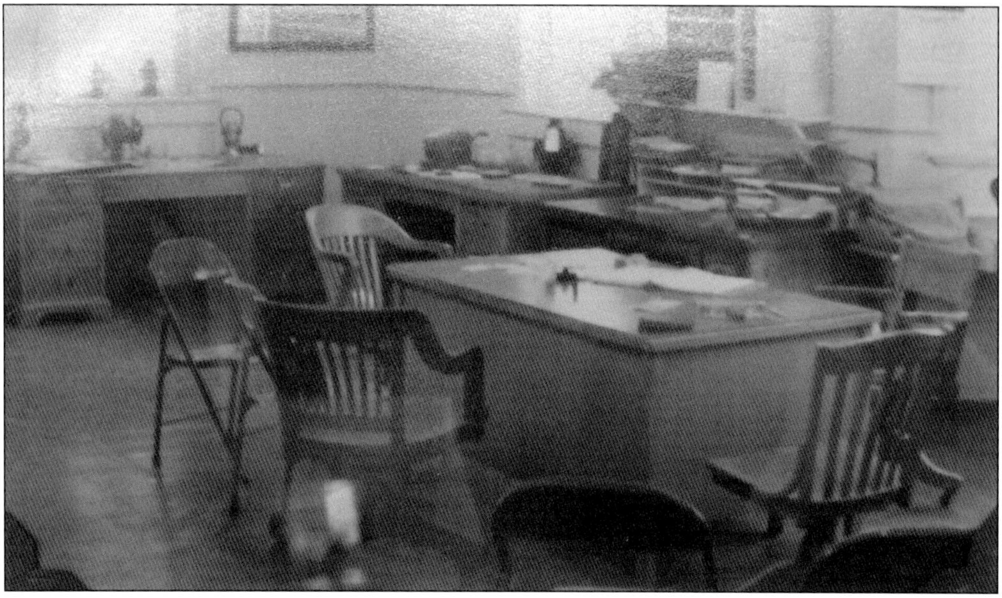

A number of Tooele residents spent their entire careers working various jobs for the Tooele Valley Railroad. Don Lee, the company's final president and superintendent, held nearly every job possible on the railroad before taking the helm in 1975, starting as an engine repairman and working his way through the ranks as a section hand, a fireman, and an engineer. He stayed with the railroad to the very end—and beyond. After the company closed, Lee continued volunteering for the railroad's museum board and helped move engine No. 11 to its new home on the museum property. In the later years of his career, Lee worked out of this office at the railroad depot. (Both courtesy of the Tooele Valley Railroad Museum.)

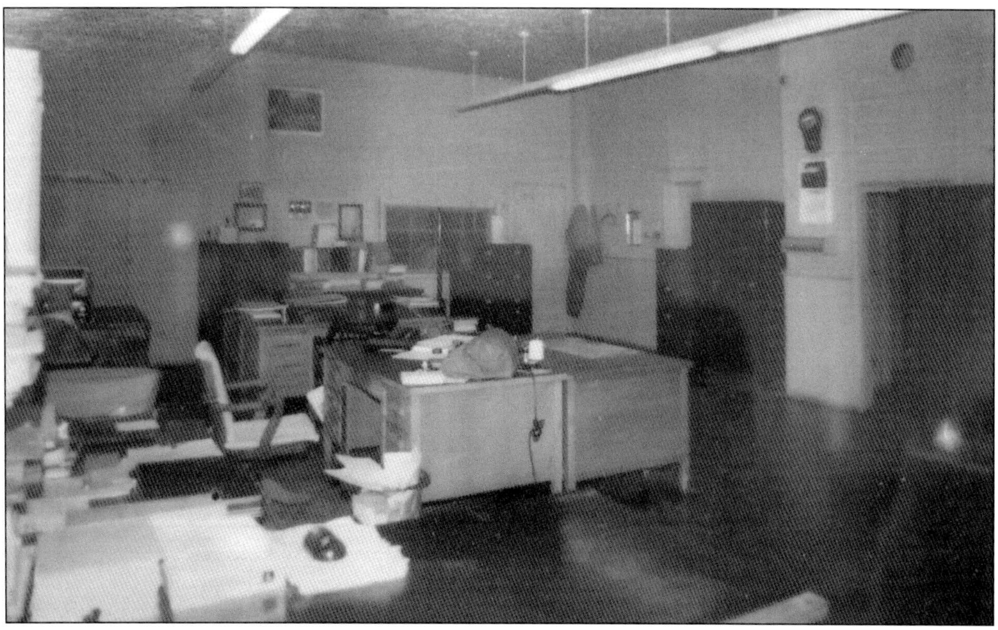

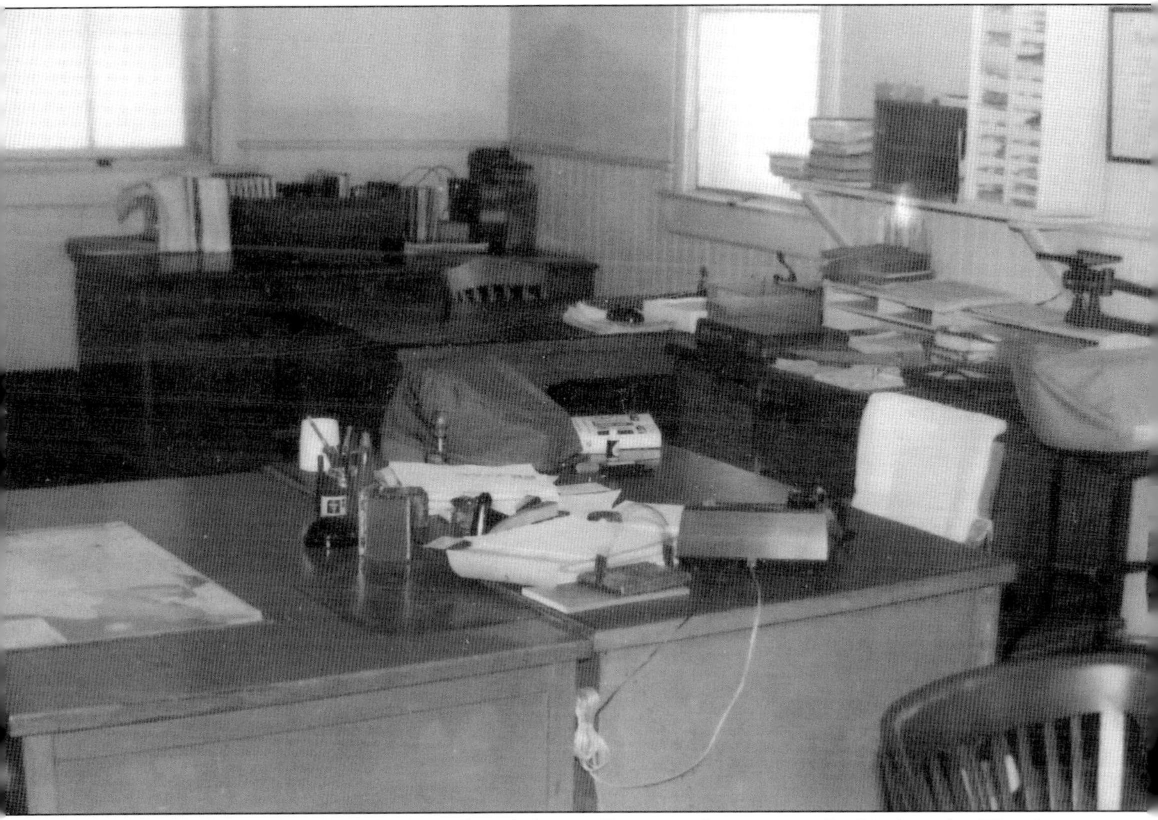

This is an office inside the Tooele railroad depot. Because the station doubled as the Tooele Valley Railway's company headquarters, it also housed space for the station agent, the timekeeper, the paymaster, a telegrapher, and two accountants. Many company records housed at the station became the property of the railroad museum after the depot's conversion. (Courtesy of the Tooele Valley Railroad Museum.)

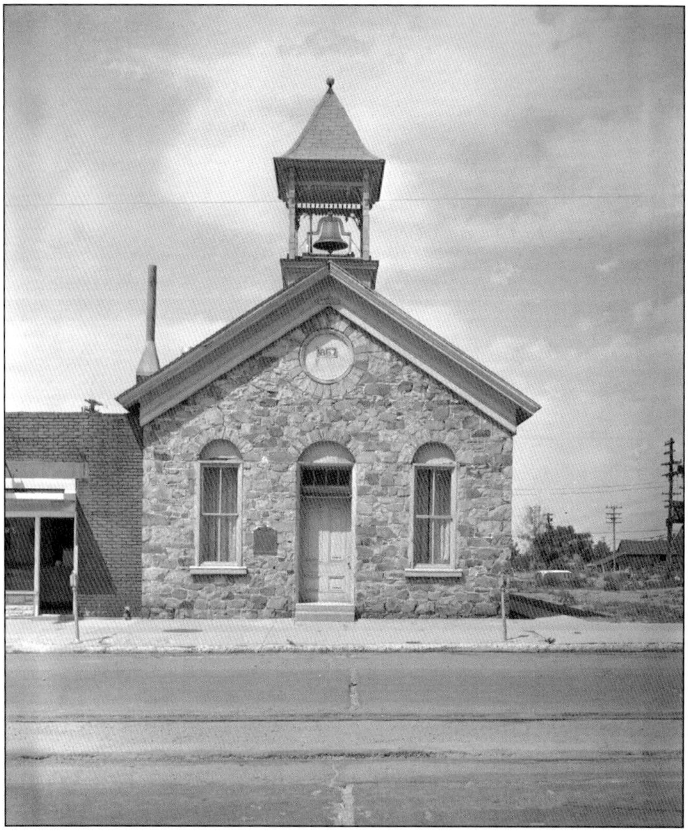

The historic Tooele County courthouse and city hall is seen here in August 1968, with tracks for the Tooele Valley Railway in the foreground. The courthouse predated the railroad by several decades, but became an important landmark on the railroad line. (Courtesy of the Library of Congress.)

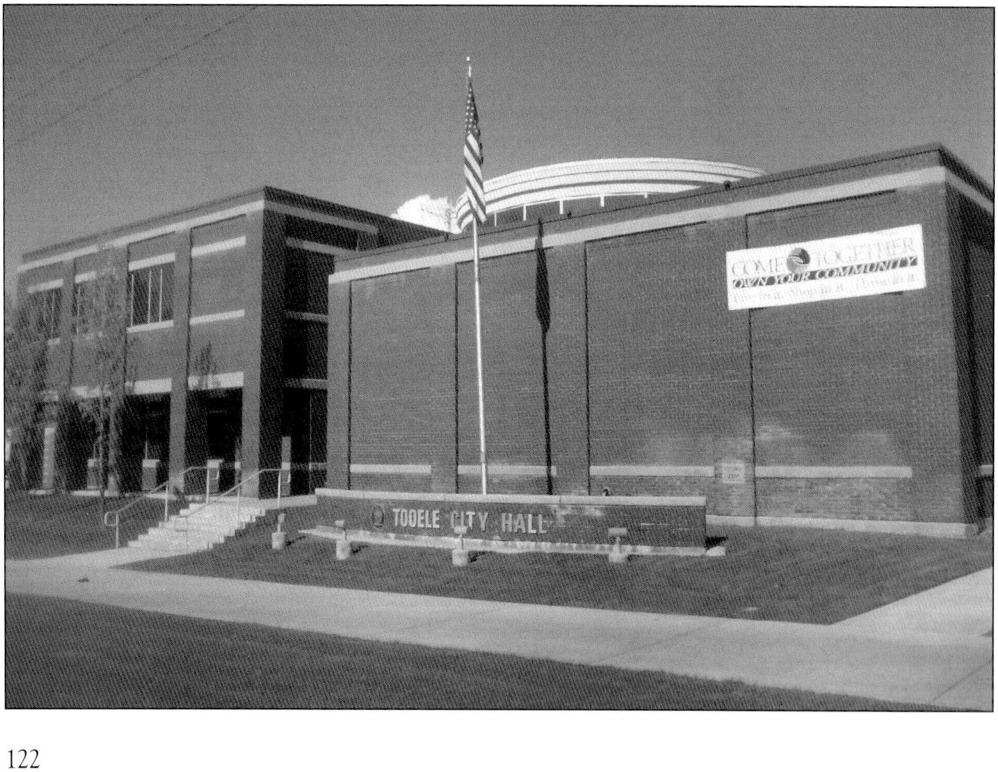

The new Tooele City Hall, built in 2005, is pictured here. The old stone courthouse now houses a museum dedicated to the Tooele Valley's early settlers. (Courtesy of Wikimedia Commons.)

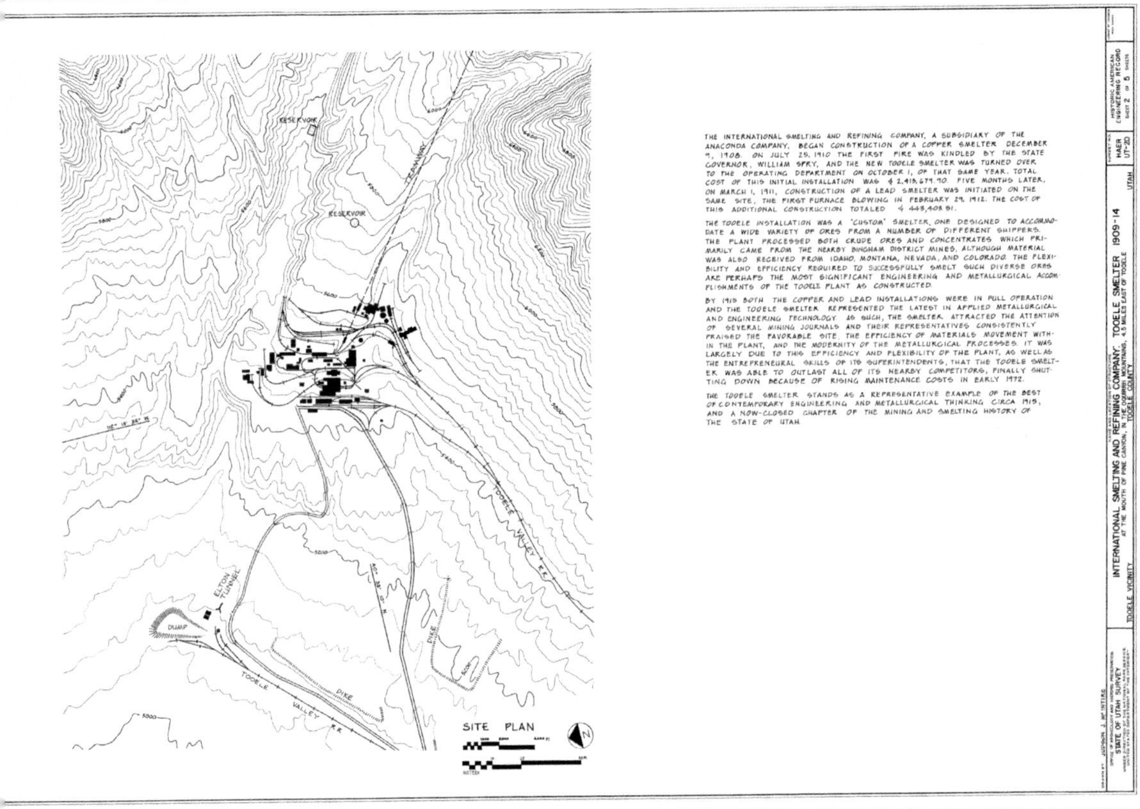

This topographical map illustrates the location of the International Smelter site relative to Pine Canyon. The position of buildings and various on-site rail lines are noted in detail. The Tooele Valley Railroad's main line and a spur to the Elton Tunnel are visible at the bottom of the image, and the elevated tram is illustrated as a dotted line toward the top.

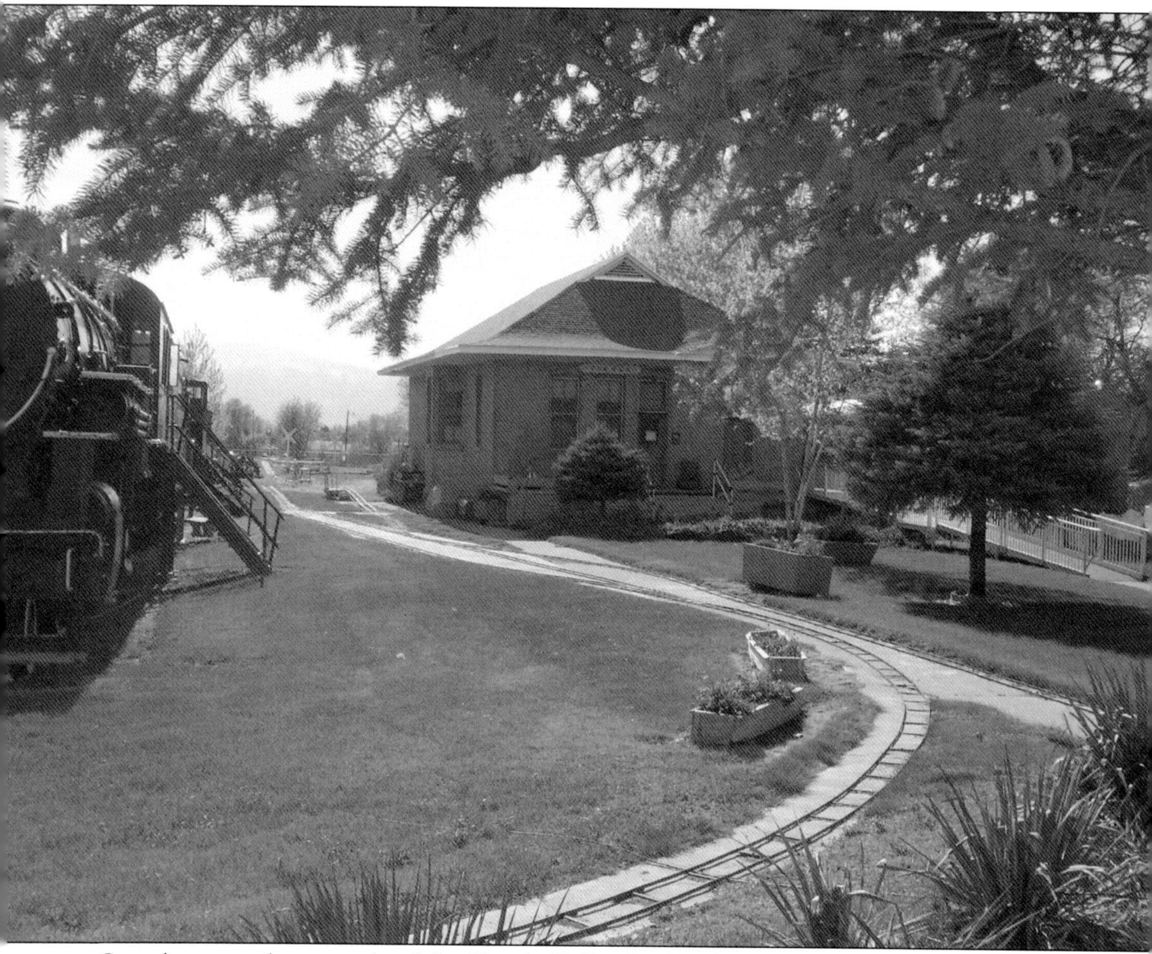

Seen here are the grounds of the Tooele Valley Railroad Museum. Many great images and artifacts, as well as steam engines, a caboose, and several passenger cars from the era of the Tooele Valley Railway are found at the site today. A miniature train ride—the tracks are visible in the foreground—circles the museum property. (Courtesy of Wikimedia Commons.)

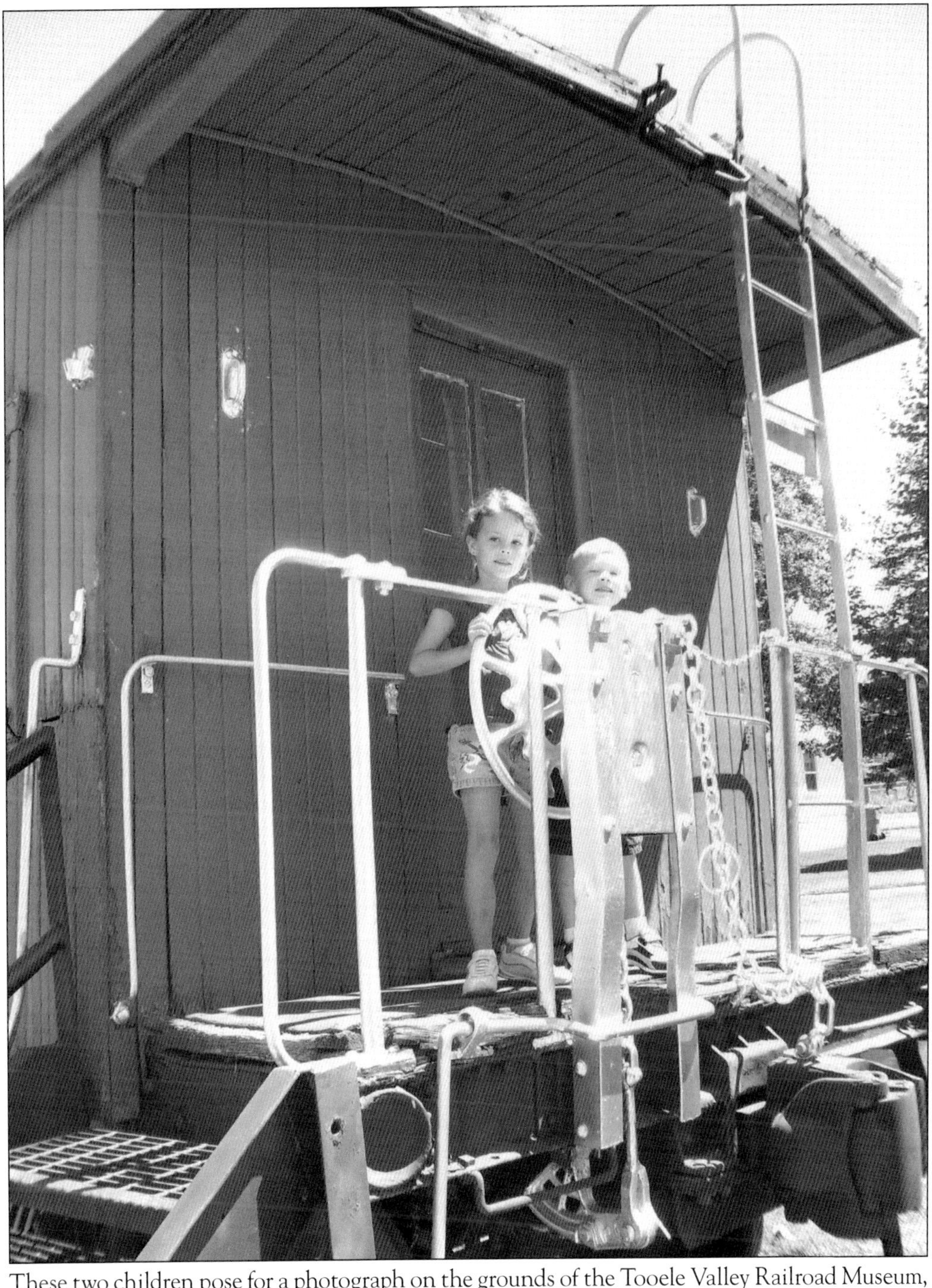

These two children pose for a photograph on the grounds of the Tooele Valley Railroad Museum, with big smiles on their faces as they climb around on the caboose. The railroad depot is not particularly large, so many of the museum's exhibits are located within the old railcars. (Courtesy of Michelle Powell, enjoyutah.com.)

Bibliography

Atkin, Claude F., Allan T. Comp, S.E. Craig, Larry Deppe, Frank C. Dunlavy, Bill Kelsey, Chris Weyland, and Orrin P. Miller. *Mining, Smelting and Railroading in Tooele County*. Tooele, UT: Tooele County Historical Society, 1986.

Tooele County Daughters of Utah Pioneers. *History of Tooele County, Bicentennial Edition*. Salt Lake City: Daughters of Utah Pioneers, Tooele County Chapter, 1961.

Tooele Transcript-Bulletin. Tooele: Transcript Bulletin Publishing, issues from 1905 to 1989.

Strack, Don. www.utahrails.net, 2013.

Terry, Jeff. "Lineside Legacy: Tooele County Railroad Museum." www.steamlocomotive.info, 2003.

Church, Michael A. "Smoke Farming: Smelting and Agricultural Reform in Utah, 1900–1945." *Utah Historical Quarterly*, Summer 2004: 196–218.

Mining and Contracting Review. Salt Lake City, 1941.

About the Tooele Valley Railroad Museum

Claude Atkin, a local historian and former International employee, first suggested that Tooele City and Atlantic Richfield jointly found a museum honoring the Tooele Valley Railway's history in 1981, at about the same time that Atlantic Richfield announced its intentions to abandon the railroad. On Atkin's suggestion, mayor Doug Sagers petitioned for the donation of Atlantic Richfield in October of that year, and Atlantic Richfield granted it shortly after the abandonment became official in March 1982. The company no longer needed it, so the city became the sole owner of the railroad depot at 35 North Broadway. Two remaining cabooses and engine No. 11 also became city property.

Mayor Sagers organized an official Tooele County Museum board on July 7, 1982, to convert the depot and find artifacts with which to fill it. Moving engine No. 11 from the memorial in the city park to this new site one mile to the east also fell under the board's jurisdiction. This the board accomplished with the help of men from the Tooele Army Depot, who arrived with a crane to lift the immobilized engine onto the back of two flatcars pulled by engine No. 104.

When the engine arrived at its new home, the failure of two tractors to move it into position revealed that, in 1964, someone had welded the engine's brakes into place. Once a blowtorch solved this problem, the weight of the engine caused another failure as it neared the end of the temporary track and sank into the asphalt on Vine Street. A fail-safe on No. 104 complicated the situation, and a tractor had to be summoned again to free the old engine.

Volunteers reunited engine No. 11 with engine No. 12 about a year later, in October 1983, when the snowplow built from the tender of the scrapped No. 12 was also donated to the museum. The plow had been left in storage at the Tooele Army Depot, which had little use for a steam powered snowplow.

A dedication ceremony on June 18, 1983, attended by locals and administrators from Atlantic Richfield, and an opening event held in September of that same year made the museum official. Tooele City continues to own and operate the Tooele Valley Railroad Museum, which is open seasonally, usually between Memorial Day and Labor Day.